Cell - 404-0128I (0121)
4013 Ahoy Dr.
Cheasapeak, VA
23321

Ruby Rollins
703-425-7404

Shda pacemaker
Ariel - cist forehead

Richard Stokes
**1-757-516-8337

7968
Gates Rd.
Suffolk, VA. 23437

Rev C[signature]

Calvin Johnson
1-757-925-5706
305 St. James AVE
Suffolk, VA 23434-5732

A Cry for Ethical and Moral Strength

By

Carl L. Sweat, Jr., D. Min.

authorHOUSE™
1663 LIBERTY DRIVE, SUITE 200
BLOOMINGTON, INDIANA 47403
(800) 839-8640
WWW.AUTHORHOUSE.COM

This book is a work of non-fiction. Unless otherwise noted, the author and the publisher make no explicit guarantees as to the accuracy of the information contained in this book and in some cases, names of people and places have been altered to protect their privacy.

© 2005 Carl L. Sweat, Jr., D. Min. All Rights Reserved.

No part of this book may be reproduced, stored in a retrieval system, or transmitted by any means without the written permission of the author.

First published by AuthorHouse 03/05/05

ISBN: 1-4208-0593-2 (sc)

Printed in the United States of America
Bloomington, Indiana

This book is printed on acid-free paper.

Forward

Humanity Can Regain Moral And Ethical Strength

Darkness Confronted By A Crowd of Witnesses

A Treasury Of Moral And Ethical Principles

These are the ideals that I embraced after reading this breathtaking book.

Two years ago I edited "Why Are Women In The Ministry?" a magnificent thought- provoking book written by my pastor Rev. Carl Sweat, Jr. Similarly, "Moral Strength" book number two, clearly and instructionally addresses in detail issues that face society. Knowing that Christ will return soon looking for a church that does not have a spot or blemish, we need to take a serious look at the lives that we lead. The time is now to seek God and to gain moral and ethical strength. The precision and style of this book presents an opportunity for readers to listen to the testimonies of others and to be enlightened by unadulterated teaching of God's word. May God receive all the glory for this book's contents and may you be spiritually strengthened through Christ's love and the vision He has given His servant to pen.

By the Editor: Marva Parker, Deaconess of Laurel Hill UCC

Acknowledgement

Writing a book is never a single author's endeavor. Similar to life, it is a joint venture supported by various contributions. Unquestionably, this book is no exception. Therefore, I extend my deepest thanks to the many authors that made this book possible through personal donations. Also, I would like to thank the editor, Marva Parker, my Laurel Hill UCC family, and a special thanks to my wife, Janice Sweat, for bearing with me again.

TABLE OF CONTENTS

SECTION I. STORIES SHARED FOR MORAL STRENGTHENING *1*

Chapter 1	Shattered Dreams 3

Moral Strength When You Lose A Child
Marion Walton: Deacon of Laurel Hill UCC

Chapter 2   Sharing More Than Looks 8
The Moral Gift Of Organ Donation
Janine Rawls and Janice Sweat: Members of Laurel Hill UCC (Sisters-in-law and wife of author)

Chapter 3   Living With Unanswered Questions 11
Moral Strength In Uncertain Time
Unidentified Source and Modified Testimony

Chapter 4   (MSM) 15
Moral Strengthening For Men That Have Sex With Men
Breness Reynolds: Sr. Programmer for AIDS and HIV seminars

Chapter 5   A Mother's Love And Son's Decision 21
Moral Strength To Continue Your Education
Diane Sweat and Brandon White: Members of Laurel Hill UCC

Chapter 6   Single And Love'n It 25
Moral Strength In Recommitting
Calveta Odom: Sr. Social Worker, MS

Chapter 7   Marriage 28
The Morality Of Preserving The Sanctity Of Marriage
David Runnion-Bareford: Executive Director, Bible Witness Fellowship

Chapter 8   My Decision To Divorce 32
Moral Strengthening For Divorce
Anonymous Writer

Chapter 9   Abusive Relationships 36
Moral Strength For Spousal Abuse Victims
City Counsel Member and Deaconess Joan K. Carter: Member of Laurel Hill UCC

Chapter 10   Love Destroyed And Regained 41
Moral Strength For Rape Victims
Rev. Jocelyn Morant: Assoc. Minister of The Church of Jesus in Hampton, VA

Chapter 11   Rape In The City 44
Moral Strength For Rape Victims
Rev. Slater Matthews, Jr.: Senior Assoc. Minister at Miracle Temple Baptist Church

Chapter 12	Abduction Of A Part Of Me 47
	Standing Morally Against Pornography
	Rev. Gloria Matthews: Assoc. Minister at Miracle Temple Baptist Church
Chapter 13	A Man That Broke Color Barriers 49
	Morals Against Discrimination
	Luther White: Deacon of Laurel Hill UCC
Chapter 14	Submitting To One Another 53
	Moral Strengthening For Marriages
	Rev. Elton R. Pryor: Pastor of Zion Poplar Baptist Church, Gloucester, VA
Chapter 15	Older Men Younger Women 57
	Morals on Relationships
	Deborah Williams: Owner of Deborah Williams Agency
Chapter 16	IF I Could Only See You 64
	Moral Strength For The Blind
	Geraldine Banks: Member of Laurel Hill UCC
Chapter 17	Virginity Vs. Spiritual Celibacy 68
	Morals of Christian Dedication
	Melvina Simon: Master of Divinity Candidate
Chapter 18	The Lord Working Through Me 74
	Moral Strength For The Incarcerated
	Rod Copeland: Member of Laurel Hill UCC
Chapter 19	Be Still And Know That He is God 80
	Moral Strength Concerning The Aspirations Of Life
	Editor: Marva Lee Hines Parker: Deaconess of Laurel Hill UCC
Chapter 20	Domestic Violence 84
	Moral Strengthening Of Relationships
	Fannie Mae Gilliam Burke: Clerk of Laurel UCC
Chapter 21	A Life Like Christ 88
	Moral Strength Is Offered When We Live Christ-Like
	Dr. D. A. Peace: Pastor of Zion Bethel UCC

SECTION II. TEACHINGS OF CHRIST FOR MORAL STRENGTHENING – A TREASURY OF MORAL PRINCIPLES 95

Dr. Carl L. Sweat: Pator of Laurel Hill UCC

Chapter 1	The Bible Viewed As A Book Rated X 97
	Morals On Viewing The Bible As Authoritative
	The Moral Problem 97
Chapter 2	The Origin Of The Struggle 102
	Morals On Poor Choices Or Decision Making

	Nothing Has Changed	102
Chapter 3	Biting Off More Than You Can Chew	110
	Moral Strength In Decision Making	
Chapter 4	Don't Let Dirt Get Into Your Eyes	118
	Morals On Fighting Back And Revenge	
	The Battlefield of the Mind	118
Chapter 5	Temptation Is Coming - It Cannot Be Deferred	123
	Morals On Fighting Back	
Chapter 6	Partiality	133
	Morals Against Prejudices And Improper Judgments	
Chapter 7	The Problem With Partiality	137
	Morals Against Prejudices And Improper Judgments	
Chapter 8	I Am Glad That You Have Come	140
	Moral Strength Against Discrimination	
Chapter 9	Thank God, I'm Jesus' Neighbor	145
	Moral Strengthening In Christian Duty	
Chapter 10	You Can't Handle The Truth	152
	Morals On Hearing And Doing	
	The Truth Can Hurt	152
Chapter 11	What Do We Give Up By Not Letting Go?	157
	Morals On Hearing And Doing	
Chapter 12	Things That Last	165
	Morals On Worship	
Chapter 13	Mastering Your Masters	171
	Morals On Spiritual Warfare	
Chapter 14	The Church Is Gone Fishing And They Are Fishing On The Wrong Side Of The Boat	177
	Morals On Missions	
Chapter 15	How To Make Your Church Great	185
	Morals For A Growing Church	
Chapter 16	Do Not Sell Your Birthright	193
	Morals For Valuing An Inheritance.	
	The Inheritance Of Our Fathers	193
Chapter 17	The Power Of Promises	200
	Moral Of The Cost Of A Promise	
Chapter 18	A New Beginning	205
	Moral Of Forgiving	
Chapter 19	Will God Forgive Me?	208
	Moral Of Forgiving	

Chapter 20	Can Men And Women Live A Perfect Life? 214	
	Moral Of Salvation	
Chapter 21	Why Did God Give The Law? 220	
	Moral Application Of The Law	
Chapter 22	It's Time To Come In For Your Curfew 241	
	Moral Strength For Living A Sanctified Life	
Chapter 23	You Want The Body, Bruise The Head 269	
	Morals In Placing Christ Head Of Your Life.	
	How does Satan plan to gain control of the body?..271	
Chapter 24	Take It To The Limit, And Don't Back Down 274	
	Moral Strength In Knowing Christ Is Ultimate	
Chapter 25	After All Is Said And Done, "The Shocker" 284	
	Moral Strength In Christian Accountability	
Chapter 26	A Cry For Ethical And Moral Fortitude 288	
	Moral Strengthening In Patience	
Chapter 27	War Waged Against Morality 291	
	Moral Strength In Knowing Truth Is Absolute	

SECTION III. DIVERSE TEACHINGS ON SEXUALITY AND HOMOSEXUALITY..299

Chapter 1	Now, No Condemnation...301	
	Rev. Paul H. Sherry: Former President United Church of Christ	
Chapter 2	BWF Executive Director's Response 307	
	David Runnion-Bareford: Executive Director of the Bible Witness Fellowship	
Chapter 3	"Homosexuality In The Life Of The Church" 311	
	Dr. Carlton Upton: Sr. Pastor of Tabernacle Christian Church	

Introduction

Within the last twenty years our nation has drastically declined in its moral strength. Obviously, the condition of moral degeneration is directly connected with the immoral and unethical decisions people make. Each day mankind is challenged to make difficult decisions that affect their relationships, finances and careers. Confronted with this constant, even the strongest of men and women periodically experience moments of weakness and require help. In knowing this constant to be true, this book inquires: Where are the voices of those that can help men and women make the proper choices? Where are the words of encouragement? (Periodically, everyone needs to be encouraged.) Where are those that have experienced what many people are going through? What moral words of wisdom can they share to solidify the weak and broken hearted 's confidence? Is there someone we can turn to, or is there an ultimate source that can lead to personal empowerment? Every now and then we all need moral strengthening.

What a privilege it is for me to reveal through this book the voices of those that are committed to sharing their experiences and dedicated to offering words of moral strengthening. It is also an honor that I not only teach Biblical principles of morals and ethics but also reveal why there is a need for individuals, families, communities, and nations to morally strengthen one another.

Section I

The first section of "A Cry For Ethical And Moral Strength" shares with the reader stories collected from some parishioners of Laurel Hill UCC and stories from persons of the Tidewater region that I have befriended over the years. Their stories are personal accounts of dark and challenging moments in their lives. Each story captures a critical time when they were confronted and had to make the crucial decision to stay strong by either doing what was morally and ethically right despite their emotions and negative perceptions regardless of the outside influences and social impact or by just waiting patiently for moral strengthening from a supernatural

God. The writers are people that are witnesses to how others can experience extreme darkness in their lives and be faced with making the most difficult decision yet still emerge virtuously and with moral fortitude. They offer their story as a testimony to you, the readers, that you may be encouraged and strengthened. They have dared to talk about their darkness so that others can be confident even during times of uncertainty.

Section II

Section two of "A Cry For Ethical And Moral Strength" serves to highlight factors regarding how principles of morality should influence the lives of men and women. It addresses the nation's moral degeneration and advocates that the Creator of all things and all people would not ask or require men and women to live moral and ethical lives without providing the means by which they can accomplish His command. He has supplied humanity with an unchangeable, unwavering and unshakable document. That eternal document is the Bible. It contains foundational principles for living a virtuous life.

Section III

The third section addresses a profound philosophy that is indicative to the notions or thoughts of most men and women and applies it to the topic of homosexuality. A Greek philosopher by the name of Thales is noted for one of the best-known statements in history. He stated that, "All things are made of water." The reason his statement is recorded as a historical importance is it not only required a daring mind to conceive a proposition containing such a general idea, but also it took gall to ascribe his philosophy to the term "all" when attempting to confine all things into certain parameters. One proposition that consistently appears to be justified by the facts of our everyday experience is that all things cannot be restricted to a single definition; various principles must be integrated for clarity and a better understanding of how things are interrelated. When addressing homosexuality many people's central philosophy is similar to Thales'. They only see life one way. They see life as people being created male or female and they must conduct their behavior within the assigned parameters. However, multiplicity and variety are the obvious facts about this imperfect everyday world. Subsequently, society, the judicial branch of government, and the religious community are at odds with regards to inquiries of morality and the ethics of human sexuality.

This final section is devoted to one of the most controversial subjects of this cultural era. Homosexuality has overwhelmingly impacted faith-based communities and has intensely influenced many facades of life. As men and women search for truth by questioning the ethics and the dilemma of morality, I submit to the reader writings from reputable authors that have extensively researched the concept of sexuality. Their analytical findings advocate diverse interpretations concerning moral principles of Christian character.

A Minister's Prayer

We begin our review of "Moral Strength" with a prayer contributed by Rev. Joe Wright, who is Senior Pastor of Central Christian Church in Wichita, KS. He beseeched his prayer at the opening session of the Kansas Senate. "The response was immediate. A number of legislators walked out during the prayer in protest. In 6 short weeks, Central Christian Church, where Rev. Wright is pastor, logged more than 5,000 phone calls with only 47 of those calls responding negatively. The church is now receiving international requests for copies of this prayer from India, Africa, and Korea. Even, commentator Paul Harvey aired this prayer on his radio program, The Rest of the Story, and received a larger response to this program than any other he has ever aired. With the Lord's help, may this prayer sweep over our nation and wholeheartedly become our desire so that we again can be called one nation under God." The prayer will always remind men and women how many have faltered in maintaining their moral and ethical responsibilities to one another and how individuals, groups, societies, and nations must regain moral fortitude.

Rev. Joe Wright to the Kansas House.

Heavenly Father, we come before you today to ask your forgiveness and seek your direction and guidance. We know your Word says, "Woe to those who call evil good," but that's exactly what we've done. We have lost our spiritual equilibrium and inverted our values.

We confess that we have ridiculed the absolute truth of your Word and called it moral pluralism.

We have worshipped other gods and called it multi-culturalism.

We have endorsed perversion and called it an alternative lifestyle.

We have exploited the poor and called it the lottery.

We have neglected the needy and called it self-preservation.

We have rewarded laziness and called it welfare.

We have killed our unborn and called it choice.

We have shot abortionists and called it justifiable.

We have neglected to discipline our children and called it building esteem.

We have abused power and called it political savvy.

We have coveted our neighbors' possessions and called it ambition.

We have polluted the air with profanity and pornography and called it freedom of expression.

We have ridiculed the time-honored values of our fore-fathers and called it enlightenment.

Search us O God and know our hearts today; try us and see if there be some wicked way in us; cleanse us from every sin and set us free.

Guide and bless these men and women who have been sent here by the people of Kansas, and who have been ordained by you, to govern this great state. Grant them your wisdom to rule and may their decisions direct us to the center of your will. I ask it in the name of your son, the living savior, Jesus Christ.

Amen.

SECTION I

Stories Shared For Moral Strengthening

Carl L. Sweat, Jr., D. Min.

A Cry for Ethical and Moral Strength

Chapter One
Shattered Dreams
Moral Strength When You Lose A Child

By Marion Walton: Deacon of Laurel Hill UCC

Laura Annette Walton was an honor student and a senior at Elizabeth City State University. All things were falling in place for graduation and preparations were being made for finding her first job and starting a career. Her parents were excited and had great expectations for their daughter. Marion said, "We were the best of friends. She was my heart and soul." Life couldn't get any better for Laura and her family. Unfortunately, it didn't.

Laura lived on campus. However, because of strong family ties she frequented home as often as her schedule permitted. One day, Laura came home and did the things that she normally did when she visited. She went to her room, put up her things, and came out to greet her mother. But something drastic happened during this visit. As she entered the living room she became faint. She walked toward her mother and suddenly fell to the floor unconscious and she ceased to breathe. Lois administered CPR and called the rescue squad. They came and rushed Laura to the nearest hospital. That night, the emergency team thought they would lose her before arriving at the hospital. I was not contacted and informed that my daughter was in ICU until noon of the next day. When I did receive word of my daughter's condition, I drove with haste to be with her. It was the longest two-hour drive I ever experienced.

When I pulled into the parking lot of the hospital, I ran like there was no time to waste. I reached her room and saw her lying there with all kinds of tubes in her mouth and nose. She was connected to numerous instruments. But in particular I noticed, one gadget that had a light with a name on it. The name said "Baby." As I looked at my daughter and the doctors and nurses informed me about my daughter's condition, that gadget and light never escaped my mind. So I asked the nurse, what is this gadget with the name baby on it.

The nurse said to me, Mr. Walton do you not know that your Laura is pregnant? And I responded, "No, I have no idea."

At that time Laura was conscious and could speak. So I drew near to her; knowing that the only reason she did not tell me she was pregnant was because she felt she had let me down, and I told her we all make mistakes but we can make it through this. You can have a child and a career at the same time. You will make it. She looked deep into my eyes as if my words were a great relief to her and relieved her of a great pressure or burden. She then asked, "Daddy, will you pray for me?" I said, "Yes, I will pray for you." I held her hand and prayed, "Father heal Laura, deliver her from her sickness, deliver her from all evil, and direct her that she may surrender herself unto you." After I prayed, Laura looked at me. She said, "Thank you and then squeezed my hand and said Daddy, I would like to be saved."

Later the next day after the doctors had called the family together because things appeared to have gotten worst, she asked me if I would contact her boyfriend because no one showed an interest in informing him of her or the baby's condition. Because of my love for her and the baby, I called the young man and he hurried from Fayetteville, N.C. to be by her side. On the fifth day, Laura was transferred from the ICU at Elizabeth City to the ICU at Norfolk General Hospital because at that time they didn't have the equipment to accommodate her condition, which was an unidentified virus that a team of specialist could not effectively treat. Also, due to her pregnancy they could not provide the level of health care Laura required.

An Angel Comes To Visit The Family

Upon Laura's arrival and admittance into the hospital, that afternoon an angel came to visit. Laura gave birth to the first baby to be born in Norfolk General Hospital's ICU. Everyone called her "Angel" because of Laura's disease, the affect it had on her body, and the baby being premature, it was probable that Angel would not make it or she would have some deformities. Yet, despite the entire mass of opposing factors, a healthy seven-month baby was delivered and she truly was an "Angel." Laura named her Marion Louise Walton.

Stuck In The Middle Of My Dilemma

I remember praying to God and asking Him to deliver my daughter from her sickness and to restore her to a reasonable portion of health. But also I prayed, Lord if it is not your will to heal her would you please save her soul. I placed my deepest conviction in the belief that she would get better and in many cases the episode appeared that she was getting better but then things would decline. Yet, as I would hold on to her hands I would hold on to my faith. The greatest challenge for me was to trust God completely. I say this because prior to the crisis that existed, my faith in Christ was being renewed. I had recently recommitted my life and service to God. So, this was a burden that I had to brave with Christ, with a new found trust, hope and rekindled fire of faith. For the forty-five days that Laura was at Norfolk General I visited each day and prayed fervently.

Loss Of A Child

One day, while I was at work I received a call that my daughter had passed. On the way there and upon entering into the room, I had mixed emotions about the entire experience of Laura's passing. It was something that no parent could accurately explain or describe. What helped me keep it together was the fact that she asked me to be strong. She said that she needed me to be strong through the crisis because her mother was not strong. I said I would be there for her, but when I saw her body on the bed with no breath I collapsed over her and began to cry. My tears flowed like a river.

When I left the hospital, for a long period of time I existed but I had no existence. I was living but I had no life. My reason to live appeared to have been taken away. The daughter that was to outlive me was now gone. We were to grow old together. She was to outlive me. I never thought I'd outlive my child but reality takes its own course. Indirectly, I blamed God. I would not confront Him directly, out of fear or reverence of Him. Yet, at that time, Laura did not have an opportunity to live. All her life she had been confined. She was in school and college all her life. She never had a chance to get out of college and live life. She had lived for 23 years but something always had her confined. I had asked God to deliver her and I stood on that faith. My relationship with Him had changed. No longer could I pray to Him for the major reason that I did not want to question God or hold Him in contempt. The first three weeks after my daughter's death my life could be associated with that of a walking zombie. I only existed. I saw things but they had no meaning. I heard the voices of others that offered their help but the voices were void. Nothing was of relevance or significance. Not even God. The only meaning in my life was the fact that when I set on the stoop of my front porch and looked at the trees, the sun, and the children in the neighborhood playing across the street or just walking together, some were the same age as Laura I would say to myself everyone else has their child but mine is gone. My reality was the one I loved was no longer here with me.

Moral Application: For a long period of time I lived in a secluded and a denied resentful state of mind. When suddenly, it dawned on me that I had prayed to God to deliver Laura from her illness but if that was not His will then save her soul. Just as if it was yesterday, I remembered a particular day; it was about the twentieth day of her stay in Norfolk General, I walked into the hospital to visit Laura. My aunts and a cousin who are evangelists were there. Laura could not speak at that time because of the type of tubes that were in her mouth. But as soon as she saw us, she was excited and grabbed a piece of paper. Frantically, she began to write on it. Then she held it up and handed it to us so that we all could read what she wrote. The note said, "Daddy, I got saved today." On her own, she had willingly given her life to Christ. The glow on her face and the joy that she revealed at that time began to strengthen me. Just the thought of that day caused me to immediately leap with joy. Christ brought me back to a place in time that He revealed to me He answers prayer. From that memory, my life started on a road of recovery, a road of healing, and a road of prayer and praise. Also, Christ used my wife as an instrument of encouragement in a time of sorrow and healing.

Today I can say I miss Laura's presence but I am comforted in knowing that she is with Christ. Life will never be the same; yet, by God's grace life can continue without the feeling of being void, or incomplete. Life carries on in completeness with an "Angel" and my family.

Carl L. Sweat, Jr., D. Min.

Chapter Two
Sharing More Than Looks
The Moral Gift Of Organ Donation

By Janine Rawls and Janice Sweat: Members of Laurel Hill UCC
(Sister-in-law and wife of author)

Janine and I are identical twins. Throughout our lives we did everything together. We played together, we laughed together, we shopped together, and we graduated high school and majored in the same field in college together. Together we were inseparable. Even during a time of darkness in my life we both cried together.

In October, 1994 my life changed dramatically. It all began with a simple head cold. I remember waking up one morning with abnormally swollen hands, but I didn't think much about it. At the time I had a cold but the symptoms eventually disappeared. However, my ankles began to swell in addition to my hands. Then I became concerned because I knew something was wrong.

A visit to my doctor confirmed something that I did not expect to hear. I went to the doctor under the impression that whatever was causing the swelling was treatable. However, my doctor said my cold went away on the outside, but not on the inside. That day I was diagnosed with Focal Sclerosis Glomerulonephritis (FSGS), a condition that causes inflammation of the kidney filters. Sadly, he looked at me and said, "Janice, we do not know exactly what causes this disease. We can slow your immune system down but the disease and its' affects are irreversible."

Medication stabilized my kidney functions for four years and within those years I tried to live a normal life. I did not share my condition with my twin sister, my immediate family, or my two children that were nine years old and eight years old. Only my husband and I were aware of my physical state. We talked and agreed not to place our families under undo pressure or stress. We prayed every day. We prayed every hour. We offered thanksgiving every day. It was a trying ordeal. For four years my husband wrote me letters of encouragement and he taped personal messages for me to listen to as I drove to and from work each day. Though we sought God's face in all things, the day came, the day my doctor stated would come, the day when the medicine could no longer help me because both kidneys would begin to fail. When that day came, my husband and I thanked God for giving me four years of reasonable health.

Now was the opportunity to unload my heavy burden. Now was the time to tell my children, my twin, and my immediate family. The disease had reached its culmination. I couldn't keep it a secret any longer. My heart had longed to tell them but I just didn't know how. But I mustered the strength to call my family and inform them of my condition. I didn't hold anything back. Not even the fact that I would soon be placed on dialysis and that a healthy matching kidney needed to be found quickly for me to remain alive.

I knew my closest match would naturally be Janine, my identical twin. However, asking such benevolence from her was more than I could handle. She and her husband were young, they had two very young girls and to ask her to take a risk for me was unimaginable. Carl stepped forward and spoke to Terrell and Janine. We sat together in my mother's home and talked about the situation. Carl ended by saying, take some time to pray and think about it. Whatever you decide to do we will respect your decision.

Surprisingly, our families never met to discuss the issue again. Once again my twin and I proved to be inseparable. Janine came to me and firmly asked, "Why didn't you tell me earlier? You did not have to go through this alone." After she asked the question, you could have heard a pen drop in the midst of the silence. Many reasons ran through my mind but at the time none were a sufficient response. Janine said this sudden notice is overwhelming. Perhaps, if I knew earlier it could have helped me prepare for this. Yet, despite my disappointment there is no time to be angry. I want to be there for you. And though I have apprehensions because I do not know what to expect, I am very aware that you need me as I need you. I began to cry and Janine cried with me. We cried and faced the operation together.

Carl L. Sweat, Jr., D. Min.

On November 20, 1998, one day after our 35th birthday, Dr. Thomas McCune at Sentara Norfolk General Hospital removed Janine's right kidney and placed it in my left side. There were no complications during the surgeries and my body accepted the transplanted kidney. Today, my sister's children say that their aunt has their mother's kidney inside her and my children say our mother would not be alive if Aunt Janine had not given mom one of her kidneys. Once again, Janine and I can smile together and say we share more than identical looks.

Moral Application From Janine Rawls: Thanksgiving for Janice and me comes everyday. I am blessed that my sister is here with me; I am here with her and most importantly that we are both healthy.

From Janice Sweat: Love and respect of another person helps you to determine when to ask someone for help. It must because you are about to ask them to make a sacrifice for another person. You are asking them to go without in order to assist someone else. Also, love and communication helps a person make the tough decision to help. Therefore, communicate with a person(s) as soon as possible to give them time to seek God and prepare for any situations. My husband and I often think how it would have been if we had shared my medical condition earlier. We find strength in knowing that we made the decision we felt was best at that time. Others that are experiencing similar crises also have to weigh things out and make the decision that is best for them and their family.

Note: The national waiting list for kidneys is long- and quickly getting longer. Of the 46,350 people on the list, just 12,500 will get a transplant this year, according to the United Network for Organ Sharing, or UNOS. Living donors are becoming more important in the process of making transplants more available to more needy people. Be an organ donor and give the gift of life.

Chapter Three
Living With Unanswered Questions
Moral Strength In Uncertain Time

Unidentified Source and Modified Testimony:

Frank was a man known by his determination and relentless persistency. These characteristics were evident to the people that came to know him and they were prominent in all aspects of his life. Early in our marriage he set his eye on a piece of land and desired to build our family home on the property. Though times were difficult because the industry he was employed with was drastically changing, nothing could hinder him from seeing his dream unfold. Without collateral he went to the local bank and convinced the banker to loan him money to build a single family home. Immediately, he started construction on our dream home. It was completed within eight months.

The changes in Frank's field were not for the best. Businesses were closing and employees were receiving pink slips but my husband was more determined than ever to succeed in the career his father had prospered and paved for him. Frank would not succumb to the fate of the industry. With all his might he kept going. The struggle soon paid off. First there were subtle signs of improvements and then the market soared. My husband and I were elated. Frank had worked so hard to stay afloat. He was more than ready to reap his portion that was long overdue to him and his family. For the next several years Frank excelled in his field. Perhaps it was God's way of giving him a little relief from the challenging years he had labored so hard. I believe God blessed him because he was a good steward.

The glory years passed by quickly; one year before the second decline of the industry began a cycle of drastic events that took place in Frank's life. During the beginning of the year Frank could not work for a few months due to a job related injury. He soon recovered; however, his trials did not end there. That same year, Frank suffered with severe migraine headaches. The day before Easter he was diagnosed with a severe brain disorder. After a couple of days spent in the hospital and a series of test, the doctors came and informed me that my husband was very ill, his disease required immediate surgery, and the procedure they would use was complicated. Also, following the surgery, months of therapy would be required.

After surgery, Frank began to regain moderate strength and he quickly recovered the usage of his motor skills. His speech improved along with his coherence. His will to fully recuperate and desire to return to work drove him to push himself. Once again his determination and motivation served to be positive characteristics of his life. They helped him to accomplish many milestones. In this case they helped him to return home and back to a moderate and independent life. Nonetheless, within a brief period Frank grew weary and became depressed. He became overly concerned about the rate of his recovery. He became anxious about whether he could actually return to work. Though his doctor informed him that he could return to work, the only stipulations were that he take it easy, don't lift heavy objects, get plenty of rest and make sure he takes his medicine but Frank continued to feel as if his career was over.

One night Frank couldn't sleep. The next morning, he told me all he could think about was losing his business and our home. I told him he shouldn't think about those types of things. The doctor said everything would be fine, just give yourself time. He said, I can't help from thinking about it. He then asked me to contact the doctor and pick-up something that would help him sleep. The next morning he said he slept well and it appeared to me that all was back to normal. Regrettably, I misread my husband's condition.

Several days later, I returned home from work and Frank was missing. I knew something was wrong because it was nearing the time that he was to take his medicine. He always took his meds on time. So, I contacted some friends in the community and asked if they had seen Frank. They said no and offered to help search for him. We all combed the neighborhood but did not find him. After spending hours searching, I contacted the local police department and informed them of Frank's absence.

They located Frank's vehicle late that night. However, discovering my husband's body would take several more hours. Within those hours it appeared to me, even with Frank's body not yet found until later that morning, that the police perceived the matter as an open and shut case. I was left feeling that their investigation was handled poorly and that they showed no interest in preserving vital evidence that might have been pertinent to investigating the death of my husband.

To this day, I accept their report as being incomplete and inconclusive. Much evidence was not included in their report, including eyewitnesses' statements. The police suggested to me that Frank had a self- inflicted wound and the wound was the cause of his death. However, when I received the coroner's report it did not suggest that the wound was self-inflected nor was the wound the cause of his death. I spoke to the coroner and police on several occasions and expressed my concerns but I did not pursue my position because rebelling was not going to bring my husband back.

Today, many questions remain unanswered concerning my husband's death. I often ask myself were there signs of depression or signs that might have indicated that Frank needed help? Did I miss the signs or did I not take heed of them? What more could I have done? What if I had stayed home that day? Would things have turned out any differently? I know Frank's death has affected my children's lives, how much and how deep it has affected them I am not so sure. I have many questions relative to what actually happened.

Nearly thirty years have passed but the memories remain. When they begin to taunt me and fill my heart with pain, I strengthen myself by saying this prayer, "Father, I do not know what took place but you know all things. Lord, there are many uncertainties in life and many things I do not know and certain things I cannot control so I ask for your peace and strength." I find moral strengthening in my confidence and assurance that there is a God and He loves us, and that He created all things and He's in control of everything. I am persuaded that He will give me peace in the midst of adversity; therefore, I have not relied on the police report or the coroner's

Carl L. Sweat, Jr., D. Min.

report to find peace or contentment. I have found strength in Christ who sees all, knows all and one day He will reveal all.

Chapter Four
(MSM)
Moral Strengthening For Men That Have Sex With Men

By Breness Reynolds: Sr. Programmer for AIDS and HIV seminars

The Center for Disease Control (CDC) discovered that census data and various statistical facts pertaining to the total populations of homosexual, bisexual or gay men were not accurate. They found that many men that were sexually active with the same gender did not classify themselves as being homosexual, bisexual or gay. Therefore, they created the term Men Having Sex With Men (MSM). The CDC and numerous researchers currently use the term MSM. Their primary objective is to dismantle the homophobia cycle. Whereby, they can gather more specific and accurate data. Organizations and institutions have identified that there are many labels associated with people that participate in non-traditional sexual behaviors. Also, that the present labels have become so prominent within today's culture that they are replacing previous traditional terms known as homosexual, gay and bisexual. If the truth could be told, it would suggest that, because of discrimination factors, the phobias, and the negative social woes connected with the traditional terms, people are attempting to redefine their sexuality.

Take for instance, a man that is married but has sexual relations with another man. He commits a homosexual act but does not consider himself a homosexual. The societal jargon for that particular person is (DL) Down Low. He lives life in denial or in secret of the homosexual act(s). Within the urban arena, there are men that are known to force other men to engage in various homosexual acts with them or others. This type of man is identified as homo-thugs for the mere fact that he threatens, pressures, or forces another man to participate in a sexual act.

If the CDC had not changed their term or definitions, an individual they might have missed in their statistical calculations of homosexual males is Breness. Breness does not identify himself as gay, bisexual or homosexual. He classifies himself as a man that had sex with other men (MSM).

An interview of Breness

Breness was born August 4th, 1958 in North Carolina. He is the second oldest of six children. He grew up as a child with great responsibilities. He and the oldest sibling shared responsibilities in assisting in the care for the younger siblings and completing the household chores. Though he was raised in a single parent home, neither he nor any family member went without the basic necessities. And though his mother and father had agreed to separate when he was a child, he had a great measure of love that radiated from his mother and grandmother.

During his years in elementary education, Breness showed signs of shyness. With dark skin and lips that slightly protruded, facial features that are not identified as handsome, and people saying unkind things to him, he suffered from a low self-esteem. More and more he became socially withdrawn. In junior high he did join the drama club and he excelled as an actor and playwriter. He enjoyed acting; however in high school he did not participate in any sports or extracurricular activities. For the most part, Breness lived an alienated life. He went to school, attended his classes and then came home.

He did have an interest in girls but after acknowledging his affection for them only to be rejected, Breness's attempts of becoming friends with females ceased. Also, his efforts to discover and share in a relationship with a female came to an end in high school. There was one special girl that he liked. He thought of the possibility that they could marry, have children, and live together for life. But he remembered when he asked her out she said no. She was not interested in him. It hurt him so badly that he has never been able to muster the strength again to ask another female out. Even, today, there are women he has an interest in but he has not revealed his emotion nor has he asked them for a date.

The Pursuer Becomes Pursued

Four years after graduating high school, Breness found himself working with a person that showed an interest in him. For the first time the affection he desired to offer another human being was now being offered to him. The joy that he felt could not be explained. Instead of being the pursuer Breness was being pursued. Yet, there was one dilemma. The pursuer was male.

Breness said to himself, "What must I do?" I have never experienced a relationship with a man. When he pondered the question, something he wanted to try when he was a kid began to stir inside of him. A slight curiosity that existed when he was younger had grown into a deep-seated desire. A second nature that wanted to test the waters on the opposite side began to take control of him. His inquisitiveness urged him on. Breness became close friends with his work associate. They found themselves communicating more intimately each day. The intense period of talking was over. Now, it was time to consummate their relationship.

One day when Breness arrived at work, before he could settle in to start his daily routine the young man asked him if he would be interested in meeting him at his house after work. Breness accepted the invitation by saying yes. It was that evening; Breness had his first sexual experience with a male. He did not consider himself homosexual then nor does he consider himself homosexual now. To him he was a man having sex with a man (MSM).

At the age of twenty-one Breness began to travel down a dark and winding path, a road that held challenges he could not imagine. For nine years, Breness maintained a relationship with the first man in his life. The relationship was not filled with the love that he sought for so long. The relationship was filled with mental abuse and instability. Because of the many existing problems, Breness became discontented and abandoned his loyalty. Two separate sexual relationships spawned from the depression of his low self-esteem and loneliness. One relationship lasted for a year. The next was a rebound encounter from his fall. It did not last long. Ten years later, Breness ended the relationship that was never meant to be. He was torn to pieces by the criticism and he had been ripped to shreds by the roller coaster ride he was taken on.

The Day I Was Informed I Had HIV

For the next nine years, from 1990 to 1998, rarely was Breness sexually active with men. Yet, when he participated in satisfying his fleshly desires it was with men he knew and with men who were total strangers. In April of 1998 Breness noticed there was a slight change in his energy level. He began to feel sluggish and tired all the time. However, he assumed it was due to his demanding position. As a mental health technician he was pouring out his heart and soul to assist handicapped and mentally disabled persons. Though he dismissed the thought that he needed to be seen by a physician, he continued to push himself. In August he turned 40 years old. Unfortunately, his birthday was not a day that Breness felt he could celebrate. The draining of his strength was progressive and the disease had begun to run its course within his body.

During that time, Breness decided to donate blood plasma. He thought it would be a good way to get some extra spending cash. Unfortunately, upon his second visit, during the processing of screening the donated blood for HIV, Breness' blood was identified positive for the HIV virus. In the aftermath, the Department of Health and Human Services was contacted and informed of his health related condition. Before they could get in touch with Breness he had returned in November of 1998 to the blood bank to give blood for the third time. But this time they had a pink line drawn through his name and told him to remain where he was because the doctor needed to speak with him. Breness was turned away from giving blood but others that came in after him were being allowed to donate. The notion that something was wrong began to hit him. Suddenly, a doctor carrying a briefcase appeared. That is when Breness became frantic. He panicked and hasted away.

Refusing to wait for the doctor to give him the results related to his blood screening, Breness went home. Regrettably, that did not help things get any better. There, he found himself continuing to get sick. Even at his job, he began to become irritable with co-workers and lash out at them. Often he would begin to sweat and he would get tired. People would ask if he was ok. He would say he was fine. Everything is alright. But things were far from being alright. In the back of his mind Breness knew something was terribly wrong. However, he was reluctant in contemplating negative thoughts.

In December of 1998 a letter was mailed to Breness' mother's home and when he visited she handed it to him. Breness read the notice. It requested him to immediately contact the sender. Breness called the man. The representative from the Health Department stated he needed to speak with Breness and that he would meet him at his job. The next day, about the 28th or 29th of December, a man pulled up to the store. Breness had been patiently waiting for him and when he identified the truck, he walked out of the store. He walked over to the truck, opened the door, got in and closed the door. The man asked if he was Breness and Breness said, "Yes, I am." Then the man said, "Breness your blood tested positive for HIV. You are a carrier of HIV."

To Breness, the news was overwhelming. He was shocked with awe. The terror of HIV left him speechless. The man then said I will need a list of all persons you have been involved with sexually. He then handed Breness a resource package and said these items are for you. Breness received the package. Then he provided the Health Department representative with persons he had sexual contact with.

The Interview Was Discontinued

Breness could no longer continue the interview. He said life changed drastically on the day he was informed he had HIV. Nearing the end of the questioning, there was uneasiness because the interview was dredging-up memories that he had hidden in the back of his mind and most of the memories that he tried to forget. He requested to end the interview. Before ending, he said he found strength in knowing that God never left him. He left God. Also, he said he does not blame God for his condition because it was not His fault. God did not give him the HIV disease. He gave it to himself. God allowed it to happen and used it to get his attention. God has taken a difficult and serious issue in Breness' life and is using it for the good of others.

Currently, Breness serves as a counselor for the Urban League in a metropolitan city in the state of Virginia. He is a member of a local church near his new residence.

Though he is a carrier of HIV and he experiences crisis with his health, he said he has the strength to face each day one at a time. Just to know that Jesus Christ died for all our sins is enough to encourage him. It tells him and should tell others with Aids, HIV and various sexually transmitted diseases that can be forgiven by Christ. They can be washed clean of their sins. This truth applies to MSM.

Chapter Five
A Mother's Love And Son's Decisions
Moral Strength To Continue Your Education

By Diane Sweat and Brandon White: Members of Laurel Hill UCC

At the age of seventeen and a rising senior at Lakeland High School, Brandon is looking forward to graduation day and he is making plans to attend college. With great aspiration for her son, a calm spirited and positive person, Diane is filled with joy and excitement because only she knows the many hurdles that had to be crossed for her son to arrive at this mark in life. Only she knows the many days and sleepless nights that had to be endured over the years. Only Diane knows the many prayers she prayed as she interceded on behalf of her son and family. Today, she looks at Brandon and notices a magnificent change. Today, she stares at her son and testifies that God hears and answers a mother's prayer.

Her son, a six-feet two inches tall young man intrigued by sports, who excels in track and field, a slim structured well-groomed teen who is admired by his peers, an intelligent handsome male revered by the younger students nearly threw his entire life away at an early age. He practically placed his future on a silver platter and handed it over to the enemy to do with it as he pleased. Most of the student-body was unaware of Brandon's secret past, how he had lived a life contrary to the morals and ethics taught by his mother, and how he found himself drifting deeper and deeper into a life of darkness and destruction that has claimed numerous sons and daughters of countless families. Brandon had shared his tainted life's story with a selective few that comprised the inner circle of his friends. Yet, today he stands with confidence and pride and freely communicates with others how he experienced adversities and overcame them.

Brandon's story

As an only child living with my mother and being raised by my grandmother and grandfather all things jelled together and everything was going well. But when I moved from the country to the city the change of environment had a negative effect on me.

I was not accustomed to the city lifestyle. I tried to adjust to the changes in my life and I attempted to make new friends but things moved a little too fast for me and I found myself getting deeper and deeper into trouble or trouble was getting deeper and deeper into me. More and more, guys that had darkened pasts, skewed views of life, corrupted impressions of others and defiled ways of living influenced me. Their ways became my ways. Their life became the life I lived. Their troubles became my problems. For nine years, my defiant thoughts and rebellious acts were inseparable from theirs. Until, one day my friends and I skipped school. One of them had a gun. We went to an open field and shot the firearm. Regrettably, the police caught us and I was detained in a correctional facility for one week. After experiencing the tragic and shocking events of seeing my mother cry during the days she visited and the sight of her tears at the legal proceedings, I decided to turn my life around. I knew that I was the cause of her pain. However, for the first time in my life, mother's pain became my heartache. I did not want to see her hurt that way again. I knew that she loved me but for some unknown reason I had not come to understand it. When the trial was over I told my mother it was time for me to make a new life for myself. It was then that my family agreed that the city was no place for me and that it would be best for us to relocate.

Diane's view of change

When Brandon was young I was a single mother, a student and a career woman. We lived with my parents. Later I met Keith and after dating for a period of time we decided to marry. Not only was marriage an enormous change for Brandon, the arrival of a baby sister would also play a great role in our new life. Because our family was increasing and I desired to care for my baby, for financial purposes, Keith and I decided to move to the city to be closer to his job. Immediately, following our move I noticed a change in Brandon's behavior. No longer was he that sweet innocent child. He became rebellious, disobedient and confrontational. Right away, I took measures to separate him from the friends he had associated with. I began to talk with him more on how to select his friends and how to identify people that try to hurt you or bring you down to their level. I prayed night and day for my son. Though I took precautionary measures, the counseling, the monitoring of his where-abouts and the praying continued for nine long and grueling years. Each time Brandon found himself in a precarious situation he broke my heart. Each dramatic episode caused me to become more exhausted and torn with pain; yet, I could not give up so I turned to God and prayed harder. Finally, Keith and I agreed that if Brandon was going to survive we needed to remove him from the existing lifestyle by relocating the family to the country.

That night I called my parents and asked if Brandon could stay with them until Keith and I sold our home. On this day I thank God for my parents because without hesitation they said yes and their acceptance of their grandson and my son into their home was the beginning of a one hundred and eighty degree turn around. They began to take him to church and got him involved in Sunday school. He also became more active in high school. It took at least one and a half years for my husband and me to sell our home and have our new home built in the country. Between that period I did not abandon Brandon. I drove to see him on the weekends and we spoke on the telephone during the weekdays. It hurt me not to see him each day or be in his company, but I was comforted in knowing our separation was temporary and for his benefit.

Moral Application: Diane Sweat: A mother must never stop talking with her children because children must feel free to be able to talk about all aspects of their lives. Always be a mother first and a friend second. Mothers should teach their children early how to set goals and how not to lose focus of their goal. We must teach our children how to distinguish people that seek to help from people who seek to hurt. We must show our children how to select friends with goals in life and how to be careful of the time they can waste in their life, because when they come to the realization that they have squandered their time it may be too late to correct their mistakes. We must teach our children to take Christ with them wherever they go. Most importantly, mothers, never give-up on your child regardless of how long or how painful your trial has been. Moreover, a mother must be willing to allow a child to experience punishment for their faults because when mothers continuously come to their rescue they will never stop their wrong doings and expect you to bail them out.

<u>Brandon:</u> Trouble is wherever you go. It is in the large cities and in the smaller cities. It's even in the country. Though the same types of people in the city are in the country, the greatest truth is God is everywhere and if you take Him with you wherever you go you can overcome trouble. A change of location can assist a person in turning their life around, but the greatest influence comes when a person chooses to place Christ first. Then an individual can develop a determination to do something positive in life. I decided to put Christ first and to stay in school. These were the best decisions I have made in my life.

Chapter Six
Single And Love'n It
Moral Strength In Recommitting

By Calveta Odom, Sr. Social Worker, MS

Have you ever played tug-of-war? In this game, you plant your feet into the earth, clinch both hands around the rope, stare your opponents in the eye and literally hold your stance for dear life, as the mediator drops the flag. You see, at 23, I distinctly remember in my mind, playing tug-of-war. I wanted to live a Christian life, but I knew there would be consequences. It would surely bring forth closure to a five-year relationship with my first and only love (*mind you, my only love at that time*). I knew our relationship would end, because my now, fiancé, had told me in no uncertain terms that if I continued to talk about committing my life to Jesus, there would be no more us. According to my fiancé, such a drastic life style change wouldn't be fair. And, I knew he was right. It would sorely dampen our love for going to clubs and dancing the night away, sharing a glass of wine, and engaging in activities only designed for married couples. What could I be thinking? I would end a relationship with a man, whom I desperately loved, and who said that he loved me, too, and indeed had recently placed a beautiful diamond ring on my finger. Our marriage plans however, were interrupted when his career took him overseas. Shortly, after his departure, I could no longer deny the longing in my heart to say, yes. Yes, Lord, I will live for you. I will love you and serve you all the days of my life. I finally felt free and my heart was at peace. No more tug-of-war plunged my mind. I needed strength and I set forth to learn scriptures that helped me deal with my situation. I encountered two scriptures soon after confessing Christ as my Savior that helped me to understand, that living single afforded us a wonderful opportunity to devote ourselves to God's work. 1 Corinthians 7:34 NLT, *In the same way, a woman who is no longer married or has never been married can be more devoted to the Lord in body and in spirit, while the married woman must be concerned about her earthly responsibilities and how to please her husband.* And Philippians 4:11(KJV) *Not that I speak in respect of want, for I have learned, in whatsoever state I am, therewith to be content.* I believe this next scripture helped me to become stronger and stronger in my Christian walk, almost like a female incredible Hulk, but in a good way. 2 Corinthians 6:14 (KJV), says *Be ye not unequally yoked together with unbelievers: for what fellowship hath righteousness with unrighteousness? and what communion hath light with darkness?* Yes, our relationship did end, but not quite as I envisioned. I did return my engagement ring, and we were officially unengaged. Yet, he continued to ask me to marry him, in fact, he asked me twice within a two year span. Each time, I responded with, but the bible says*, Be ye not unequally yoked with unbelievers.*

As I sought to trust God, with all my heart, and to seek His will, (God's will is His Word and His Word is His will). I honored God in my Christian walk. I presented my body holy before God and my former fiancé. I was single, happy, and content. As I embraced my decision to remain single, I grew and matured in the ways of God. I was living single and love'n it. So can you.

A Tidbit of My Life Today

My former fiancé told me I would never have anyone who would treat me like he did, nor offer me the financial means like he could. Well, I only boast in Christ Jesus, the author and finisher of my faith, that those words of prophecy did not come true. In fact, my husband of 15 years, *(I was single for five years)* whom I am desperately loving more and more each day has more than provided for my financial needs, more than made me feel beautiful in his eyes and on top of that ladies, I even got a larger diamond ring the second time around! Praise God from whom all blessings flow! We also have two beautiful children.

If you can image God's hands interlocked and then your hand interlocked just underneath His, then you can envision how I viewed marriage. I had to know that my relationship was pleasing to the Lord. I didn't just pursue an answer from the Lord myself. However, after diligently seeking the Lord, I wanted covering. I was on a mission. I knew my father wanted the best for me (and all of his eight daughters) so I had to have my father's blessings. If not,

I knew I could not marry this man. My father and mother gave me their blessings. Believe me, I also had the blessings of my pastor, and the Bishop.

I had a special request for my mate that I had only shared with the Lord. There was a special prayer and request that I had shared "only" with the Lord regarding my husband to be. And that was, that he would love the Lord more than me. I believed if this was so, I could trust him to treat me right.

When I met my husband, the first time he came to visit me, he said these words… I told the Lord that whoever my wife would be, I wanted her to love the Lord more than me, because I believe, I could then trust her to treat me right.

As you can image I almost tripped over my feet standing still. Not really. But, know what I was thinking, maybe I'm about to experience a detour in my life's plans. Remember, three weeks had only passed since beseeching the Lord for three more years of singled bliss. I had already made plans to start traveling (to visit a Bible College in Texas), and I felt mission fieldwork would soon follow.

Chapter Seven
Marriage
The Morality Of Preserving The Sanctity Of Marriage

A Pastoral Letter: To the Churches of the Connecticut Conference of the United Church of Christ

October 10, 2003

Dear Pastors, Elders, Sisters and Brothers in Christ;

It is with great urgency and a passion for the spiritual integrity and well being of our churches that I am writing to you. As the indigenous church of New England, our witness to the truth of God's word and gospel of our Lord Jesus Christ is critical.

In just a few days your delegates to the Connecticut Conference autumn meeting will be considering "A Resolution in Support of Legal Marriage for Same-Sex Couples" submitted by the First Church of Christ, Congregational, Middletown, CT.

If you approve such a resolution it will be the first official setting of the United Church of Christ in which such a resolution will be formally adopted. It is important that we all consider the realities regarding the sanctity of marriage before such an action is discussed.

God, very clearly and emphatically, gave us marriage as a gift between a man and a woman. It is the first covenant out of which all other covenants find their origin. The essential nature of marriage, *"a man shall leave his father and mother and be united to his wife and they will become one flesh"* is unambiguous (Genesis 2:24). In fact the relationship between man and woman is the very context in which humanity enjoys God's creation blessing. When *"God blessed them and said to them, 'Be fruitful and increase in number; fill the earth and subdue it"* (Genesis 1:28), He was unequivocal.

Jesus speaks in powerful affirmation of this truth. *" 'Haven't you read,' he replied, 'that at the beginning the Creator "made them male and female," and said, "For this reason a man will leave his father and mother and be united to his wife, and the two will become one flesh"? So they are no longer two but one. Therefore what God has joined together, let man not separate.' "* (Matthew 19:4-6).

This reality is reflective of the very character of God himself in his relationship to us. "*Husbands, love your wives as Christ loved the church and gave himself up for her to make her holy, cleansing her by the washing with water through the word, and to present her to himself as a radiant church, without stain or wrinkle or any other blemish, but holy and blameless. In this same way, husbands ought to love their wives as their own bodies. He who loves his wife loves himself.... 'For this reason a man will leave his father and mother and be united to his wife, and the two will become one flesh.' This is a profound mystery – but I am talking about Christ and the church.*" (Ephesians 5:25)

The truth is not vague or confusing. It is at the core of our faith, not the periphery. Marriage is marriage. It is an ordained reality in the natural moral order that supercedes all humanly devised agencies and institutions such as governments and religious organizations. The effort to humanly redefine marriage by political activism, votes, and persuasion is a vain exercise in idolatry. Such actions only serve to degrade the credibility of those governments and organizations that participate. If the citizens of Connecticut determined that your symbolic Oak Tree was exclusive and mobilized a vote to include all pine trees in the definition of what it meant to be an oak, it would be equally meaningless.

The resolution presents a very weak and isogetical Biblical defense. The love of Jesus in his every expression is transformational. He speaks to the issue of self-discovery and self-actualization that would enable us to rationalize our sin in a definitive manner. "*...and anyone who does not take up his cross and follow me is not worthy of me. Whoever finds his life will lose it, and whoever loses his life for my sake will find it." (Matthew 10: 38, 39) "If anyone would come after me, he must deny himself and take up his cross and follow me. For whoever wants to save his life will lose it, but whoever loses his life for me will find it.*" (Matthew 16:24)

Jesus speaks clearly to the notion that he has overturned the Old Testament law when he warns us, *"Do not think that I have come to abolish the Law or the Prophets; I have not come to abolish them but to fulfill them. I tell you the truth, until heaven and earth disappear, not the smallest letter, not the least stroke of the pen, will be any means disappear for the Law until everything is accomplished."* (Matthew 5:18)

The assumption that the statements in Leviticus belong to some "Purity code" along with detailed dress instructions to the priesthood is incorrect. Leviticus chapters 18 through 20 in which the prohibition against sex outside of marriage is described in detail, including the prohibition against same gender relations, is clearly a moral code for all the people. The sections begin with *"The Lord said to Moses, 'speak to the Israelites and say to them: I am the Lord your God'."* The introduction verses make clear three times that the choice is between the cultural values of the open and affirming societies of Canaan and Egypt and *"I am the Lord your God. Keep my decrees and laws, for the man who obeys them will live by them. I am the Lord."* (Leviticus 18:1-5)

This teaching is paralleled in Romans 1:18-32, which is a vivid description of the paradigm shift in our own culture. Every teenager in my classes who reads this passage without additional commentary immediately exclaims, "This is what is happening today in our society."

Welcome one another from every lifestyle, situation or condition with the transforming love of Jesus Christ is a primary aspect of our mission. We must recognize within ourselves the barriers we erect in our own attitudes and prejudices that make our churches exclusive. Yet this does not relate in any way to redefining what God revealed in His Word. It does not change the mandate of the gospel for repentance and transformation from sin. It certainly has no connection whatever with any attempt to redefine such intrinsic aspects of the natural moral order as marriage.

If the resolution submitted by the Middletown church should find acceptance it will violate the essential "united and uniting" mandate of the United Church of Christ. It has the liability of placing the Connecticut Conference in a state of apostasy, in which it would have separated itself from the orthodox consensus of Christianity. It would be an act of schism that will add to the fragmentation and dissolution of the United Church of Christ. It would set the Conference apart from united interdenominational body of churches in your state. Separation whether it happens on the right or the left does not honor the body.

We urge you to honor Jesus Christ as Lord in this decision and to reject this overture to legitimize the licentious practice of our self-indulgent culture.

Yours in the Grace of our Lord Jesus Christ,

David Runnion-Bareford
Executive Director
Biblical Witness Fellowship

Carl L. Sweat, Jr., D. Min.

Chapter Eight
My Decision To Divorce
Moral Strengthening For Divorce

Anonymous Writer:

First I would like to thank Pastor Sweat for believing that I had a story to share and then for continuing to push me to share the story. I would like for my identity to be withheld so that I am free to share my story in its fullness and also to protect those involved.

I married at a fairly early age in my life believing that the vows made were till death us do part. My reasons for marrying included love but it also was an escape mechanism. I wanted to leave home. I wanted to share my life with someone who cared. I wanted to establish my own family and shower them with all the love and affections within my power. My grandparents raised me and to this day I credit my ability to love and give of myself to my grandmother who demonstrated everyday what true love and forgiveness was really about.

Today I look back and try to figure out what went wrong, where did I fail, what could I have done differently to save my marriage. I tried doing the little simple things to make my spouse happy but it seemed as if that was not enough. I always tried to serve hot meals regardless to the time, day or night. I tried to keep our home neat and clean. I occasionally purchased little gifts to say "I Love You" but for some reason the relationship continued to deteriorate and became physically abusive. We tried counseling, I tried counseling but it seemed as if nothing helped. For a week or two we would be ok and I really thought it would work. Then we were back to our fighting and fussing mode all over again. It was a constant on and off situation.

I have to give my pastor at that time credit for being a true man of God and for not allowing man to sway him one way or another. Whenever we or I went for counseling he would listen then talk with us and would always close with a prayer and say, "Do what you have too". Sometimes I would ask, "Do you think I should leave or I can't take anymore" and his reply would still be "Do what you have to, to protect yourself". Never, not one time did he say leave or it's time to leave. I am ever grateful to this day, for you see only I could make that decision. Little did I know that once that decision was made that what I thought was hell was only a small sample of the hell to come. Friends, family, co-workers and yes even the church turned their backs on me.

You say the church, how could the church possibly turn against you? Well the church is made up of the people and when one allows, permits and sanctions the actions of those within its body to cause harm or hurt to another, then we as the church have turned against that person. Some examples of how cold and cruel church people were: Whispering in small groups when one is around, getting up and move from the pew when one sits down, excluding you from activities, refusing to speak or shake your hand and the list goes on. Were their actions caused by fear? Did I pose a threat because I was separated or divorced? Is it that you don't really know what to say or do around me anymore?

Divorce is a grievous and painful experience. It affects all involved: the children, parents, friends and yes, even the church. Our children act out or withdraw themselves in a little shell, parents blame each other for what is going on, friends sometimes side with one or the other and create a whole new set of problems and our church turns its back for now, according to its doctrine we have sinned. I ask of you what happened to forgiveness, what happened to repentance. Thank God for His Grace and Mercy.

It is my belief and interpretation of the Holy Word that Christ meant for marriage to be a oneness, a lifetime commitment and it is that belief and others expectations that almost destroyed me. When I made the decision to divorce I had no idea that my life would change forever. You become a hermit, not by choice but by others actions towards you. I still remember how I would search the scriptures, listen to others quote their interpretations; how I would pray and question God-"Why me". I still wonder what happens to the little things in life that can make or break us. What happens to the touch, the smile or a simple whisper "I love you" or "I'm sorry".

When I look back and reflect upon all that I've been through and the time in my life that divorce occurred, I say "Thank You Lord", for I know without a shadow of a doubt that if all of this had occurred in the last 5 years I would be dead. In today's society there seems to be no room for forgiveness or no respect for one's life. I felt when my marriage was falling apart that truly my spouse wanted me dead, but I know that people today no longer value a life. Spouses have become more violent and will destroy the entire family just to get even.

I've been there, I know what it feels like to be alone, no where to run to, no one to talk to, I know what its like to want your spouse dead or to take one's own life just to rid one's self of the pain. Because of my divorce my children suffered, my spouse suffered and I suffered and even though I have found peace within, I still see the effects on my children. They don't trust fully, they will never take the abuse that I took and they tend to avoid close relationships.

I believe God allowed me to pass this way to help another find their way. I constantly counsel and share my story with others not because I want to but because I'm asked. God wants me to assure them that when they think everyone has deserted them that He is still there caring for each of us. If my life's story will help them see that if they trust and don't give up, God will see us through. It may not be what we want or when we want it but He's still there proving His love over and over again. Now some would say if I had gone through all that drama I wouldn't ever love anybody again. Well I said the same thing but it was my pastor who again through God's divine wisdom said "Close the door, lock it if you must, but don't throw away the key. There will come a time when your heart has mended and your soul is right that you will want to unlock the door and live again.

Those words meant nothing to me for more than 5 years. Then something happened. I began to smile again; I began to feel alive again. I wanted to share my love with someone again. No, it didn't happen overnight and yes I was afraid but I prayed and asked God for guidance. All my old fears returned: Am I causing this individual to commit adultery if he marries me, Am I fit to be his wife, Do I have anything to offer and the list goes on. Divorce had stripped me of my faith, my trust, and my belief in my self. My self-esteem was zero. My fear of how others perceived me had caused me to isolate myself from society. Then one day while looking in the sky I saw God's sign, I saw His rainbow, I saw His promise. I was completely surrounded by His love. I'm thankful and blessed that I found someone who believes in me for who I am, not who they want me to be or who others might think I am. We will never be able to please everybody but if we please God and each other then we will make it.

The road to recovery hadn't been easy but it's been worth it. To be able to help someone else along on this journey, to put a smile on someone's face, to show you care. Yes it's worth it. To others who have gone through divorce or those who may be considering it I can't say what's right or what's wrong for you. Only you can make that decision. I can say however, don't let others put you or your spouse down. It's a journey that only you and God can take together and survive. You may take your journey alone, but if you want to succeed, then pray and let God guide you on your journey. He won't talk about you, He won't leave you alone and yes even if you make a mistake, He'll be right there to forgive you. I know this from experience and not only will He forgive you but He'll remove the hurt, the anger, the hate, and the pain. He'll restore you unto Him and fill you with His Divine Love; that love that gives and gives and keeps on giving.

Yes, I still believe that marriage is meant to be a oneness, a lifetime commitment. What is that lifetime? It may vary. Each individual's life is unique.

Carl L. Sweat, Jr., D. Min.

Chapter Nine
Abusive Relationships
Moral Strength For Spousal Abuse Victims

By City Council Member and Deaconess Joan K. Carter, M.S: Member of Laurel Hill UCC

God is our refuge so faith and submission become the basis for our strength even in the midst of our troubled times. The Almighty is there to be the Light to lead us in the right direction as we travail situations which seem to overwhelm, frighten or limit our clear thinking. Some times we find ourselves in relationships gone badly.

Abusive Relationships is a subject that I know of primarily through my many years in the field of social work. What has been consistent for me in working with people who are in abusive relationships is that theses relationships do not discriminate. They are a part of every social group. The potential for abuse in a relationship however, tends to increase in the lives of those who are in the throws of substance abuse, extreme poverty, political and social disenfranchisement and when limited opportunities are a regular consideration in one's life. The shear grind of life often times diminishes one's strength and skill to choose what is best for oneself.

From a theoretical and academic sense, I am familiar with the subject of abusive relationships because of the need to study its causes, symptoms, the course it takes and behaviors associated with an abusive relationship. I am also familiar with the resources which are available to prevent, reduce or eliminate this destructive behavior in ones life.

Even with this background of professional acumen, I found myself, on more than one occasion, in the midst of a potentially abusive relationship. How does that happen! In short, excuses about my own behavior and the behavior of the other person. Frequently we tend to diminish the clues and make excuses in the name of love, to rationalize away all of our good senses. While relationships tend to capture a great deal of our being, real life continues to happen. We get hurt and bruised by life. Things don't go our way, we get out of sync with God's direction, and we lean to our OWN understanding. The next thing you know the devil has his way and abuse may be the insidious road that leads us on a journey that can be extremely harmful.

When one finds him/herself in something called an abusive relationship, the relationship which must precede the human relationship is that of oneness with God so that we may draw upon Him as the head of our lives. After all, He forgives us before we even forgive ourselves. There is HOPE!

Within our spiritual realm, LOVE, GRACE and FORGIVENESS are the promises that bring us the freedom to set the necessary boundaries for healthy relationships to thrive.

In the *absence* of the spiritual realm and lacking the skills to protect your self from harmful relationships, choices are made which allow another person's perceived love to direct our behavior and responses. When another person becomes more important in your life than God who promises that you are made whole and in his image, you are likely to slip into the area of abuse in your intimate relationship.

As an example, in most healthy relationships, two people negotiate and agree on what will work for them. The slippery slop to abuse occurs when the mate, as proof of his/her love for you demonstrates controlling tendencies, i.e. suspicious about your friends and acquaintances, the monitoring of your time away from home or your mate increases his/her tendencies to make decisions about what you are to wear and the like.

When discussing abusive relationships one wonders, "Is there anything redeeming about an abusive relationship?" The root word for abusive is *abuse*. In its most simple form it means to maltreat. The root word for relationship is *relate*. In its simple form it means to connect emotionally with another person. Putting those two things together, we are maltreated by someone to whom you are connected to emotionally. What betrayal!

Let us go further. Imagine that the abuser is the primary source of your support for finances, housing or the parent to your children. Beside that, what would happen to you if you were alone? You have always heard that, "a half of a man is better than no man at all", or a man might wonder, "who would take care of these children if not her"? What is one to do?

There are examples of challenging relationships between men and women in the Holy Bible. You decide, through the Holy Spirit, if the relationships herein described were abusive. Perhaps we could talk about Leah, Jacob's first wife as described in Genesis, Chapters 29 and 30. Do we perceive that that was an abusive relationship? Leah is married to a man who does not love her. He loves her sister! She knows it, he knows it, and her father knows it. Divorce is not an option in this story due to the custom of the day. Leah is the *object* of Jacob's affection and his wife. Leah has a child, a boy, and this, she believes will make the difference. He will now know that she loves him. He will now love her. Leah did all she could to get Jacob's attention. She perhaps looked her best at all times, cooked the best meals, her house was spotless, and the children were well behaved. We know the outcome of Leah's life with Jacob. Was that an abusive relationship? Read the Bible with God's guidance in your heart to see His plan and purpose for this situation. Leah, like us is one of God's children and we don't often know of His greater plan for us.

Life, like abuse is not so simple and none of us can say what we would do or not do about it. We must continue to pray about our life and allow God to give us the strength to endure. There are no easy answers.

For another example, we again look to Genesis. In chapter 38: 1-30 the story of Judah and Tamar is anchored in the woman again being manipulated by the men in her life. Judah is the son of Leah and Jacob. Judah's oldest son was Er. Judah arranged for the attractive Tamar to marry Er. Er was evil to his wife, as stated in the Bible and God saw fit to kill him. Judah then arranged for another son Onan to marry Tamar as required in the Jewish tradition. This way, the oldest son Er would have descendants. Because Onan knew the children could not be claimed as his own, he did not allow his sperm to enter Tamar doing intercourse. This displeased the Lord and God killed Onan too. Judah then sent Tamar back to her own father until Judah's youngest son could grow up to impregnate her. The youngest son finally grew to adulthood and Tamar knew that Judah had not arranged for them to be together. Tamar then creates a way to become pregnant. She understands that Judah is coming to her town. She covers her face with a veil and sits down at the entrance to the town and pretends to be a prostitute to her father-in-law. He comes upon her and asked how much she would take to give her body to him. They negotiated a price but Tamar is shrewd. She said she would take his staff, seal and cord as a pledge until he delivered the goat they agreed upon as payment. When Judah sent his man servant to deliver the goat, no one could find this nameless woman. About three months later, Judah got word from the community where Tamar lived that she was acting like a whore. She was now pregnant and no one knew who the father was. When Judah sent his men to have her burned at the stake, she sent word to her father-in-law that "I am pregnant by the man who owns these things. Look at them and see whose they are; this seal and its cord and walking stick." Judah was caught! What he had done in the dark had come to light.

In similar terms today, a promise is given by the man in your life whom you believe will honor you, whether through marriage, engagement or a long term intimate relationship. You find out in the long run that you have become dispensable. The promise is broken. You no longer fit into his plan. How does being "sent away" or ignored by him feel. How is this situation abusive? Betrayal again comes to mind.

The implication of this topic to men and women of today is that if you ask God for deliverance from this situation, John 8:36 tells us, that He will not forsake us or leave us alone. God also has other words for us to under gird us and protect us from harm. In second Corinthian, 8:11 the Bible tells us that Love is patient, love is kind. Love is....God. With God's love and our self love, we set boundaries for our bodies, mind and spirit as a reminder to those who present themselves to us as potential mates that we are worthy of good treatment or honor. These individuals will respect us because we respect ourselves.

To prevent an abusive relationship in your life, we will need to continuously work on ourselves. This is not to suggest that abusive relationships are our fault. Not at all! It merely suggests that we, through God have the capacity to be careful about how we present ourselves to others. During playful time with a love interest, do we set boundaries such as not accepting punching or hitting ever? Finally, do we pay attention to the behavior and verbal comments of others while in our presence? Do we politely challenge men who speak disrespectfully of women or challenge women who speak disrespectfully of men in our presence? Do we leave the gathering as a signal that we do not concur with certain behaviors? These are simple yet effective ways of assuring that an abusive relationship is not in your future. If you are already in a relationship that is veering in the wrong direction, there is time to escape this relationship before you get too deeply involved. Quite frequently, as earlier stated, the abusive person has revealed him/herself to us on more than one occasion through behaviors that we may have chosen to ignore or just go along with believing that the other person may have treated others a certain way but would never do the same to us.

When you are involved in an abusive relationship, the first step following the awareness of your situation through Jesus Christ is to then seek professional assistance through your minister or some other reputable outside resource. In Virginia you may call the Family Violence and Sexual Assault HOT LINE at 1.800.838.8238

Remember, you cannot change the abuser but you can act to protect yourself by prayerfully thinking and planning ahead.

Chapter Ten
Love Destroyed And Regained
Moral Strength For Rape Victims

By Minister Jocelyn Morant: Associate Minister of The Church of Jesus in Hampton, VA

I am a mother of seven, a public school teacher, a thirty-seven year church organist and now an associate minister at The Church of Jesus in Hampton, VA. I am a 1977 graduate of Norfolk State University. I also have done master's work in school administration as well. However, I am happy about the seven lives God entrusted to me to nurture and direct with His guidance. It is an honor to write on moral strengthening because I have been a victim of rape and molestation during my lifetime, to include times during the years of my being in the Church. Had God not been such an important part of my life, I just do not know what could have happened to me.

First of all, let us define rape. The Random House Dictionary of the English language, second Edition, unabridged defines rape as the unlawful compelling of a woman through physical force or duress to have sexual intercourse. One thing I can say is this; it is a terrible and dangerous thing to be the object of someone else's immoral lust or sexual gratification. Most people do not even know what is going on until the perpetrator has already completed the attack. This can even be confirmed in scripture.

Tamar's Story

King David had a son named Absalom and one named Amnon. Absalom had a sister named Tamar. The brother, Amnon fell in love with Tamar and lusted after her until he was vexed and sick. One of his friends (cousin actually) named Jonadab came up with a plot to rape Tamar. Jonadab told him to lie down and make himself sick so that when his father, David came to him, he was to request that Tamar could come and feed him so he could get better. At this point David did not know what Amnon had plotted. This reminds me so much of what I went through during much of my childhood years because I had older parents who did not quite understand what was meant by rape or being molested. However, this is similar to the subtle way my relative did me as well and then threatened me if I did not keep it to myself.

To get into the story in scripture, Tamar went to Amnon's as her father David had told her. It was there that she found out how Amnon felt and what he desired to do to her. Tamar tried to remind him that this was terrible evil for an Israelite to do, but he forced himself upon her causing great shame to be upon her. Amnon had broken the Law of Moses then after he did this evil, he began to hate her more than the supposed loved he had for her in the beginning. Tamar, because of her shame hid herself and rent her clothes and put ashes upon her head and the Bible says she remained desolate in her brother Absalom's house.

King David got wind of what had happened and instead of following the Levitical (Lev. 20:17) solution (death) for what had occurred, David brushed it off and did nothing because he loved Amnon. This angered Absalom so he set out to take matters into his own hands by plotting to kill Amnon. Two years later, Absalom used David for his purpose just as Amnon had done to get to Tamar. Absalom loved his sister and he was determined to destroy Amnon for what he did to Tamar, his sister. Absalom's plan to use his servants to kill Amnon while he was drinking and making merry worked. When the king found out about Amnon's murder, Absalom flees. King David's pride would not allow him to accept Absalom back, even though he mourned for him greatly.

Joab, one of David's servants knew how much the king missed Absalom so he plotted to reconcile them using Tekoah, who was a wise woman in their province. Joab told her what to tell the king, but he realized that Joab had put her up to the plot. King David eventually sends for Absalom to return, however, they did not see each other for over two years until Absalom sent for Joab so he could go to the king and tell him that it would have been better for him if he stayed in Geshur with his grandfather, at least they were talking and being family. After Joab told David what Absalom had said, King David sent for Absalom and they were reconciled but Absalom never forgot how David had done him and Tamar.

If David had only done what the law required as stated in Leviticus 20:17, David would have only lost one of his sons, but because of his disobedience in handling the matter, he lost both of his sons in reality. More than likely, Absalom would not have felt he had to be so rebellious and distrustful of his father if he had seen him execute the required judgment for the evil act that Amnon had done against Tamar. Here we can see how sin gone unpunished can cause love to be destroyed. However, the Holy Spirit is able to help us to regain our ability to love without dissimilation even after someone has terribly wronged you.

My Story

I had four of my children as a result of rape. At first, for a while, I could not see why these things were happening to me. God has now restored the love I could have lost towards those who trespassed against my person. The wonderful thing is to see how God has taken these same people and filled them with His spirit just as He did me. I have been able to understand and know that God is Sovereign and can use whom he pleases to complete His plan. Most children of God do not actually realize what they say to God when they say, "you can use me how you wish, I'm yours"! I know that I did not at first. Sure, what was done to me was lawfully as well as morally and ethically wrong. This is why having the Holy Spirit is so important because, it will help you to see others as God sees them. He loves everyone no matter what they've done and as with all of us the only thing in our lives that makes us worth anything is that Jesus has come into our lives and is changing us daily through His word and spirit. After all, that's what everyone needs to have make a difference in our own and other lives' around us.

When we learn more about Christ we learn more concerning our relationships and us. When we learn to forgive then we learn that Christ can take our worst experiences and utilize them to strengthen us. They become the parts of our lives that make us whole. They are incorporated and not dispelled from life because those same horrid problems now become the topics and reflections of God's love and strength.

Carl L. Sweat, Jr., D. Min.

Chapter Eleven
Rape In The City
Moral Strength For Rape Victims

By Minister Slater Matthews, Jr.: Senior Associate Minister at Miracle Temple Baptist Church.

In an editorial titled "Justice Denied" District Attorney Bill Fitzpatrick was noted as being one of the toughest criminal attorneys. He prided himself on his low tolerance and his success record within the Division of Criminal Justice revealed it. However, Melissa could convey otherwise.

Late one evening April 9th, 2001 Melissa was at a house party in Syracuse. That night shortly after she had lain on a bed in the house because she had too much to drink, an assailant raped her and violently beat her. It took the Syracuse police over ten months to locate and apprehend the rapist. Richard Lodman was no stranger to the police.

Because Melissa did not yell for help, fight back or put up a struggle for her safety, the D.A. Gary Dawson did not charge Lodman with a felony, first-degree rape. Instead he charged him with a misdemeanor, sexual misconduct. With regret, Melissa agreed to the charge because Dawson promised her that Lodman's jail time would run consecutively with a previous violation. In the end she was left feeling she was lied to. The city judge's verdict was against consecutive detainment. He ruled that the defendant serve only ten months in jail. Melissa, her parents and friends, and the citizens of Onondage County wanted to know, where was the man that prided himself on being tough on crime when this case took place? How could someone's immoral decision that is devised to hurt another person go virtually unpunished?

Popular opinion today tends to assume that cities by nature offer a lower quality of life than do suburbs, small towns or rural areas. In fact some people have made getting out of the city a goal of their lives. But the Bible does not endorse the idea that cities are inherently evil, or that life is necessarily better away from the urban landscape.

Actually scripture seems to hold cities to a higher standard of justice and morality than rural areas. For example, the Old Testament law held that if a woman was raped in the country, the man who raped her was liable for death according to (Deuteronomy 22:25-27). [25]But if out in the country a man happens to meet a girl pledged to be married and rapes her, only the man who has done this shall die. [26]Do nothing to the girl; she has committed no sin deserving death. This case is like that of someone who attacks and murders his neighbor. [27]For the man found the girl out in the country, and though the betrothed girl screamed, there was no one to rescue her. It appears that the man only shall die if the violation (rape) takes place in the countryside because it is presumed that the woman was forced against her will.

Rape in the City

But if a woman was raped in the city, she, too was liable (Deuteronomy 22:23-24). [23]If a damsel that is a virgin be betrothed unto an husband, and a man find her in the city, and lie with her. [24]Then ye shall bring them both out unto the gate of the city, and ye shall stone them with stones that they die; the damsel, because she cried not, being in the city; and the man, because he hath humbled his neighbor's wife: so thou shalt put away immorality from among you.

The logic behind the seeming double standard was based on the assumption that a woman in the city must have consented to the sexual act since she could have called for help. In the city with neighbors all around, such a call was expected to be heard and people were to respond to a cry for help. The law of rape assumed that city neighbors were beneficial and responsive. They were to stand up for the law of God. The standards of physical purity were much higher in Israel than among the neighboring people. Canaanite worship involved prostitution and sensuality.

In the Hebrew code more was expected of women than of men, and the penalties exacted of women were correspondingly more severe.

The women were regarded as property in whom, first the father and then the husband held a right. Regarding any common case of abuse or violation of chastity, the man had to only pay a fine to the woman's father. Nevertheless, over a period of time women have gained a self-identity and achieved certain rights. Currently, the law reflects a measure of reverence for their dignity. However, some questions continue to exist. Are we standing up for godly ways where we live and work? Are we good and godly neighbors to people around us when they call out for help, protection, and justice?

The truth of this matter is, whether we live in a highly populated metropolitan area or a quiet town, God wants us to fill that place with His presence. He wants us to do something about evil, not just walk away and let it destroy people whom He loves.

Moral Application: Unbridled sexual passion or personal pleasure makes a good slave but a poor master. When men and women focus primarily on self-gratification, the results can be destructive, not only for us, but also the people around us (Titus 3:3). Granted, biological needs such as food, sex, and sleep is important. But when we allow these needs to dictate or control our lives, they tend to become vicious addictions that destroy us. The Song of Solomon give words of wisdom "Do not stir up, nor waken love until it pleases" (Solomon 2:7, 3:5, 8:4) the message seems to be to wait! Like a free-spirited horse, sexual passion can be powerful and beautiful, but to keep it from running away it needs to be fenced in by commitment, discipline, and service toward one's mate. Our sexuality is not our own; it is a gift from God to be treasured and used for His glory.

Chapter Twelve
Abduction Of A Part Of Me
Standing Morally Against Pornography

By Minister Gloria Matthews: Associate Minister of Miracle Temple Baptist Church.

Saturday, March 14, 1998, six-year-old Carrie was playing with her puppy Jazzman in the back yard while her mother washed clothes inside. Around 9:30 am. Janette Rummburg paused from her washing to go outside and check on her only child, only to discover that Carrie had been abducted. Hysterically, she dialed the emergency number 911 to report that her child was missing. She then contacted her husband at work.

Three years had passed and the detectives had no clear leads on the case. But in September of 2001, Steven and Janette received a call from one of the detectives that was handling Carrie's file. He informed them that photos of a girl that appeared to be Carrie were found on a pornographic web sight and the evidence led them to a known pedophile that was presently in their custody and being interrogated. After obtaining a warrant, the detectives along with the police searched the suspect's home. They found more pornographic pictures of children; some of the pictures were of Carrie. They also found nudity videos recorded of Carrie and many children previously reported missing.

Though the man was prosecuted for numerous crimes, the case was touchier on the Rummburg family because they never found Carrie nor any of the other children that were identified on the photos and videos collected from the man's home. In the court room Janette said, "This man abducted a piece of me and I will never be whole again. He abducted a piece of my family and it will never be complete. A piece of us will always be missing." Steven's testimony consisted of the following statement: "Have you seen these persons? Have you seen this child?" Our country is inundated with fliers, posters, and pictures on the back of milk cartons all because of the pornographic addictions of men and women."

The prosecutor called on his special witness. She was a well-noted social behaviorist and psychologist. Her statements were as follow: Sex alone is not pornography. Pornography, as defined by today's social culture, is something or anything deemed "obscene" or offensive to moral decency and moral modesty. In less than three decades pornography has grown into a giant immoral industry worth 12 to 13 billion dollars.

Yet, the basic objection against pornography that continues to be retained within the American culture is the fact that it presents sex divorced from love, affection, and moral responsibility. Also, pornography demoralizes and devalues people by objectifying human beings. Psychologist perceives that pornographic material influences many people and projects stimulating images that reduce individuals to lower levels of animalistic behavior.

Sociologist believes that one of the greatest and foundational protest against pornography is linked to religion. Cultural beliefs and moral practices are connected and rooted in the fundamental conceptions of religious principle. Communities of faith view the human body as a temple and sex as a God given gift that is confined to the bonds on marriage. Thus, they contend against pornography because is violates the sanctity or relationships and privacy intimacy.

Dr. Vuctir B. Cline in his report concerning the effects of pornography in every case found that men and women became hooked on sex related telephone conversations. He used for his study the dial- a-porn sex line and found that it had an addicting effect on people. Police statistics indicate that an increasing number of young people have an addiction to pornography, more teens are becoming addicted to sexual stimulating drugs, and the youth that are being convicted of sex related crimes have pornographic addictions.

She closed her comments by saying pornography is a growing problem in various societies and once a person becomes addicted or influenced by it they must seek rehabilitation and we must do all we can to help them.

Chapter Thirteen
A Man That Broke Color Barriers
Morals Against Discrimination

By Luther White: Deacon of Laurel Hill UCC

In 1953 at the age of 21 years old, I received a letter from the United States Government that started with the word "Greetings". As I continued to read the letter I discovered that day that I was drafted to fight in the Korean War. I left my parents and the farm to go to Camp Braking Ridge in Kentucky for basic training. From there I was shipped off to Korea. When I arrived at Korea, low and behold, both countries had agreed to a ceasefire and one week later the war was over.

While I was there all the men were mixed together, the Hawaiians, Philippines, Koreans, Turkish, and Whites. As the months went by I became accustomed with being among and living with a mixed race of people. For eleven months, we did all things together. We talked, we showered, and we ate, and became close friends. It was as if race, discrimination, or prejudice never existed. War had broken the color barrier.

Hawaii was the home of the 25th division, which was my battalion. I was transported there and remained there for two years and a few months. While I served the military in Hawaii no segregation existed among the natives or among military men. The racial problem had escaped me until I left Hawaii in 1955 and arrived back in the states at Fort Mead, Maryland.

Fort Mead, Maryland was the Army's debriefing discharge location. It was the last stop that I would see many of my buddies. After we were discharged out of the military, we all got on different buses headed to our own hometowns. I got on the bus headed to Richmond VA. God fixed it so that when I got to the Richmond bus stop many of my buddies that trained with me during basic training were getting off various buses. They remembered me and I remembered them. Though we served in the war, we had not seen one another since our basic training. Some had served in France, some had served in Germany, and some had served several places.

Return Of The Racial Problem

We all went inside the Greyhound bus station to get our tickets so that we could catch our different buses home. One of the guys said let's have dinner together before we catch our bus home and we all agreed. We went into the restaurant, sat together and ordered our food. The waitress brought back my buddies' food but I was still waiting. We waited awhile and one said say grace so that we could eat. Another said, "No, we'll say grace when White gets his food. He called the waitress over and said our friend's food has not been served. The waitress said he would not get his food here. He has to go around to the black section. There he could get his food. Then it hit me, I didn't recognize it but I was the only black in my group and I was sitting with them in the white section of the restaurant. It did not dawn on my buddies. But after her words, we discovered we were back in America.

After serving my country, after risking my life for the protection of all men I returned back to a place that devalued me and segregated me because of the color of my skin. The five white guys that were sitting with me got angry. They refused to eat or pay for their food. They cursed and fussed at the waitress, manager, and some of the people. They threatened to throw their food at the manager for not serving me. The manager said, "I didn't make the rules." If you want to change them, go to Congress. Then he called the police. That's when I said, "Look I do not want to be the cause of any problem." I got up and went around to the other side. Low and behold, the section was filled with black people, soldiers and civilians. I got my food, set at a table, and ate. When I had finished my food, I walked out of the restaurant, sat on the bench and waited until the bus bound for Suffolk, VA arrived.

Becoming The First Black Bus Driver

After living in Connecticut and working for Pratt Whitney Aircraft for a few years, my wife and I returned to Suffolk, VA. I gained employment as a truck driver for the Suffolk Lumber Company. For five months, I submitted many applications for other employment but no one had contacted me to offer me a job. Yet, something began to happen in Suffolk that turned things around for me. The bus boycotts that were taking place in Alabama and Georgia caught hold in Suffolk. The blacks in Suffolk said they were not going to ride any city buses until Suffolk hired a black bus driver. One day, Mr. Earl Russell the owner of the Suffolk City Transit stopped by my house. He had my application in his hand and said White, are you still interested in driving for the city? You know the current situation; blacks are refusing to ride the bus until I hire a black driver. You can become a driver if you go to be certified. The class takes three weeks. Then I will put you on the payroll. He said it would take three weeks. Yet, the instructor for J.O. Jones certified me in three days. So I became the first black bus driver for the city of Suffolk, three days after Mr. Russell offered me the job. The strangest thing about my experience was that many whites seemed just as excited as blacks about having an African American bus driver. Two years later Suffolk added another black driver. Two years after that they hired one more black driver. Now almost all their drivers are black with the exception of a few whites.

Becoming The Third Black Policeman

I drove the city bus for five years before my wife Mildred and I decided to relocate to Franklin, VA, a town that was about 20 miles from the city of Suffolk. They were experiencing a similar problem. Franklin had two black police officers and the chief was looking to hire another. So I submitted an application. The police chief came to me and said we are in need of an additional black policeman and your application stands out. Every one I talked to had nothing to say but good things about you. I would like to offer you the job if you are still interested but you must qualify by passing a test. I told him I wanted the job and I took the policeman's test. The chief said I only missed one of one hundred questions. I was hired as a policeman for the city of Franklin at the age of thirty-five years old. I served as a policeman until I retired.

Moral Application: When I was a child plowing fields, I would see Greyhound and Trailway buses passing by on the highways. I prayed one day that I could learn how to operate those buses. Not only did God bless me to learn to operate buses, he gave me the jobs that only whites were hired to do. I even looked in the sky and said Lord I surely would like to know how to operate an airplane. God not only heard me but he allowed me to become a student pilot and I flew small planes. Despite the color lines in life I have been able to accomplish many great things in life and at the age of seventy-one I can say the world does not owe me anything. Jesus gave it all to me and I would not change my life's experiences with any man; whether they were struggles or victories. In life people must rid themselves of the color factor. If we are going to make it, people must stop seeing one another as black, white, green, or yellow. What men and women must strive to do is qualify themselves for whatever they would like to do, because when you prepare yourself and become qualified then you have the opportunity to be employed just as the next man or woman. Go to school; trade school, some form of apprenticeship, or college. Get an education and become qualified for the jobs available. Learn to be independent and not dependent on people. Have something to offer. Secondly, always remember that you are as good and as important as any person in the world. Never let people make you feel any less than your true value to Christ; the one that died just for you. Finally, always present yourself properly and represent the Kingdom of God. Live by high moral and ethical standards. This way not only will you give respect to others but you will gain the respect of all people. This is how the color line is broken.

Chapter Fourteen
Submitting To One Another
Moral Strengthening For Marriages

By Minister Elton R. Pryor: Pastor of Zion Poplar Baptist Church, Gloucester, VA

Ephesians 5:25 Husband love your wives, even as Christ also loved the church, and gave himself for it.

Titus 2:5 To be discreet, keepers at home, good, obedient to their own husbands, that the word of God be not blasphemed.

Society has dictated to humankind a way of dealing with matters concerning marital relationships in a manner that is not Christ-like. There seems to be a lack of value in what the word says concerning relationships. It seems that before we allow the word to speak to us concerning a matter in our lives, we turn to the ways of the ungodly, sinner, and scornful to solve a problem that God has given us instructions as to how to deal with. (Reference Psalm 1) As we choose our mates we often do not consider the fact of learning the ways of our mates. Some things never surface until later in our marriage, which are often not dealt with in a manner that is pleasant, loving or pleasing to God. As stated in the New Testament many times, the writers exhorted believers to engage in specific activities that would enable the body of Christ to function effectively and to grow spiritually.

Renewal

Renewal is to be noted as a Biblical Perspective. It is the essence of dynamic Christianity and the basis on which Christians, both in a corporate or body sense and as individual believers, can determine the will of God. This was made clear by Paul as he wrote to the Roman Christians – "be transformed by the renewing of your mind." (Romans 12:2) As two become one there must be some renewing of one's way of thinking, living and reasoning. We become members of one another as was stated in Romans 12:5 "So we who are one body in Christ, are individually members one of another." We must learn that two people must become as one when they unite in marriage. We cannot feel that one is more important than the other. In so doing, it will only bring about division in the relationship. A great effort must be initiated to create unity among two diverse people. The most important ingredient in unity is that of Love. It is a very important element in keeping the relationships functioning properly. The body of relationship cannot or does not function automatically. Marriage must consist of the following traits:

1. There must be a degree of spiritual maturity: In order to become mature, believers must be taught the nature of the body of Christ. We must acknowledge Christ as head over everything. (Col. 1:18)

2. There must be devotion to one another: (Romans 12:10) "Be devoted to one another in brotherly love." As we are devoted to God, we can find that it is easy to devote to one another. Knowing Christ is to know love, for Christ is the center of love.

3. There must be honor for one another: (Roman 12:10) "Honor one another above yourselves." We are not to try to lord over or rule over one another as we have some type of ownership. We must always try to put forth the effort to go the extra mile in making one feel good about themselves as well as their decisions.

Unity

We have to strive to be of the same mind with one another. We let our differences of opinion rule in trying times of our relationships instead of reasoning with one another. We are also faced with the concerns of not excepting one another. There is in our society a problem with persons accepting one another's faults and shortcomings, for we all have some. No matter how we view persons we should consider the fact that we are all born with a nature that will allow problems within us to surface. (Romans 12:5) "So we who are many, are one in Christ, and individually members one of another." We all belong to God, and are very much a part of one another. We cannot function all by our self; we need one another to make it in life. Sometimes bad experiences and past hurts, let downs, and disappointments cause us to misjudge persons. We cannot allow the past to dictate to us the future.

This way of thinking will sometimes cause us to think of ourselves as more important than others, which will create unethical results in a relationship. We must be certain to try to work hard at trying to create unity with one another, instead of sowing seeds of discord and bringing about confusion. The opportunity should always be given to bring about peace in any given situation, for we will be blessed by exemplifying the attributes of Christ. We find that the primary reason for disagreement in relations is that we are putting emphasis on something that the Bible does not emphasize. We tend to rely on old wise tales, male ego thoughts and assumptions, and information from un-godly counsel. This has created more problems in relationships than enough. We are quicker to listen to someone outside of the relationship than we do to our mates.

The Key to Happiness

One must know that the key to happiness in relations is Christ. For Jesus is love, and if we do not know him, we do not really know love. (1Corinthians 13:11) Love for others is the most significant key to unity and effectiveness in relationships. They do not function automatically. There must be a degree of spiritual maturity in order to function as a unit. When one is spiritually mature this will lead to concern, humility, patience, sensitivity, freedom and unity. Romans 12:10 states: "Be devoted to one another in brotherly love in honor preferring one another." This could be translated as showing love and affection. Our attitudes and actions toward one another should be evaluated and weighed according to the word of God.

There are often difficulties in identifying with one another at the feeling level. We find it difficult to express emotion towards one another. This could be because of the fear of rejection, family background, angry or resentful feelings, or lack of trust. Feelings of hurt or distrust will cause one to become frustrated or resentful which would cause one to be disillusioned or misled and cause problems to worsen our relationship. We must learn to honor one another above ourselves. Jesus Christ was the prime example when

He walked among men as He set the supreme example in honoring others above Himself.

We must learn to be of the same mind with one another. Being of the same mind helps us to function better as a unit. We must also learn to accept one another just as Christ accepted us in order to bring praise to God. We should not sit in judgment of one another for this violates our personal rights. Submission to one another is in essence a synonym for obedience. In its most general use it means to yield to one's admonition and advice. In Christ all believers have the potential to submit to one another out of reverence for Christ.

Chapter Fifteen
Older Men Younger Women
Morals on Relationships

By Deborah Williams; Owner of Deborah Williams Agency

The choice of the subject "Older Men Younger Women" was particularly interesting to me because I currently am aware of two couples involved in similar scenarios. Initially, I will discuss three such relationships given in the scripture and will follow with:

1. Current ethical and moral concerns of society

2. Observations of individuals whom I know personally that are involved in the "Older men
Younger Women" relationships.

3. Application

Now King David was old; advanced in years, and they put covers on him, but he could not get warm. Therefore his servants said to him, "Let a young woman, a virgin, be sought for our lord the king, and let her stand before the king, and let her care for him; and let her lie in your bosom, that our lord the king may be warm." So they sought for a lovely young woman throughout all the territory of Israel, and found Abishag the Shunammite and brought her to the king. The young woman was very lovely, and she cared for the king, and served him; but the king did not know her. (I Kings 1: 1-4 NKJV)

When Older Men Seek Younger Women

The relationship between King David and the young woman was somewhat unusual. It is obvious that she was young enough to be a granddaughter to him. It appears that the primary purpose of the relationship was to keep King David warm under the covers. While the scripture clearly indicates that the relationship was not sexual, the servants made it very clear that their desire was for the king to have a beautiful young virgin by his side and went to great lengths-- to Shunam, to secure her. King David, earlier in life, had been involved in an affair. As a result of the affair, he suffered great losses within his family as well as the respect and integrity he had achieved over a period of time. It is possible that King David had a change of heart, and that at this stage of his life, his heart was "fixed" or established to live a holy, pure life.

Throughout the eons of time, men often desire beautiful women, especially if the man is very successful; by their side is a young gorgeous woman the object of a prideful display. It seems to add to their egotistical arrogance. As king of Israel, the servants wanted their king to have lovely women by his bedside. They may have even speculated that as he assessed her loveliness, it would make him feel better or perk his spirit up as she waited on him and cared for his personal needs. Apparently, King David valued her virginity and as a result, she had the opportunity to carry that virtue into marriage later on.

When Younger Women Express Interest In Older Men

The second example of the "Older Man Younger Woman" is Boaz and Ruth. (Ruth 2:5) Then Boaz said to his servant who was in charge of the reapers, "Whose young woman is this? (Ruth 3:9-11) And he said, "Who are you?" So she answered, "I am Ruth, your maidservant. Take your maidservant under your wing, for you are a close relative." (10) Then he said, "Blessed are you of the Lord my daughter! For you have shown more kindness at the end than at the beginning, in that you did not go after young men whether poor or rich. (11) Now my daughter, do not fear: I will do for you all that you request, for all the people of my town know that you are a virtuous woman.

Boaz referred to Ruth in chapter 2 as "the young woman" and later in chapter 3 he called her "my daughter". Based on the latter statement, it is possible that Ruth was as young as a daughter to Boaz. He fit the old man picture very clearly. The very first time Boaz saw Ruth, she captured his attention but he did not pursue her (2:5). It appears that the heads of older men turn when young beautiful women are around. Research indicates that men are deluded into thinking that being with a young woman will actually make them appear younger than they actually are.

We are aware of how the mid-sixties ushered in the women's liberation movement. Well, Ruth was somewhat advanced in her era. In modern day terms, she actually asked Boaz to marry her (3:9). After a quick assessment of Ruth's youth, beauty, virtue and loyalty, Boaz promised her he would grant her request to marry her if the closer relative did not honor the opportunity. A very wealthy and prestigious man himself, Boaz determined to follow the custom concerning redeeming and exchanging. After confirming the exchange with the close relative who could not accept the offer without losing his own inheritance, Boaz --the old man, married Ruth--the young woman and they appeared to have lived happily ever after. Morally, this relationship was good, it was handled in a manner deemed ethically sound, and the couple adhered to the rules of society. The difference in age did not appear to have been a concern in that particular period of time.

Tell Me An Old Old Story

It is an old, yet modern story we all have heard at some point in time. A beautiful young woman meets an older, successful, married man. They become involved in a sexual affair and hope their liaison will remain a secret. Emotions and moral decency are suddenly forgotten as they engage in the passion of the moment. The successful married man violates his previous ethical vow of faithfulness made to his spouse at the altar. Society as a whole continues to view adultery as immoral.

On college campuses, in corporate offices, at Capitol Hill and in other settings, young women have long provided a source of gossip and speculation as they secretly engage in the Old Man Young Woman relationships. They sense they have options and a better sense of identity and self-respect, but are they likely to pin their dreams to this older man? Will this hamper their efforts as they move forward in their careers? Many have suffered demise, as the private liaisons became public knowledge.

As feminism coincided with the sexual revolution in the mid 60's, it became easier in many respects, for women to take risks in matters of the heart in unhealthy relationships even when advised to do otherwise. Many have been hurt, used and abused, however, sophisticated, educated women still reject the notion that they are naive.

A view of adolescent/younger women 18 years old or less, reveals that when they are involved with men who are substantially older than they are, differences between partners in such factors as maturity, life experience, social position, financial resources and physical factors may make such relationships inherently unequal. Young women may, therefore, be vulnerable to abuse and exploitation by their partners. This long-standing concern is reflected in the fact that every state prohibits sexual relationships between adults and minors in many circumstances, although individual state laws define the crime of statutory rape differently. State laws defining age of consent and statutory prohibitions on sexual relationships between minors and adults set varying age limits and age differences, and usually apply to adolescents aged 16 or younger (Family Planning Perspectives, 1999,31(4):160-167). Sadly, many times the young woman is drawn to the older man as a father figure and feels he will nurture and care for her in a way she has never experienced only to be subjected to the disappointment and abuse.

Current Moral Concerns of our Society

One of the ethical and moral concerns of society today is the fact that relationships between young women and older men have produced a high proportion of babies born to teenage mothers-- adult men fathered many. As a result, high welfare caseloads and costs impact society. The need to revamp pregnancy prevention services to include older fathers and to rigorously enforce statutory rape laws to deter pregnancies between older men and younger women is currently being reviewed to lessen the cost of federal funding for such matters.

What is the disadvantage of the older men younger women relationships in campus life and in the work place? Are there any advantages? Whatever your choice, the fact remains that these relationships are existent and are very real. In the corporate world, even with the sexual harassment laws, they seem not to have abated.

Rosemary Agonito, author of "Dirty Little Secrets in the Workplace" consultant on workplace gender issues had this to say about it. " It's a real ego booster for older men to have younger women interested in them. And younger women see these powerful men as an entree to better things---It's still the case that too many women define themselves by the male they are attached to".

A study of college campus relationships between older faculty men and young women shows that it is, in fact, the younger women who pursue the older male on faculty! They are persistent in their pursuits and the underlying causes are many. Values and principles taught by parents seem to take flight as the pressure to succeed at any cost surges to the surface. Society as a whole feels it is the professors, or the men who are the most aggressive; however, in many cases the female students are the seekers of such engagements. Are their motives a better grade, a promotion, a scholarship or a father figure? The question cannot be accurately answered because stimulus of motivations may be different. As many schools seek to deter fraternization, prohibition of such relationships may be a good idea to slow down the ill effects of such acts.

Personal Observations of Known individuals involved in Older Men Younger women Relationships

I knew a younger woman who briefly dated an older man and later married him. She was 15 years old and he was 23. They married in 1934 during a period of time when women married young and society thought nothing of the matter. Observation of the liaison revealed her to be somewhat submissive. She cooked meals each day, cleaned the house and took care of the children. Her thoughts concerning the male participation in the chores were that a woman should be grateful for "anything" the husband did at all regarding chores at home. She also felt that because the children were actually of her blood that the children should be preferred over the man if a choice had to be made. The husband on the other hand, treated her like a daughter. Basically, he had to teach her to cook and other things because she was only a child when they married. Arguments were usually over tidiness or the children. However, the arguments were always with normal voice tones never the "raised" pitch.

Overall, it was a good marriage and the couple was married over 60 years prior to the death of the wife in December 2001. The older husband is still alive at 92, and remains single. Women are actually chasing after him at age 92!

The second scenario is a 23-year-old woman who is currently cohabitating with a 50-year-old man. She is a successful businessperson who is somewhat of an independent thinker. Her positions have varied from self-employment to other commercial jobs. Because the younger woman is a personal relative, it was very disappointing to hear of the matter. Initially, on the first date, she had no idea the older man was as old as he was. Her thoughts were, maybe 35 years old. It was hilarious to her upon discovering his age and said she would not see him again---we thought! Three years have passed and they remain together. I personally attest to the fact that the younger woman was raised in a Christian home, which opposes cohabitation prior to marriage. Moral values and principles, which were instilled during the childhood years, were totally ignored. Her argument is that younger men are deceptive, lazy, immature and ill responsible. She also feels more secure in the relationship because the older man is ready to marry and settle down. They both struggle with the "age" issue; however, the struggle has been a little more difficult for her. As a result, she fears marriage. He appears to respect her and has asked for her hand in marriage over and over again, placing an engagement ring on her finger, also, relocating with her after she was promoted. The rest of the story remains to be told.

Questions have to be addressed such as, how is the health of the older person? Will he be sexually responsive to her needs, or capable of fulfilling them? Will he want additional children from their marriage; she has none? If marriage is a choice, how much longer will the older man live after the vows are taken? Will the younger person be content? Will the relationship be balanced --- and so forth? Many feel such relationships are outrageous and that the younger person is somehow missing the youthfulness shared in "same age" or closely aged relationships. They also fear manipulation by the older person because of more experience.

Moral Application: There are two passages of scripture that come to mind concerning the above discussion: Flee also youthful lusts! (II Tim. 2:22) And it is better to marry than to burn! (I Cor. 7:9) Yet, rejection of the truth is a very popular fad of our current society, however, it is not new. Male and female relationships would be healthier if they were based on biblical principles, regardless of the age difference. Even Sarah was approximately 10 years younger than Abraham.

We can see how, many times, thankfully not always, as in my first example, younger women are hurt, deceived, or even worse. Older men, already coarsened, to the disappointments of life, rebound more quickly---as if nothing ever occurred. "As younger women sort through their rationales for making the choices they do, what they need most is better guidance from older or more experienced women. When women go out and lead the same promiscuous emotionless sexual lives as men, the consequences can be heartbreak, sexual disease, pregnancy, and "overall coarsening of love and relationships with men" (Dr. Danielle Crittenden, freelance writer on women's issues). Young Woman, Older man, give it a second or even a third examination, life is full of consequences!

Chapter Sixteen
IF I Could Only See You
Moral Strength For The Blind

By Geraldine Banks: Member of Laurel Hill UCC

Geraldine Banks celebrated her birthday this year. She turned the sixty-third page in her book of life. Life has been filled with many joys and challenges, said "Jerry." One of the greatest adversities I had to confront and continue to struggle with is being blind. For the past thirty-six years I have been journeying through life in darkness. At the age of about twenty-two, life was bright and full of light and hope. When one day, I was typing at work and suddenly the paper I was typing turned pure white. I saw no typed characters. The sheet was empty of all printed alphabets and numbers. So, I informed my supervisor that I was experiencing a problem with my vision. She allowed one of my co-workers to take me to Columbia Presbyterian Hospital. They examined my eyes and the doctor advised me that there was a problem with my eyes but he could not identify my specific disease.

After five years of visiting specialists the disease eluding their medical knowledge and after witnessing my vision fluctuate from deteriorating each day, at the age of twenty-eight I was diagnosed with an eye disease referred to as Retinitis Pigmentosa "R.P." and I was certified as being legally blind. Within the five years, I had started preparing for the lost of my sight by attending the "Light House." It was an institution commissioned by the state of New York for the blind. It helped people learn various skills and trades. Also, it trained each individual how to live in a society designed and developed for people with vision not people with visual impairments.

I started my training at the Light House when I was twenty-three and it was at that time that I learned to except my visual impediment because I saw so many people with worst conditions. It made me say thank you Lord. There was one particular person I met that stood out from the rest. Her name was Marie. She was a Polish woman that suffered with a form of glaucoma from the age of fifteen years old.

She was totally blind and was given a Seeing Eye dog for assistance. How she gained my attention was, I noticed how hostile she was toward everyone except me. From the very first day I arrived at the Light House she treated me with kindness and we became very close friends. My teacher Mrs. Sexton, who was a native of Suffolk, VA, said, "Jerry, God must have sent you here because we have not been able to get through to Marie."

Marie was from a dysfunctional family. Against the family's will, she had married a black male and had three children from the marriage. They lived with Marie's parents in Pennsylvania but when times got tough they moved in with the husband's family in New Jersey. While there the husband became addicted to drugs and later died from an overdose. Marie and the children moved to New York City, but the entire time she was living there she neglected to register her children in school. Someone noticed it and reported her. The court ruled in favor of the husband's parents to care for the children and gave them custody. For a long period of time Marie had no one, not even her children. She was left alone in the huge city of New York. I believe this is how she became so defensive, withdrawn from others and hostile. Then a person told her about the Light House and this is how I met her. Marie's behavior taught me how to accept my condition and my behavior began to teach her how to accept the things that had happened in her life. I would invite her to my house. She got involved with my children. And Joseph and I would take Marie to New Jersey to see her children. We were friends then and even today we communicate with each other.

Undoubtedly, any person that deals with blindness must learn to be flexible and adjust to their surrounding. This was some of Marie's difficulties as well as mine. At first I wanted life to remain the same or at least that my vision would remain until my children graduated from school. I was a bit apprehensive in accepting the change that was taking place in my life. As the light dimmed in my eyes the fire of prayer kept burning in my heart. I stayed in constant prayer and tried to live life as independent as possible. Adamantly I resisted aids for my impairments. However, those days came to an end when I bumped into a steel beam as I was walking in the subway making an effort to commute home. That day I had to have stitches to close the gash on my forehead.

The next day I started mobility training in the streets using my folding cane and my prayer changed to Lord what ever the path is that you would have me to travel allow me to travel it safely. I began to take my children to the Light House so they would know what their mother and many other visually impaired people confronted. I took them to the Bronx to a school that taught blind children and children of blind people. They oriented my children as to how to cope with my blindness and how to assist me. I believe the experiences and teaching of my children during a vital time of my life caused them to be over protective. Even to this day they remain concerned and caring of my needs.

Yet, through this struggle many have not been so caring. When I sought employment the employers would not hire me because they did not offer the insurance needed to cover my disability or they did not have equipment for the visually impaired. When people would be in my company, they failed to understand that though I could not see them my hearing sense was heightened and I could hear their rude and ungodly remarks. They did not comprehend that their body motions or tones of speech were signs and revealed their attitudes and emotions towards people with disabilities. But there was one that cared until the end. That was Joseph Banks. We were the best of friends. He had never seen me with my cane and because of my initial struggle with independence I would tell myself Jerry you can do this, Jerry you can do this and I tried without revealing to others my challenge. He would notice from time to time me knocking something over in the house but he did not pay much attention to it. One reason was because I would become frustrated and cry. The first time he saw me with my cane he cried, because he did not know that my sight had gotten worse.

A deeper relationship was in the making. Each morning he would walk me to the bus stop and see me off to work. He was always there to help me make sure that my clothing matched. He made himself available to be my guide. He would read the Bible, the Sunday school quarterly, and newspaper to me. In all things and at all times he made his life a life of availability and help to me. My husband was a light in the darkness. He became my eyes. And after he passed I truly discovered how much I had grown to depend on him because he spoiled me.

Though life is different without my children around and my husband, I have been able to make it through this darkness by being surrounded with family and friends. People that love me and adjust their schedules for me when I am in need and I adjust my needs to their life's schedules. I have been able to make it by recognizing how to not become over dependent and too independent. I am defeating blindness by keeping a positive attitude and keeping busy because if you lose hope and stop being active you will slip into a state of depression. I have been able to see the light in the midst of darkness by staying in prayer. Christ has been my light in the darkness and he has made ways out of no way. He has opened doors that people shut because I was handicapped. He is the strength of my life.

Lord, "Your word is a lamp to my feet and a light for my path." Ps 119:105

Chapter Seventeen
Virginity Vs. Spiritual Celibacy
Morals of Christian Dedication

By Melvina Simon: Master of Divinity Candidate

I was born in a little town called Melfa, Virginia on the Eastern Shore. My mother had no idea that at my birth an unexpected surprise would spring forth. On that day she had identical twins. We turned out to be more than a hand full. Our lives are filled with wonderful memories as well as challenging experiences. Since my mother was a single parent, after graduating from high school I went into the military to further my education. Despite the many opportunities life has afforded me, my life took on new meaning the day I received Christ as my personal savior. From that day on I have aspired to know more of Jesus and sought to know more about true celibacy. What does it really mean to live a celibate life in Christ?

True Virginity

In researching the subject of celibacy (virginity) this particular topic can be discussed from several different approaches. Celibacy is to abstain from sexual relations, a person who is unmarried or remains unmarried, especially for religious reasons. One approach could be Mary, the young virgin who was overshadowed by the Holy Ghost and conceived a son called Emmanuel. Matthew 1:23 Behold, a virgin shall be with child, and shall bring forth a son and they shall call his name Emmanuel, which being interpreted is, *God with us*. Luke 1:35 And the angel, answered and said unto her, The Holy Ghost shall come upon thee, and the power of the Highest shall overshadow thee: therefore also the holy thing which shall be born of thee shall be called the Son of God. Mary a virgin (celibate – having never known a man), pure and innocent experienced an immaculate conception and brought forth Jesus our wonderful Savior who saved the world from sin and redeemed us back to the God the Father.

Another approach is a person abstaining from sexual relations for several different reasons, *No. 1*. The person is unmarried and who unlike so many others had decided that sex is permitted only in

A Cry for Ethical and Moral Strength

marriage, and lives a celibate life until marriage. *No. 2.* A person decided to live a celibate life for religious purposes. *No. 3.* A person who has been hurt by divorce or other circumstances and chooses to lead a celibate life to protect one self from future hurts and disappointments. In Matthew 19: 10-12 Christ's disciples say unto him, if the case of the man's is identical with his wife, it is not good to marry. But Jesus responded by saying, "All men cannot receive this saying, save they to whom it is given. For there are some eunuchs, (Those unable to have sex or unable to have children for metabolic reasons) which were so born from their mother's womb: and there are some eunuchs, which were made eunuchs of men: and there are eunuchs, which have made themselves eunuchs for the kingdom of heaven's sake. He that is able to receive it, let him receive it." In this passage of scripture Jesus is talking to his disciples about how divorce was never intended by God in the beginning, if a man puts his wife away except for fornication and marries another, he commits adultery. The disciples' response, "if this is the case, then it's better for man not to marry." Jesus' answer suggests that all men cannot accept or live a celibate life. For some eunuchs were born, some were made by men and others choose, but whosoever is capable of embracing this way of life receive it.

It is interesting to know that even Jesus points out variances in being a eunuch or celibate person. He makes it very clear that if you are capable of living a celibate life by all means do it. Perhaps one reason for so much controversy and scandal existing within the Catholic Church could be underscored by their interpretation of celibacy. Currently, many priest have been convicted and some accused of sexually abusing young boys. The Catholic community must consider that Jesus stated if one is capable of living a life of celibacy then by all means be celibate, but if not recognized, you have an option with the opportunity to serve God faithfully. It may prove to be permissible for priests who cannot vow to a life of chastity to be allowed to marry. For it is better to marry than to burn. 1 Corinthians 7:9 But if they cannot contain themselves, let them marry: for it is better to marry than to burn. If you can't contain yourself then marry. Make intimacy honorable before a Holy God who made all things and they were good. He also gave the gift of sex in the context of marriage.

In today's society we have become a nation of just do it. If it feels good to you then go for it. No matter what the consequences are. Romans 6:23 For the wages of sin is death. There are consequences when man decides to break his or her vows with God to live immorally and apart from God. Then the question may be asked, if more people would choose to be celibate either until they marry or to continue for religious purposes would there be such an alarming increase of sexually transmitted diseases. Is part of the epidemic decline of more unmarried people leading celibate lives a break down in the morals and ethics of our great nation? The principles that our forefathers intended this great nation to be founded on – in God we trust. Today, that which was previously considered immoral is being portrayed as morally acceptable. Divorce is on the rise. Families having no fathers to set the example of how a girl, his daughter, should be loved and cared for are becoming more and more prevalent. Her father telling and showing her how special she is and that her innocence and virginity is a gift from God to be cherished until she marries a special man and for the first time a husband and wife are to discover together the beauty and enjoyment of sexual intimacy; that's the way that God intended for it to be.

Today, young boys are growing up without role models to show them how to treat women with respect and as the weaker vessel. In addition, the results of the sexual revolution have increased sexual assaults and rape, not only of women and girls, but also young boys. It seems that the word *no*, no longer means *no*. The average age of young people having sex or experiencing sexual encounters is 11 years old. It is like trying on clothes at the mall the way teens are having sex with different partners. Aids have reached an epidemic rise among blacks, whites, and other nationalities, male and female. People sexually active are not using discrimination or discretion concerning the selection of their partners; age, race, gender, religion, or economic as determining factors. They have sexual relations with several partners anywhere, anyway, and anyhow. Thus, there will be no discrimination when payday comes because the wages of our sins is death.

Spiritual Abstinence

Although the previous approaches of celibacy have been portrayed from a physical perspective and of intimate relationships, there is another approach that deals with celibacy from the spiritual connotation. In this view one may look at celibacy through the revelation of spiritual relationship with God. Man and woman's virginity or better said purity to God is to abstain from committing fornication with other gods or man made idols and live a fully dedicated life to the Creator.

When Jesus discussed the topic of marriage in many respects His definition paralleled the Church's relationship to God. The Church is the called out ones – those set apart to God for His divine will, as a bride is engaged to her fiancé for she is promised to him. She is committed to him. Each individual that makes up the "Church", the body of Christ is to live a life of celibacy. They are to abstain from contact with others in an intimate relationship that would jeopardize his or her relationship with the one he or she is promised. Each believer called into the church is supposed to be engaged to Jesus our bridegroom. Though our status may be married, widowed single, divorced, the church should be totally committed to Christ. We are set apart to Jesus for him alone, leading a spiritually celibate life fully persuaded that nothing shall separate us from the love of God. Pledging total allegiance to the cost of the cross that we as the church died to anything that would lead us astray from being prepared for the bridegroom.

Jesus' disciples' men, who lived with him everyday, ran out on him at the end, betrayed him, even denied they ever knew Him. These same disciples who claimed that they would never leave him, that they were totally and fully committed to him became spiritual adulterers. Matthew 26: 35 Peter said unto him (Jesus), "though I should die with thee, yet will I not deny thee." Likewise also said all the disciples. They committed that they would die with him before they denied him. They pledged total allegiance and virginity to

Jesus. Yet, when the time had come they left him. What happened to those that were chosen by Jesus to become fishers of men, those who were supposed to be committed to him?

God's Faithfulness Man's Faithlessness

What about the Church today being in the image of God; Born again believers that so easily forget how the doctor can't explain how the last test result reported *"no cancer,"* the shock that there's still a roof over your head, when the check miraculously appeared in the mail the same day as the eviction notice, your eldest son accepted Christ after you had been faithfully praying for years for him? So soon we seem to forget how God has been faithful to us through our trials and tribulations. We turned to everyone else for help and advice before we came to God the Creator who is an all knowing and all wise God. We trust our friends' words, who themselves are also having some kind of problem or situation more than we do God's word (Psalms 1). We place our confidence in all kinds of things instead of the God who never lies to us nor lets us down. God, who promised to be with us and to never leave us wants us to have faith and not doubt that everything will work out for our good. But when situations don't work according to the time or way we think that it should then we become impatient. We take matters into our own hands. This is when we commit adultery.

The church is supposed to be the bride of Christ. We are promised to be betrothed to our groom. In Revelation 19:7-9, Let us be glad and rejoice, and give honor to Him: for the marriage of the Lamb is come, and his wife hath made herself ready. And to her was granted that she should be arrayed in fine linen, clean and white: for the fine linen is the righteousness of saints. And he saith unto me, Blessed are they that are called unto the marriage supper of the Lamb, and he saith unto me, "These are the true sayings of God." The Church, the bride of Christ, is to make herself ready for him. The relationship is to be a spiritually celibate one not allowing anything or anyone to jeopardize this intimate relationship. Believers, the church, are promised to be the beloved Christ. We are to be prepared to marry Him; having our garments spotless and without blemish for the wedding, by being arrayed in fine white linen- the righteousness of saints. This does not suggest that a servant of God cannot be married, but it implies that believers are to abstain from becoming physically and spiritually defiled.

Is the Church playing the role of a harlot? It may seem like the church is not the church of old. It may even seem like we aren't totally committed to our God as the saints of old. It may also seem that we are whoring after other gods. Time may have changed and we may do things a little differently from the way grandma and the saints of old. But one thing about God is He is Immutable and He never changes. The methods may change but not God. He will always have a remnant. There will always be a ram in the bush that's prepared and is totally committed to the promise of the betrothal to the bridegroom, Jesus. The remnant bride, the church, is making herself ready by leading a celibate, spiritual life, abstaining from the very presence of immorality, being fully persuaded that neither death, nor life, nor angels, nor principalities, nor powers, nor things present, nor things to come, nor height, nor depth, not any other creature, shall be able to separate us, the remnant church, from the love of God, which is in Christ Jesus our Lord.

Carl L. Sweat, Jr., D. Min.

Chapter Eighteen
The Lord Working Through Me
Moral Strength For The Incarcerated

By Rod Copeland: Member of Laurel Hill UCC

I was born in Suffolk, VA at Louise Memorial Hospital on February 3, 1963. The late Mr. Raymond and Etta Copeland were my parents. Both were hard working Christian people that started praying for me prior to my birth, because they were 40 years of age and they did not cease praying for me until their death. I grew up thinking that I was my older sister's child because people said my parents were too old to have a child. My father retired from the Norfolk Naval Shipyard and my mother retired from the Suffolk Public School system.

As the youngest child, my life was smothered with love from my mother and father. Nothing honored them more than to attend a Forest Glen High School football game and a Virginia Union University football game just to see their baby boy run for a touch down. Nothing could have been finer until my drug problem finally caught-up with me and became my addiction or habit.

I can remember so vividly my first experience with drugs. On that day, I had time on my hands, so to pass the time away I went and sat in my father's van. My older brothers drove the van to the shipyard. They carried passengers to work. I noticed in the ashtray something that appeared to be a joint. In the early 70's, drugs were the things to do and I wanted a part of it. This was my opportunity. So I grabbed it, placed it in my pocket and went to a secret place. For the very first time, I got high. As I grew in age and statue, one of my brothers would hire me to babysit his son while he and his friends would go to dances. They would gather together smoke weed and have drinks before they would go to the dances or parties. I would clean up by drinking their left over beers that were piled up. I would make sure the house was clean by searching it for weed that was left. Those nights I smoked, drank and got high.

Getting high began to become a regular thing for me to do. It now was a part of my life. I concealed my drug related activities from my parents by doing the things that a young teenager was supposed to do. I went to church, did well in school, and was a well-mannered young man. I did my chores of cutting grass, worked in the garden, and feeding the pigs. Yes, I had a wonderful childhood and exciting teenage years.

My parents didn't think I was doing hard drugs. I believe they knew that I was drinking some beer but weren't all the guys? My mother told me that the Copeland men were known for three (3) things: women, liquor, and money. Keeping the traditions going, I was involved with these traditional family addictions. Mentally or physically, it really didn't matter what I had to do to keep the lifestyle, I became accustomed to living, and going. I was a Copeland and the way that I carried myself caused me to have many friends that respected me. Also, I had a lot of lady friends. They say that hindsight is twenty - twenty vision. As I reflect on my life, I say to you it is true. Because, I have to admit that the life I led and the mindset that I had caused me to make some of the biggest mistakes.

It was not long before the smoking reefer and drinking beer escalated to a higher level. My drug experiences evolved to snorting cocaine, drinking liquor, and the worst of all things created. I do not desire to mention its name. However, I learned how to cook cocaine and how to free-base cocaine. Free-basing is when you add fire and baking soda to powder cocaine. This form is a derivative called "ready rock." This addiction leads men and women to do some of the most ungodly things anyone could imagine like lying, stealing, cheating and using people to their advantage. Going with the crowd and trying to be a big shot started me to trust no one, not even myself.

When I got arrested on January 11, 2002, this should have awakened my senses. Instead, I stayed in jail (Western Tidewater Regional Jail) for 3 days. I slept the entire period. When I called my father to come and bail me out, the phone kept ringing and ringing or it was hanging up on me. After the passing of my mother and discovering I had a drug problem, my father previously warned me if I went to jail for using drugs he wasn't going to come and get me out. So I called all four of my brothers and my only sister. They said the same thing…call "Pop." I knew that I had to get chewed out by him, but

I put pride aside and gave him a call anyhow. The love of a father surprised me. He actually listened. Even when I let him down and did something that he told me not to do, he came down to the city jail and bailed me out.

You want to know how I rewarded him for helping me? I started right back, smoking and selling rocks because I still wanted to get high and needed money to finance my addiction. But it would soon become my demise. I stayed out of jail until September 23, 2002. On that day I arrived at court in the City of Suffolk and to my surprise and stubbornness the judge sentenced me to jail because I didn't spend $12.00 to have my TB shot taken. My heart dropped to the floor, when he said, bailiffs arrest this man and take him down to WTRJ. I was incarcerated until my next court date, which was scheduled for October 2002. I had an African American public defender, whom I thought was just a pawn for the Commonwealth Assistant Attorney. I explained to my lawyer that I wasn't a convicted felon before until January 2002. I had been arrested previously on the charge of possession of cocaine in 1999, but the charge was dropped because the State didn't have enough evidence to prove me guilty; however, the case triggered the investigation that led to my arrest on January 11, 2002. So, I end-up staying in jail until October 2002.

The presiding judge released me. All I had to do was report to my assigned probation officer. I believe the judge's decision really made the Assistant Commonwealth Attorney upset, because he said in his 20 years practicing law, he had never seen a man released upon having 9½ grams of crack. I have to say that God was really on my side; yet, the struggle with drugs was taking its toll. I believe the impact of the chain of events in my life had a great influence on the life and the death of my father.

He was and still is the best friend that I could ever have. I was just glad that I could be at the funeral without handcuffs, because he had stated that he didn't want me at his funeral with police security and me being in handcuffs. God is good all the time. He answered my prayers by allowing me the opportunity to be sitting with my brothers and sister. My father died on Thanksgiving Day, November 2002. You want to know how I honored my best friend that had a strong love for all of his children and great dreams and expectations for us? Well, after my father was eulogized and buried I turned to the only companion I thought I knew and had. I returned to something that gave false hope and security. I was back in her arms again. I reverted to smoking crack. I returned to doing drugs even though I knew doing drugs was wrong.

After the death of my father and getting tangled up into drugs again, I stopped reporting to my probation officer. On January 2, 2003, I saw two police cars rolling up my driveway, while I was attempting to open the door of my truck. I didn't even realize that I had my stemma in my pocket and when the officers got out of their cars to arrest me, I knew that if I had run to try to escape that this part of my life would never end. Without a struggle, I surrendered into their custody. When I was arrested I thought that once I went to jail, I could bond myself out, but to my surprise, they had me this time. My road had come to a dead end. Drugs had taken everything from me and I did not see it. It stole my college education. I had a full athletic scholarship granted by Virginia Union University and in the last semester of my senior year I surrendered my graduation for the love of drugs. It took my home that my grandmother willed to me. The house is mine but I abandoned it because I did not value my inheritance. Drugs took my children. My little girls have never seen their true father. The person I was when they saw me was a stranger. Someone I did not know. It even took the mother of my children away from me. We got trapped in the cycle of drugs. And now it was claiming the most precious aspects of an individual, which were my freedom and my autonomy.

It was time for me to grow up and pay the piper's price. It was time to serve in prison. At first, I was mad with the world, I, Roderick K. Copeland was in the "cub" for good. After being in jail for about four months, I had a revelation. I was in confinement on restriction, because I had gotten into a fight. A troubling feeling of conviction, sorrow, and weariness came all over me. I just cried out to Jesus, I'm tired of being tired; I can't do this by myself. Please come into my life and take all of my iniquities away from me and show me the way, Lord. At that time of about 3:00 a.m., I got real cold and the bars started to shake, and a shadow came into my cell and my bible that I was reading just fell to the floor, with a loud sound. I looked around and I knew that I didn't knock the book off that stool, so I just assumed that Jesus had given me the answers to the questions I had asked of Him.

No longer was I mad about my situations. I kept writing to my sister, Janis to come and see me. And after mailing numerous letters to her, she finally came to see me. And to her surprise, when she saw me, she had seen how good God had been to me. My skin was so clear and bright that it had to be God shining through me and proving his mercy and grace was for real. See, I was born with an ailment called eczema, dryness of the skin, which causes my skin to crack, peel and bleed. This was the first time that any of my immediate siblings had seen me. I just told her, just because a person is in prison doesn't mean that they shouldn't be visited. I read this in the Bible, that if a man is sick, send him to the doctor to be healed and no one should be left alone to suffer. I believe some Christians need to re-evaluate their lives and help the needy when they are hungry and talk to these kinds of people about being real Christians. Jesus died on the cross to pay the penalty of our sins with his blood.

Yes, there's a great hope in my life because Jesus found me while I was locked up in prison and I believe he can find any one that is in prison in other ways of life. Your prison may not be jail, it may not be drugs, it can be depression, it can be loneliness, it can be a low self-esteem, it can be a financial burden or it can be the shackles of a sickness. Regardless as to what your prison may be, God will come and visit you. He will give you strength in the darkest time of your life.

I believe Jesus gave me all the opportunities in the world to do right, but I continued to choose drugs. Now, with my body being clean for over 1 year and 3 months with God's will, I believe I can continue my college education and continue to minister about what God is doing in my life and hopefully, just spread the good news about the Gospel. After leaving jail on October 13, 2003 I had written and gotten accepted in a program called Youth Challenge, Inc. founded by Brother Troy Collier. With constant reading of the Word and prayer,

I believe that a spiritual cleansing will continue to take place in my life and I will emerge victorious in the battle of my drug addiction. When I said that sinner's prayer and cried out whole-heartedly, I don't have any cravings for cigarettes, liquor, or crack and this can only come from the grace and mercy of Jesus. With time to think about what I want to do with my life, I plan on marrying my fiancée, and taking care of my three beautiful daughters and continue to worship my Lord and Savior. I just want to be ready to spread His word and lead people back to the church and away from the life of worldly dreams.

Moral Application: My moral advice to anyone on drugs or any kind of situation that is drawing them away from morality and godliness is to change your friends, scenery, and lifestyle. I believe some people do not want to see you clean or sober and serving the Lord. Again, my advice is to get away from those types of people and continue to pray and ask the Lord to help you make the right decisions. You can't serve two masters, no way, no how, just believe that Jesus is the only way, the truth and the life to bring about change in your life.

Carl L. Sweat, Jr., D. Min.

Chapter Nineteen
Be Still And Know That He is God
Moral Strength Concerning The Aspirations Of Life

By the editor: Marva Lee Hines Parker, Deaconess of Laurel Hill UCC

Nearly twenty years ago, I started fulfilling my lifelong career dream. Years later I discovered that my plans were in direct opposition of the divine plan and purpose of God. For a while I traveled a journey that started out my way but did not end the way that "I" thought or could have imagined it would. When I reflect on the journey I say to myself, "He knows what is best for me!"

It all started when I enrolled in Morris County College in Dover, New Jersey. My intent was to become a licensed Registered Nurse. After completing the fall semester Therbia, my husband, and I discovered that I was pregnant with our first child. We were extremely excited and ready for Natasha because we had been married for five years. Unfortunately, the issue of my pregnancy promoted a financial dilemma with the college. I could not receive MCC scholarship funds while pregnant, so I withdrew my enrollment and dedicated myself to the family. Soon after our firstborn, Therbia Jr. was added. Fifteen years had come and gone. Within those years I contemplated and attempted to return to school but my efforts did not go as planned. I had to sacrifice for my family; however, I longed for the opportunity to complete my college education.

Therbia was offered employment in Virginia and said that we were relocating to what I then called "Suffering Virginia." It was not a choice I would have made but he was my husband and I loved him. The move was a major adjustment in my life. Despite the fact that we both were born and raised in VA, I didn't like being here. I cried from the time I started packing to move from New Jersey until we arrived in Suffolk, VA. Though the move was agonizing, as I look back, I have discovered that it was the window of opportunity that God had given me to return to school.

A Cry for Ethical and Moral Strength

The children were in elementary school, family was near by, and the community was closely knitted. With these advantages, I was able to work not one job but three jobs and return to school again. However, one of my jobs was with the Suffolk School System and it began to have a heavy influence on the path of my education. For several years, I took courses here and there. Finally, it all worked out. I graduated from Paul D. Camp Community College in May 1998. I was happy and ready to take on the world. Immediately, I began attending Norfolk State University, matriculating in the evenings with a major in Interdisciplinary Studies and a minor in Early Childhood Education. Now my intent was to change the world as a teacher, not a nurse. Regardless of the obstacles, I traveled many evenings sometimes four times a week from Forest Glen Middle School to Norfolk State not knowing if my vehicle would start when I exited the building at ten o'clock each night.

In the year of 2000, I graduated from NSU as a Suma Cum Laude 3.9 GPA Honor graduate. The miracle of it all is that I was offered a fulltime position with the Suffolk School System prior to my graduation. Though I was elated, little did I know that my expectations and plans still did not quite line up with God's.

From May of 2000 until August 2004, I took the Praxis Math examination so that I would pass "The Test" and receive my state teaching license. I prayed and fasted consistently. I planned, studied, received the assistance of college tutors, and went to math workshops at Old Dominion University but to no avail. Each time that I took the Math portion of the examination, I felt confident that I had passed but when I received my scores I was a few points short of passing. I began to ask God, "Why this and Why now? Every thing's going so well." I became angry, frustrated, embarrassed and wreaked in self-pity because I was supposed to pass the test with ease and receive my license. Why not? I was recognized as one of the brightest of my graduating class. I didn't understand what was happening. Suddenly, it culminated and the bottom dropped out of the dark cloud that hung over me for four years. In June 2004, Suffolk Public Schools could not and did not renew my provisional contract as mandated by the State Department of Education.

By the time all of this took place, God had not answered any of my questions but He was molding me for His purpose and shaping me according to His will. Between the four year spans of time, God I asked Him many things. Yet, one stands out more than others. I asked Him to use me for His glory. Though my body was physically drained, though issues with my family arose, and concerns with my spiritual life emanated, in answering that particular request, through a painful and challenging process, I believe He revealed to me how to truly trust Him, how to believe that He has my best interest at heart, how to believe that He loves me and my family, and how to believe that He will always provide for us.

After packing four years of classroom materials in boxes and preparing to move on in life once again, this time it was not so painful. This time it was not agonizing. I had gained strength through my darkest moment. When I left Driver Elementary School on June 16, 2004, I had informed all my coworkers, who were feeling sad, that I was leaving; they were feeling sorry for me but I assured them that I was going to be alright. Trust me when I say that, saying those words did not come as easy as they flow now. But God had given me an inner peace that surpasses understanding, articulation, and expression. Nevertheless, what the devil meant for my bad, God used for my good.

During the summer of 2004, the inner peace that He gave me challenged me to "Be still and know that He is God." That was one of the toughest assignments that I have had to complete. As I began to do just that, my family and friends began to ask me when I was to start looking for a job. As hard as it was for me to be patient, to wait on God and not call local school systems, each time that faint thought crossed my mind I quickly regained my strength and encouraged myself to be still.

Unexpectedly, one day in August, three weeks prior to the starting of the new school year, I was sitting at my kitchen table sipping coffee and looking at the newspaper when I noticed an announcement for a third grade and seventh grade teacher at a Christian school in Suffolk. I did not respond to the ad that day but days later it continued to be announced. It just seemed that the paper was everywhere that I was.

It was as if this was the opportunity that I would know He is God. Now was the time to step out on faith. So, I called the school on a Tuesday, received the application on Wednesday and Monday I received a call to come for an interview. I went on Tuesday and was called on Thursday for a final interview, which took place the same week on Thursday. Out of many applicants, on Friday morning the principal contacted me and offered me the third grade teaching position.

It is true that in life some discover God's will early while others find out much later. Yet, regardless of the process we all must come to realize that He is in control and desires that we all reach our greatest potential. Even when things appear dim and seem to be growing darker, "Be Still And Know That He Is God." I trusted and He gave me peace and strength. You can trust Him and He will see you through. Knowing that God has placed me according to His divine plan and will, and accepting that I am now where God desires for me to be, I am happier than I have ever been in life. I love Suffolk and I am making plans to receive my state teaching license.

Carl L. Sweat, Jr., D. Min.

Chapter Twenty
Domestic Violence
Moral Strengthening Of Relationships

By Fannie Mae Gilliam Burke: Clerk of Laurel Hill UCC

"Husbands, love your wives, even as Christ also loved the church, and gave himself for it." *Ephesians 5:25*

Domestic violence refers to physical, sexual, emotional or psychological abuse between marital partners, former partners and to other adults who are, or have been in a close relationship. Both men and women may act violently toward each, but women are more likely than men to be injured or murdered by their partners.

Domestic violence leaves long-lasting effects on its victims and their families. For many years, domestic violence was considered "a private matter" but today social scientists and experts recognize it as a dangerous social problem

There appears to be no single reason for domestic violence. Many offenders have a history of abuse. Other causes may be stress caused by unemployment, sexual difficulties, job loss and low self-esteem. Domestic violence crosses racial, socioeconomic and educational barriers. There are few set perimeters for abusers. They may be black or white, rich or poor, poorly educated or well educated, young or old.

Domestic violence has to be one of the most insidious and destructive types of behaviors. For the victim, it can be embarrassing, degrading and humiliating. The embarrassment of talking about such a personal and damaging encounter causes the victim in some instances to delay, avoid or just rationalize their way out of seeking professional help or assistance from agencies or the authorities. The victim often thinks, this can't get any worse, it has to get better. But without some type of serious intervention, the violence increases.

It is estimated that as many as 4 million women suffer abuse from their husbands, ex-husbands, boyfriends or intimate partners in the United States each year. One of the reasons this number is so

A Cry for Ethical and Moral Strength

high is that people have become more comfortable talking about and reporting the problem. This was not true for our mothers' and grandmothers' generations.

Because there is no typical abuser, abusive relationships do share similar characteristics. In all cases, the abuser tries to gain power and control over his partner. He may try to gain control through anger or by making threats. He may also use physical violence, such as kicking or punching. Or he may use sexual violence, forcing you to have sexual intercourse or to engage in sexual activities against your will. Abusive behavior can be broken down into categories and you can use this checklist:

A. Being jealous and possessive

B. Being nice, then irrational and upset

C. Throwing and breaking things

D. Making humiliating comments

E. Isolating you from family or friends

F. Controlling the money

G. Blaming all problems on you

H. Locking you out or not letting you leave

I. Hitting you or forcing you to have sex

Unfortunately, the abuser never sees himself as doing anything wrong. He seems incapable of putting himself in the shoes of the abused. He is able to defend his actions by saying things like "she made me do it" or "she enjoys being slapped around." So untrue, absolutely no one enjoys being abused. The wife often tries to do all that is possible to make the relationship work and last ("Whom God has joined together, let no man put asunder"); to set an example for the children and your children's children, (" My son, keep my words, and lay up my commandments with thee"); she rationalizes and remains silent to restore peace and harmony in the home environment. Things are more likely to get worse than better.

The most common reason for not leaving an abusive relationship is financial, especially for women with children. They don't think they can survive on their own. Some women may not leave because they see the situation as their fault. Older women may stay in an abusive relationship because of their perceived need for companionship. As bad as it may be, the relationship is familiar and comfortable.

Abuse does not happen just once. It happens in a cycle that continues for years. This cycle portrays behaviors the abuser uses to control his victim. Everything is going fine. Then the tension starts to build and there are episodes of anger over some silly statement made or over something that was not done. The wife tries to calm the situation but the situation escalates. He yells, hits or performs some violent act. Sometimes, he is remorseful, says he's sorry, wants to make up and then everything is okay until the cycle starts again with the tension building. What's interesting about this cycle is, as time goes on, the violence gets worse and OK periods start to disappear. Eventually, the quiet times disappear altogether and are replaced with constant battering. Many violent relationships exist for years in this stage of the cycle. Studies show that many women-women who have been killed or have serious illnesses as a result of battering had reached this continuous state of constant battering.

"Train up a child in the way he should go; and when he is old, he will not depart from it" *Proverbs 22:6*

Domestic violence reminds me of a watch battery that just keeps on ticking. It not only affects the abused but children are just as deeply affected. Boys who watch their mothers being abused are more likely to abuse the women in their lives; their girlfriends and their wives. Girls who live in families where abuse occurs are more likely to be attracted to boyfriends and husbands who are abusers. It is true that children learn what they live. Children are likely to think that men use violence to get what they want out of any situation and that this is the way that members of the family are supposed to act. Children in such families have nothing to compare their families with and accept certain types of behavior as the norm. Unless serious intervention and education is employed, a vicious cycle is created that passes from generation to generation to generation. The watch just keeps on ticking.

> "Be ye followers of God, as dear children; And walk in love, as Christ also hath loved us, and hath given himself for us an offering and a sacrifice to God for a sweet smelling savour." Ephesians 5: 1,2

I am a total believer of the "little girl syndrome." This syndrome expresses belief that deep within all women dwells that *little girl* who never dies. 1 Corinthians 13:11 reads "When I was a child, I spake as a child, I understood as a child, I thought as a child; but when I became a man, I put away childish things." When we become adults, we are expected to assume the role of an adult with all of its responsibilities and obligations. But deep down inside of us lives the *little girl* who enjoys a hearty laugh, who giggles with her girlfriends, who takes great joy in the company of those she truly care about her. The *little girl* who dwells in all women enjoys the simple pleasures of life. Women *must* do everything possible to nurture and protect that *little girl*. While her duties as a woman and parent will require much of her energy and time, she must diligently work to keep that *little girl* alive and well; spiritually, emotionally, psychologically and physically. Like Satan, who seeks to kill and destroy, domestic violence eradicates the *little girl* who lives within all of us.

If you are in an abusive relationship, make sure you have an emergency plan. In case you need to leave quickly, pack a suitcase and leave it with a friend or neighbor. Set aside enough money for your escape. Keep important documents handy so you can take them with you. Know where to go and how you will get there.

Psalm 31:24 says "Be of good courage, and he shall strengthen your heart, all ye that hope in the Lord." There is LIFE after living in a violent relationship. Be strong enough to sever relationships if you have to and move on with your life.

Chapter Twenty-One
A Life Like Christ
Moral Strength Is Offered When We Live Christ-Like

By Dr. D. A. Peace: Pastor of Zion Bethel UCC

John 10:10, "I am come that they might have life and that they might have it more abundantly."

LIFE:

A. Is a road we must travel, like it or not.

B. Is like a mirror: if you frown into it, it frowns back, if you smile, it sends back a smile.

C. Is a one-way street and you are not coming back.

D. Life is the – between the time we come and the time we leave.

Many of us who call ourselves Christians and claim to be living Christian lives are merely inflated bodies, drifting with the Godless winds of our times. Our only purpose for living seems to be the pleasing of our wants, our lusts of the flesh and our insatiable hunger for pleasure. A certain man who labors five days a week, buys a little food and some liquor, that he might eat and drink over the weekend relaxes in his easy chair and in a half drunken stupor declares, "Man, this is life."

A certain youth who has no other purpose in life than to work hard that he might buy a fast car and live a fast life with the fast crowd in the dens of iniquity where he is robbed of physical stamina and spiritual power, exclaims, "This is life."

A certain young woman, who has ignored the Christian way of life and has accepted the Hollywood formula for bountiful living measures the values of life in terms of bust, waistline, hips and makeup. When this underfed, reduced, thoughtless one can secure a job where she can display her jewels of flesh, the claim is, "This is life." Or when we can move our glorified bodies into a split-level

A Cry for Ethical and Moral Strength

house and split over families because of our split personalities, boast of our failures, make a joke out of every law of common decency, the claim is again, "this is the life; or when we spend all our spare time chasing anything or everything that can give us a thrill, that produces pep, but robs us of spiritual power and the will to be representative children of God on this planet, a voice thrilled by canned joy exclaims, "This is life."

Then we feel weak and void of holy power, no longer do we lift our eyes unto the hills from whence cometh our strength, but into the medicine cabinet from whence cometh our tranquilizers. After we have swallowed a few pharmaceutical boosters, we relax and exclaim, "This is life."

Is this really the life of which Jesus spoke? Can life really be lived, apart from some tasks, some duty, some obligation, some labor, that strengthens the soul and glorifies God? Is a person really living when he has no reason in life other than to eat, drink, live in a fine house, wear fine clothes, die and be placed in a fine casket and be buried in a fine grave plot?

Is God's only purpose for creating us to have us grow up and grow fat, die and be fertilizer for the earth, and cause vegetation to grow more beautifully where our decaying carcasses lie.

Could this possibly be the only purpose for existence? Should we conclude that the material things, the things we can see and touch, are all that matter? To me something about what Jesus said about life, that touches my soul precludes any positive answer. I must say no. I must say no. It is said, we live in deeds, not years, in thoughts, not breaths, in feeling, not in figures on a dial." After many folk spend many years on this planet, all they have to show for their life is a birth certificate attesting that they came and a death certificate assuring that they have gone. Yet, my lord and yours says, "I am come that they might have life and that they might have it more abundantly." This is life Jesus style.

A person's life cannot be enriched unless that person is God conscious. A person cannot enrich his life by constantly investing his spiritual and material resources in the nonessentials of this world. If a person would enrich his life, he must invest in divine necessities. Our businessmen and women must be told that in the divine economy the welfare of people takes priority over profit. Our politicians must be made aware that the welfare of the people takes priority over their selfish ambitions. Church leaders and officers must be made to know that a right relationship with God is more important than holding an office. No one can live the abundant life without Christ. Man can never be what he ought to be without God. Man plus Christ has always equals victory. Man and Christ equal creative and purposeful living.

A person may be successful according to the standards of the world and a failure according to the commands and demands of Christ. Abundant living is not merely successful living, but victorious living. Jesus didn't come that we might have success, but more exactly, that we might, through him, attain to victorious living. The young rich ruler went to Jesus one day desiring to know how he might enrich his life. He wanted to know what good thing he could do to attain that quality of life called eternal (eternity begins now). He was already successful. He was rich and he was a ruler. He was rich in things, but lacking in soul food. He needed an operation.

Jesus told him to go and sell what he had, give to the poor, and to follow Him. It was selling out time, because what he had, had begun to corrode his soul and this makes it difficult for any person to maintain a proper relationship with his God. The young man said to Jesus, "I don't believe you"; and walked away and kept his fleeting success and perishable riches. He walked into everlasting oblivion.

Life is enriched as we properly set our affections. No person who is a fool about the things of the world can ever have an enriched spiritual life. The tent maker from Tarsus advised us. "Seek those things which are above." Taking a hold of the intangible and invisible possessions gives meaning and purpose to life and human existence. Such is the experience and discovery of the reality of Jesus Christ. Abundant living or life Jesus style is that quality of life that enables us to go the second mile. We don't come into abundant life on the first mile. Egotism-selfishness-greed-jealousy-deceit are on the first mile. It's on the second mile that we discover true spiritual values. Love-joy-righteousness-brotherhood. It's on the second mile that the spiritual constitution of the soul finds strength.

It's on the second mile that we learn how to leap the barriers of racial hatred.

It's on the second mile that we meet the companion who is a burden bearer.

It's on the second mile whose yoke is easy and whose burden is light.

It's on the second mile that we experience the mysterious reserves of life, that sustain us, when material things have fled and sickness hangs a drapery or darkness about us, friends question our integrity, life Jesus style enables us to still worship at the altar within our lives with the words of Job, "the Lord gave and the Lord has taken away; blessed be the name of the Lord." Life Jesus style is a shared life. This is a shared life. No man discovers the true values of life until he shares his life. We don't really learn how to share until we learn how to turn loose our time, talent, and money.

We serve a God who shared. There was no need for God to be absolute and eternal goodness all by himself. Therefore, "God so loved the world that he shared his son." We are reluctant to share because we are afraid of losing what we have. Jesus, our Lord, has taught us that the best way to have is to let go. This method "He who loses his life for the kingdom finds it again", it seems not to fit into the scheme of thinking of the 20th century. And so, we are afraid.

But I've got good news for you. He who invests his life in the service of God and in creative and redemptive good will, invests in the gift edged securities of heaven, and the market has never been known to fluctuate, he invests in a spiritual bank where the assets always exceed the liabilities. If you are afraid of losing your life, I've got good news for you. The empty tomb is heaven's guarantee that you'll find it again. Yes, I've got good news for you. Share your life because eye has not seen, neither has ear heard, nor has it been revealed, all that the Lord God Almighty has in store for you. This is (Life Jesus style).

Moral Application: We are accountable to God for this life. We are not our own, for we have been bought with a price. God did not give us life that we might drift aimlessly through a span of years, die, and leave behind us as monuments, super highways, green country sides, jet planes, automobiles, houses, and this life. When we come to the end of our earthly pilgrimage sojourn we must stand before the throne of the righteous judge of all the earth, we will hear him say, "give an account of your stewardship," "What have you done with your life? Day-hour-month-year.

I don't want to have to tell Him about our guided missiles and misguided human beings. I don't want to have to tell Him about my academic achievements and laurels that men of the earth heaped upon me. I want to be able to tell Him that I used my life to lift up Christ and to guide somebody to the Christian way. I want to be able to tell him that I lifted somebody who had fallen, comforted somebody who was sad, fed somebody the bread of life, guided some wayward sheep back to the fold, and was a friend to somebody who was friendless. I want to be enough like Christ to give a positive accounting of my stewardship.

What kind of accounting did Christ give of his life? I believe that upon his return to his Father in glory, seated on the right side, he could say: (Jesus could say:) You gave me a dark night on which to be born and turned it into eternal day. You gave me a stable into which to be born, and I consecrated it into a shrine forever. You gave me the dust of the earth and I used it as a pharmaceutical plant and created a salve that opened blinded eyes. You gave me your word and devils had to flee, the sick were made well, the lame were made to walk and the dead to live and talk again. You gave me a well curb for a resting place, and I used it as a pulpit from which I preached a sermon that started flow of an eternal fountain in a woman's life and water broke out in dry places and a whole country was evangelized from there. You gave me a few unpromising men and I made them to become fountain stones in the Kingdom of God and permanent words of eternal truth. You gave me a seamless robe and I used it to wrap born and unborn generations into your plan of eternal salvation. You gave me the garden of Gethsemane as a resting ground and I used it as praying ground. You gave me a cross, and I used it to break the enslaving chains and to help bridge the chasm that separated man from God, and left words for on coming generations saying, "If I be lifted up from the earth, I will draw all men unto me." "At the cross, At the cross." You gave me a borrowed tomb into which to be buried, and I made it to become the gateway to eternal glory. This was his life and may our lives be contributive and fulfilling. Take my life and let it be.

Carl L. Sweat, Jr., D. Min.

SECTION II

Teachings Of Christ For Moral Strengthening:
A Treasury Of Moral Principles
Rev. Carl L. Sweat, Jr. D. Min: Pastor of Laurel Hill UCC

Carl L. Sweat, Jr., D. Min.

A Cry for Ethical and Moral Strength

Chapter One
The Bible Viewed As A Book Rated X
Morals On Viewing The Bible As Authoritative

"Woe to those who call evil good and good evil, who put darkness for light and light for darkness, who put bitter for sweet and sweet for bitter. Woe to those who are wise in their own eyes and clever in their own sight. ...who acquit the guilty for a bribe, but deny justice to the innocent. ...for they have rejected the law of the LORD Almighty and scorned the word of the Holy One of Israel. Isa 5:20-22,23,24

The Moral Problem

Ethics can be defined as a question into the principles and problems of morality. However, as mankind inquires into the state of morality, it becomes apparent that the resolution to the world's current moral problem cannot be discovered by designating which particular act, trait, institution, body of faith, tradition, or law is correct or incorrect. The current problem concerning living a moral life and making ethical decisions is less complex and more general than we perceive it to be. Predominately, it is found within the principle upon which we have judged thoughts, acts, and deeds to be right or wrong.

If we could somehow gauge or measure this current generation's specific reference points of moral reasoning, we would discover that, to many, the Bible is perceived to be Rated X. It is considered a book off limits. Politically, it is Rated X because legislatively it is banned from federal, state, and municipal facilities. Religiously, it is a Rated X book because it lists an insurmountable amount of the "do-nots" of life. Do not do this, do not do that, or you can't do this, you can't do that. Socially, the Bible is Rated X because it is rarely read in many homes. Primarily countless individuals view it as a worthless book that is outdated and has no relevance in today's contemporary world. It is Rated X because of the perception that any sensitive subject acquainted with it is socially taboo. The normal view of subjects such as marriage and pleasing your partner, divorce and engaging in a new life, virginity and a healthy sexual relationship, alcohol for physical conditions and well-being, disciplining your children, dating and social relationships, etc. is that they are forbidden, unmentionable, or even unthinkable issues. A profound reason why the Bible is regarded as being Rated X is because it's perceived by many as a document that promotes the prohibition of freedoms of life. To some individuals, institutions, and bodies of faith it oppressively restricts the life and freedoms of individuals. However, Paul said, being Christian or living by the word of God is not so much about the things you can not do (limitations), it is more so about the overwhelming freedoms you are granted; yet, we are not to allow our freedoms (liberty) to cause us to sin.

The complex nature of moral education and the controversy among various institutions and bodies of faith associated with identifying and sanctioning a given act as being morally acceptable or immoral is a major concern. The struggle in characterizing virtuous and non-virtuous behavior is intense and prevalent in our present generation. Though modernism has distorted boundaries of ethics previously defined within the pre-modernism, post–modernism has now introduced an array of new challenges of itself.

Questions to Ask and Decisions to Make

Questions, Questions, Questions! Ethics may be defined as an inquiry into fundamental or complex principles affiliated with the multiplicity of problems and the solution of morality. The concept of certain ethical principles is the precept which men and women use each time they morally judge their or others' behavior and character. The question is how do men and women obtain a particular level of moral literacy? Is the knowledge of good and evil gained through the process of rationalism, as the Empiricist believes? Is the concept of morality an inborn feature of the human character, as expressed by Intuitionist? Is moral conduct sanctioned within the commandments of God as the religionist suggest or does the society in which a person lives dictate the moral code and make them binding under the auspices of politics.

Decisions, Decisions, Decisions! How do individuals obtain knowledge of the do's and the don'ts? Is there an authority regarding morality? What sanctions the things that are good and those that are evil? What is good in the moral sense and what is evil in the immoral sense? What are the motives behind the actions of men and women and what are the motives affected by the consequences of our behavior? Where do we go for information? Where do we go for answers? Is there something we can reference, a document that is proven to be resourceful, or a manual undeniably beneficial to all mankind?

Objective

Morality and ethics are very broad in scope. From various fields and subject topics, we shall review a problem or problems and reveal that the Bible speaks to our current condition. It is not Rated X. Meaning, it is not restricted or off limits concerning the subject's material on morality or the approaches it recommends for resolving immoral thoughts, motivations, and acts people commit. Neither is it Rated X concerning the in-exhaustive topics it addresses with foundational counseling pertaining to moral conduct. The Bible is not Rated X with regards to an assortment of diverse information relative to morality that a person may seek for clarity and enlightenment. It does not censor from us anything that is needed for men and women, boys and girls to make sound moral and ethical decisions. Jesus said, "I call you friend because I have not withheld anything from you." And because He loves us, the answer that you seek to the many questions that we all share concerning the good and the bad, the just and unjust, and the right and the wrong things to do, to say or even to think can be found within the Bible.

The Bible is inclusive not exclusive. It is not Rated X in reference to a particular type of people, their age, sex, or the ability of a person; it offers advice for moral living. Yet, because it is not exclusive to people or to moral subject topics, it is consistent to the title of this book. The Bible is Rated X in that it is considered a binding document between man and the Creator. It is to be used in the administration of counseling, advising, judging, and disciplining persons concerning moral, ethical decision making and moral conduct. The Bible is Rated X in that it clearly distinguishes the things that are categorized as good and the things that are classified as evil. It is Rated X because it plainly distinguishes those things that are immoral in the sight of

God. It is Rated X because it differentiates morally and ethically the dos and the don'ts of life. It is Rated X because it promotes moral education of the youth and literacy of adults.

According to the spiritual and social training the Bible offers, its rules, standards, precepts, ordinances and statues are presented in many forms. They are offered through story telling, psalms, parables, poems, historical records, and examples to X out and deter immoral conduct. Though we should have (PG) Parental Guidance in all matters of the Bible, as stated by Moses when he recommended that the parents teach their children Deut. 6:7-9 "Impress them on your children. Talk about them when you sit at home and when you walk along the road, when you lie down and when you get up. Tie them as symbols on your hands and bind them on your foreheads.

Write them on the doorframes of your houses and on your gates." Also, there is a teacher given unto men and women that they may discover truth relative to morality and salvation; that helper is the Holy Spirit.

Neither Ignorant nor Silent

In an attempt to pursue some of the implications of human behavior, I have taken some of the most common concerns and religious questions exactly as they are murmured among Christians and Non-believers and presented them to various people that they may respond to the readers of this book in an effort to demonstrate that the Bible is neither ignorant nor silent to any moral or ethical problems the human species face. Within the Bible are the brilliant responses of God that people seem to ignore or overlook. These textual passages address the all too familiar and unfamiliar questions of virtues posed by layman, clergy, and the unsaved. The referenced text and stories of this book can make sense only to believers and unbelievers alike who seek answers to issues of the Bible labeled X among religious and social communities or they are rarely spoken of.

Jesus said if any one has an ear let him hear and in all of your getting get understanding. How fascinating to know that there is staggering knowledge of mankind and his or her daily predicaments; yet, only if he or she would be willing to seek the way of perfection, and if the Bible could be included as a part of each person's moral reference point could such knowledge be gained. In this book, believers and unbelievers will discover messages that are geared to his or her heartfelt questions. It utilizes straightforward language that conveys the uncomplicated relativity of moral and ethical ideals.

Chapter Two
The Origin Of The Struggle
Morals On Poor Choices Or Decision Making

Nothing Has Changed

Believe me when I say Adam's children have not changed so follow me to discover if my implication is of a positive or condemning nature. If we would examine our world today, we would discover that it exists and operates in a state of continuous change. Look around you. What do you see in the drama of our time? Has our world been set on a relentless course steered by entrepreneurs, scientist, computer technicians and inventors? In laboratories around the world, researchers are busy creating technologies that will change the way we live our lives. They settle for nothing less than improving and transforming forums of communicating, computing, medicine, manufacturing, energy infrastructure, and our transportation systems. Surely, their motto must be "Out with the old and in with the new". Why? Because humanity has accepted the mentality that everything must change and that nothing should be allowed to stay the same.

The truth of the matter is some form of change has affected everyone's life. Yet, amidst our contemporary and modern life today, there exists a consistency of the primeval world. Though the exterior of our world is changing, the interior of man remains identical to the disobedient couple that lived in the Garden of Eden. If we could communicate with Adam today our words would be, "Adam, your children have not changed."

The use of technology has made this world more convenient. It has transformed some of the impossible into that which has become possible. Because of modernization, people are living healthier, longer, and more comfortable lives. However, when considering man's great successes, accomplishments, and his milestone of achievements in vast arenas, if we would survey the state of our world in view of the current spiritual condition of man and woman we would find nothing has changed. Similar to Seth's group, Adam's son today, there exist only a selective few that truly love and walk with God striving to do that which is right and just.

Compared to the descendants of Cain, many people today have departed from the righteous will and way of the Creator. Because of their departure from morality and God's presence subsequently, jealousy, murder, crime, idolatry, sexual deviances, covetousness, power struggles, profit, and hatred currently abide in our world. All these dishonorable factors are carried on at the expense of our brothers and sisters and such unethical and immoral thoughts, behaviors, and motives have proven to be destructive to our relationship with God and man. The harshness of reality is the parallelism of our present position to an ancient event.

Understanding that man has not changed, but knowing he still has a great need for a great God, can we presume that our end will be consistent to previous historical accounts concerning the judgment of man? We look upon that which is taking place in our world and shake our heads in awe as we witness the degeneration of men and women identical to our past. Surely, you remember how the descendants of Cain merged with the descendants of Seth and influenced them immorally to the point that all men and women became corrupted mentally, in their imaginations, and emotions. Because of their poor ethics and immorality God destroyed all life. Adam, your children have not changed!

Within our present world, truth is becoming relative while morals and ethics are being tossed out of the professional, political, economical, social and religious windows. The name of God is being dismantled or taken out of public and private settings. Families are no longer teaching their children morals, ethics, and how to live holy or the way of the Lord. Corruption and evil is spreading throughout our land. The light in man is growing dimmer because people are influenced by the world and how it has defined the "the good life." It appears that men and women love the darkness more than the light.

A Thirst for Knowledge Supercedes Morality

In this new information age, men and women thirst for knowledge and desires to further themselves by seeking to become a highly educated society of people. However, after all of our getting and having, God is justly displeased because we are not conducting ourselves any more morally, ethically, or godlike than our forefathers. I dare say, yes if anyone would ask, if we are better off than those of the past. The thirst for knowledge has not withdrawn itself from the life of man or woman. Temptation; the challenge of doing good or evil has not retreated to a corner. No, what it has done is weaved and entangled itself into our lives.

Knowledgably, the way mankind's change towards his or her thirst for knowledge concerning what's good or bad (evil) for self, another individual, society, our economy, and even spiritually, which has caused him to sin, is his or her struggle or war against it. What we do when moral choices confront us and how we respond should give a clear indication as to whether man is transforming and transitioning. History gives a long and clear record of how men and women have confronted and handled choices of morality and immorality. Each instance of our reaction to what is considered "moral choice" can be compared to how men and women of the past responded in similar situations. Then an accurate evaluation of the development and change of mankind can be equated. In comparable instances what men and women decide in various situations really has not changed over the years.

Now the serpent was more subtil than any beast of the field which the Lord God had made. And he said unto the woman, Yea, hath God said, Ye shall not eat of every tree of the garden? And the woman said unto the serpent, We may eat of the fruit of the trees of the garden: But of the fruit of the tree which is in the midst of the garden, God hath said, Ye shall not eat of it, neither shall ye touch it, lest ye die. And the serpent said unto the woman, Ye shall not surely die: For God doth know that in the day ye eat thereof, then your eyes shall be opened, and ye shall be as gods, knowing good and evil. And when the woman saw that the tree was good for food, and that it was pleasant to the eyes, and a tree to be desired to make one wise, she took of the fruit thereof, and did eat, and gave also unto her husband with her; and he did eat. And the eyes of them both were opened, and they knew that they were naked; and they sewed fig leaves together, and made themselves aprons. And they heard the voice of the LORD God walking in the garden in the cool of the day: and Adam and his wife hid themselves from the presence of the LORD God amongs the trees of the garden. And the LORD God called unto Adam, and said unto him, Where art thou? And he said, I heard thy voice in the garden, and I was afraid, because I was naked; and I hid myself. And he said, Who told thee that thou wast naked? Hast thou eaten of the tree, whereof I commanded thee that thou shouldest not eat? And the man said, The woman whom thou gavest to be with me, she gave me of the tree, and I did eat. And the LORD God said unto the woman, What is this that thou hast done? And the woman said, The serpent beguiled me, and I did eat. And the LORD God said unto the serpent, Because thou hast done this, thou art cursed above all cattle, and above every beast of the field; upon thy belly shalt thou go, and dust shalt thou eat all the days of thy life: And I will put enmity between thee and the woman, and between thy seed and her seed; it shall bruise thy head, and thou shalt bruise his heel. Unto the woman he said, I will greatly multiply thy sorrow and thy conception; in sorrow thou shalt bring forth children; and thy desire shall be to thy husband, and he shall rule over thee. And unto Adam he said, Because thou hast hearkened unto the voice of thy wife, and hast eaten of the tree, of which I commanded thee, saying, Thou shalt not eat of it: cursed is the ground for thy sake; in sorrow shalt thou eat of it all the days of thy life; Thorns also and thistles shall it bring forth to thee; and thou shalt eat the herb of the field; In the sweat of thy face shalt thou eat bread, till thou return unto the ground; for out of it wast thou taken: for dust thou art, and unto dust shalt thou return. And Adam called his wife's name Eve; because she was the mother of all living. Unto Adam also and to his wife did the LORD God make coats of skins, and clothed them. And the LORD God said, Behold, the man is become as one of us, to know good and evil: and now, lest he put forth his hand, and take also of the tree of life, and eat, and live for ever: Therefore the LORD God sent him forth from the garden of Eden, to till the ground from whence he was taken. So he drove out the man; and he placed at the east of the garden of Eden Cherubims, and a flaming sword which turned every way, to keep the way of the tree of life.) Gen 3:1-24

The same attempts at handling the problem of deciding to do what is right or wrong today are approximately the same efforts of mankind centuries ago. In the recent past and even in the ancient world some men after making the wrong "moral choice" hid their sin. Like Adam and Eve, whose first response to the problem of "moral choice" in their life was to hide themselves from the presence of the Lord. Many men and women today, because of poor moral decisions maintain lots of skeletons in their closets. They attempt to hide the sin in their life from the awareness of others and God. But God knows all things and He said what goes on in the darkness will come out in the light. The fundamental problem of making poor moral choices lingers and the tactic of hiding sin has not changed. They both remain inadequate responses.

Notice that Adam and Eve not only hid themselves but they also covered their bodies because they discovered that they were naked. Many today apply the same technique. Because men and women realize that sin is wrong, they try to cover up or conceal their poor choice. Why? We have to remember that Adam said "I was afraid…" Our father and mother witnessed the shame and the sorrow that sin can expose unto men and women. They did not want to be subject to such a degrading and embarrassing condition. Perhaps men and women today cover their sin in fear of the threat of being viewed by others and God as disgraceful or immoral if their deeds are revealed.

Yet, Christ said in I Jn 1:8-10, If we claim to be without wrong decisions, we deceive ourselves and the truth is not in us. If we confess our wrong decisions, He is faithful and just and will forgive us our sins and purify us from all unrighteousness. If we claim we have not made immoral choices, we make Him out to be a liar and His word has no place in our lives. No man or woman should endeavor to hide or cover their sin and believe that acts of deceit would afford them an opportunity of being perceived godlike or moral. Despite confidence in our resourceful capacity and ingenuity to weave or conjure ways of evading sinful dilemmas, no works of man is sufficient for the covering of his or her sins or for salvation.

Adam's children have not changed because in today's world, they are still utilizing the futile and childish method of blaming others for their personal misfortunes or poor choices. How useless their reaction proves to be in the Garden of Eden. Both unsuccessfully attempted to shift the blame on another. Adam even blamed God. What commonplace of immorality we find ourselves today. Whereby, men and women will try to blame their divorce on their spouse. They will try to blame their frustrations, hates, prejudices and lack of trust on their parents' uprearing or life's experiences. They will blame their addiction to drugs on society or their environment. Some blame God for their failures. Some blame Him for sin being in the world. Many blame Him by asking why did you allow these situations to take place? Some blame God for the loss of a loved one. Though Adam blamed Eve and God, and Eve blamed the serpent, the truth remains that God was very aware of the encounter and each was given an opportunity to repent and give an account for their sin(s). God judged them in accordance to their personal choice. The word of God states that every man and woman will have to stand before Christ, be it at the judgment seat or the great white throne judgment, and give a personal account of the moral, immoral; ethical, unethical; right and wrong thoughts, actions, and motives he or she has committed while in the body. Paul reveals the prominence of morality in his statement, "whether good of bad." in II Cor.5:10.

The Image of God in Us.

Each human person is created in the image of God. Yet, what does it mean to be created in the image of God? The diversity of such a study primarily rests within the terms "Godliness" and "Godlikeness". Thus, the contrast of the image of God is "Godlessness" and "Ungodliness". When confronted with living our life in the image of God we discover that we are to act and react in love and righteousness. Such living or life style is considered moral and ethical behavior. The truth is there is nothing wrong with doing what is right or good. It is a part of our character. We are created to live morally and ethically and anything contrary is unacceptable.

The truth is, as an ordinary human being, with the help of the Holy Spirit we are required to reach our highest potential or become our most complete self. Our heavenly Father, in whose image we are created, calls all to excellence in thought, action, and motives. We should ever be mindful of God's requirements of mankind and understand that the image in which we are created is to control all that we do and say in life. It is this image that serves as the foundation of all ethical principles and moral conduct. Thus, if anyone's problem is one of Godlike integrity rather than Godlike purity or rationality, then indeed he or she can be so thoroughly emboldened by the demands of Christ that they will have to do something about what He says. It is therefore worth considering what man does as opposed to what Christ desires man to do.

Roman 1:20, 21 reveals that there should be no doubt in the clarity that God makes Himself known to all. For the majority there is no confusion whether or not God exist. Even Jesus did not have to face the dilemma of whether there is a God or not. There is not a greater time than now in this immense informational and evangelical age when men reasonably attest that there is a God. Although scripture does attest that God has never been seen, the most amazing contribution to the revelation of God and his image is the poetic and artistic picture inscribed in our hearts and on the pages of God's words. We are introduced to Him by the use of innumerable metaphors, typologies, symbols, and parables. In their abundance, all are cumulative efforts to depict the principle image of the Creator and the moral character He conveys.

If we could agree that morality, all that is good, right, and just, is comprised, given relevance, and defined by God's image then we discover through Psalm 19 that God has revealed Himself to all men and women through creation, the law, man and prayer. However, Romans 1:18-23 reveals that there are those who pervert the known image of God. They do so only to serve their immoral gratifications.

Rom 1:18-23 For the wrath of God is revealed from heaven against all ungodliness and unrighteousness of men, who hold the truth in unrighteousness; Because that which may be known of God is manifest in them; for God hath shewed it unto them. For the invisible things of him from the creation of the world are clearly seen, being understood by the things that are made, even his eternal power and Godhead; so that they are without excuse: Because that, when they knew God, they glorified him not as God, neither were thankful; but became vain in their imaginations, and their foolish heart was darkened. Professing themselves to be wise, they became fools, And changed the glory of the incorruptible God into an image made like to corruptible man, and to birds, and four-footed beasts, and creeping things. (KJV)

Moral Application: Let us turn from the old way of responding when making moral choices. Let's center our thoughts and mind on that which is honest and just. Let us please God for a change. Let's stop denying our involvement in immorality. For we all are guilty in some form or another of unethical acts or deeds. As children of Adam and Eve, many have not outgrown the childish characteristics of disobedience, denial and blaming others. Though we have grown in age and are increasing in maturity, intellect, and in physical statue, and though we are heavily influenced by the change of our modern world, we tend to be a little more sophisticated than a child in the manner of our disobedience, denial, and blaming others for our immoral conduct. Adam's children have not changed but through the power of Christ; men and women can be changed, transformed and transitioned.

Chapter Three
Biting Off More Than You Can Chew
Moral Strength In Decision Making

"For when for the time ye ought to be teachers, ye have need that one teach you again which be the first principles of the oracles of God; and are become such as have need of milk, and not strong meat. For every one that useth milk is unskillful in the word of righteousness: for he is a babe. But strong meat belongeth to them that are of full age, even those who by reason of use have their senses exercised to discern both good and evil." Hebrews 12-14

How long will men and women continue to romanticize immorality? Will they continue to exist under some infatuated influential illusion centered on having and getting? Will their vain imaginations and non-contrite desires of the heart largely go unquestioned? All too often men and women have bitten off more than they can chew, swallow, or even digest. For the most part, when they see something they like their heart yearns, craves, or obsesses for the phenomena. The result of uncontrollable obsesses or longings are the inability to implement proper decision- making. Mankind has become habitual offenders of being irrepressible to his or her emotions. Characteristics that we should be controlling are dictating our behaviors. Society and the world at large has recklessly run amuck. Having and getting have become the predominated factors in all areas of the human life. Similar to Eve in the garden, regardless of the repercussions to ourselves, others, and the world, men and women continue to bite off more than they can chew. Naively, many people have not explored their ignorance relative to vast temporal and eternal blessings. They surrender by not relinquishing innate and conscious desires. Surely, we can agree Adam's offspring have not changed. For like him and Eve, in our own selection process, we continue to risk our lives, and we persist in sacrificing much for so little.

From the earliest times of history, a war has been fought within the minds of humanity. Our minds have been the ultimate battleground of the enemy. It is there that he attempts to cause men and women to lose focus, disbelieve, question, make immoral decisions, and even challenge the word of God. Initially this tactic is recorded in Genesis the third chapter. Whereby, the father of lies engaged the first

A Cry for Ethical and Moral Strength

woman in spiritual warfare. He devised a plot that would deceive humanity and caused them to act unethically and immorally against God by aspiring for something that would cost them significantly more than what they were able to pay. Regrettably, mankind lost the battle. For the first of seemingly infinite times to come, humanity chose to do the wrong thing and bit off more than they could chew. The consequences were irrevocable. From that day forth our world began to spiral downward, out of control.

Was The Tree in Eden a Tree of Morals and Ethics?

Throughout the ages, men and women have questioned, does the Genesis scripture refer to a literal tree? Was the fruit an apple, another type of fruit, or does it represent something else? Was the tree of an evil essence? Did God create evil? Was eating of the fruit destructive? Was the serpent real or does it symbolize something? Who or what was the serpent? The fundamental truth to such perplexing questions is contained primarily within Genesis. Yet, progressive clarity can be derived from various books in the Bible. Irrespective of various schools of thought, be they literal or allegorical, conservative, or liberal interpreters of the scripture, the mystery of Genesis chapter 3 carries an ultimate message that conveys God created a perfect world, a godly world, a holy world, and a world prepared for ethical and moral conduct, thought and decision making. He created man and woman and placed them in a literal garden with literal trees eastward of Eden. In Eden every tree was pleasant to the sight and good for food. However, God commanded that man and woman not eat of the fruit of the tree of the knowledge of good and evil. Yet, Adam and Eve were disobedient.

It would elevate our curiosity if we would momentarily ponder upon this tree with the consideration that knowledge of good and evil perhaps equates to morals and ethics.

Moral defined is: "Of or concerned with the principles of right and wrong in conduct and character; teaching or upholding standards of good behavior: conforming to the rules of right conduct; sexually virtuous; judged by one's conscience to be ethical or approved;

capable of distinguishing between right and wrong…" New Webster's Dictionary, Modern desk edition; Delair Publishing Company, Melrose,IL. P332

Nothing was wrong with the tree and it was there for a purpose. Consolation should be unto mankind in knowing the providence of God and the awareness that He would never do anything that places man or woman in a tempted position. "Let no man say when he is tempted, I am tempted of God: for God cannot be tempted with evil, neither tempteth he any man: James 1:13." We are also to be exalted in spirit in knowing that the Creator creates all or any one thing for the fulfillment of His divine decree and will.

If truth seekers would truly review the basic principles of God's word, they would find that God's definitive plan was for Adam and Eve to achieve a morally ethical, and a pure godly, mature state. This position was designed to surpass innocence and be quite similar to the angels. The position similar to the angels is to derive and sustain life eternal, which would be gained from the tree of life, and to know morality (good and evil), which would have been gained from the tree of the knowledge of good and evil. To have life eternal is to know God. It is to know Him intimately and have a relationship that places Him first and pleases Him. Because, above all, "… in him we live, and move, and have our being; Acts 17:28." We should love Him with all our heart, soul and mind because He first loved us, created us, provides for and sustains us and has given His life for all.

All Things At the Appointed time- Why They Could not Eat of the Tree?

God had an appointed time for Adam and Eve to eat from the tree of the knowledge of good and evil but that time had not arrived for them. They did not know when the time would come neither does this generation know. All God wanted them to do for the time being was to be obedient by living out that which he had imparted unto them and putting Him first in their life. Then all things would have been added unto them, even the tree of knowledge of good and evil. Remember God found Job, Noah, and Enoch to be righteous men, not because they knew all morality, everything good and bad, but because they attempted to live life by the things that God shared with them. They held their limited revelation dear to their heart that it would never depart from them. Their efforts were counted just, perfect and pleasing in the sight of God. However, Eve and Adam desired knowledge/revelation beyond that which God intended to give them and held them accountable for it at that particular time. Thus, their decision and act was found immoral, unjust, and unpleasing to Him.

God continues to request the same of men and women today when he says, "But seek ye first the kingdom of God, and his righteousness; and all these things shall be added unto you Matt.6:33." Though the tree of knowledge of good and evil was created for Adam and Eve, which is clearly stated within verse twenty-nine of Genesis chapter one, it is later that readers become aware in Genesis chapter two verse nine of more detailed information concerning how God delayed mankind from partaking of this particular tree's fruit. For the fulfillment of His divine plan, in so many words, He directed Adam and Eve to wait patiently for further instructions on when they could eat of the certain tree. Look carefully at the words, "And out of the ground made the Lord God to grow every tree that is pleasant to the sight, and good for food; the tree of life also in the midst of the garden, and the tree of the knowledge of good and evil. It becomes apparent that each tree was beautiful, good for eating and made for mankind. Yet, the quandary to them and us is when will they have been permitted to partake of the tree of knowledge of good and evil (morality)?

We do not know how long Adam and Eve had been in the Garden of Eden or the duration of God walking and talking with them in the Garden, nor the extent of their conversations with God. However, the question lingers, why could they not eat of that specific tree at such a particular time? Paul says in Hebrews 5:12b-14 that infants and babes must first consume the milk of the word because the principles of the oracles of God must be learned and because children are unskilled in digesting the word of righteousness. Yet, after they become full of age (mature) they may partake of the meat of the word because by reason they would have exercised their senses (spirit) and become skilled or prepared for the discerning of both good and evil (morality). Paul's statement confirms that God's daily teachings would have prepared Adam and Eve for the eating from the tree of knowledge of good and evil; however, they prematurely partook of the tree. Whereby, they bit off more than they could chew and violated the will of God, His appointed time.

Notice in the J. account of the Bibles' creation story, God refers only generally to mankind's liberties pertaining to every tree. He says, "Behold, I have given you every herb bearing seed, which is upon the face of the earth, and every tree, in which is the fruit of a tree yielding seed; to you it shall be for meat." However, in the P. account of creations God speaks more in particular relative to Adam and Eve exercising their liberties concerning every tree.

In some respect Paul clarifies the Genesis exposition when he indicates that children of God can abuse their liberties. He suggests that all things are lawful unto believers but within themselves they are not expedient. He implies that all things may be lawful but believers are to never be brought under the power of any phenomena. No one is to be subjugated by any phenomena for it causes them to transcend the boundaries of God's word and divine plan. Adam and Eve were free and had complete dominion over the earth; yet, they allowed their freedom to entice them to bite off more than they could chew. One should ask himself or herself three essential questions before exercising their liberties. The first contemplation should be, is what I am about to do beneficial? Secondly, the contemplation should be, is what I am about to do detrimental? The third contemplation must be, is the decision I am about to make or the act I'm about to commit pleasing to God?

If we maintain these three basic regards within our moral and ethical decision-making processes many men and women would react proactively concerning their attitudes, motives, fleshly desires and emotions. They would not behave immorally or with disregard in reference to the repercussions of unethical decision making/ disobedience. They would recognize that all we say and do bear a great significance on life and creation. They would arrive at the understanding that Satan would like individuals to think because humanity lives under the dispensation of grace, they can live freely and do as they desire by pleasing self or man instead of seeking first the kingdom of God. No one can have their cake and eat it too; however, some think they can commit good and evil and still be saved or are bound for the kingdom of God. How soon they discover by questioning their acts that Satan is a liar and we cannot inherit the blessings of God after practicing immorality.

Moral Application: In view of the fact that Adam's children have not changed, the excitement is in knowing that God has not changed. Throughout history God has been there for us despite our displeasing responses and decisions concerning the knowledge of good and evil (morality). The glory of all our past failures, misfortunes, shambled relationships, and shortcomings is the forgiveness of God. It was in the garden that immediately upon the fall of man, God, whom knows all things including good and evil, responded to Adam and Eve's dilemma morally by extended grace in a dispensation of innocence. Though God morally applied the ethical principle of rebuke when He judged them and cursed the earth; He also executed the ethical principle of the law when He said "I commanded thee that thou shouldest not eat?"; the ethical principle of relationship when he said "Where are thou?"; the ethical law principle of innocence when He asked, "Who told (trick or influenced)thee that thou wast naked."; many more ethical principles or laws can be discovered in Genesis; yet, the message most prominent in this lesson is God discerned and continues to morally choose which ethical laws were best for the application of our crisis. It becomes obvious that the Holy Spirit within believers is ready and willing to reveal unto us which ethical principle(s) on which to base our moral decision.

"What Would Jesus Do?"- Moral Decision Making

To be frank with you, I would suggest that I strongly convey that applying the correct law(s) of ethics as the foundational principle of our moral decision is a very complicated process. It is a process that requires help from the Helper at all times. Ethical principles are rooted in various arenas of law types and the challenge we face is selecting the correct laws or law types as the foundation to our moral choice. The difficulty is properly identifying which branch of ethical law truly addresses your present issue.

Often, we make moral decisions ethically established in Catechistic law, administrative law, judicial law, etc., when the Helper (Holy Spirit) desires and directs us to please God by choosing to act, at that time, on the principle of social law, the law of grace, the law of mercy, etc. At times the proper ethical principle or pleasing God means basing your decision on grace, later pleasing God may mean making a moral choice found in judicial statues, ordinances, or policies, even later moral conduct may mean responding out of practices of tradition, for even Christ stood to read the Word of God because it was the custom of the awaiting congregation.

Regardless to which ethical principle or law we struggle to incorporate in our moral decision making process we must do so with the sincerity and motivation of love. Throughout the Bible, Jesus teaches us this truth. Our brother and friend who keeps nothing from us at any time could not be boxed in by the Scribes and Pharisees or bound to any one procedure other than love. He revealed that there is no cookie cutter format for moral decisions. Moral decisions at all times and in all events are complex and require sound maturity and discernment of what is right, just, and pleasing to the Father. They are the keys for those that seek to behave godlike and to please Him, including those who live by the example of Christ, for in all things He pleased the Father. Thus, in all things we must ask ourselves, "What would Jesus do?" and try to imitate His actions and decisions.

What Jesus would do, does do, and is still doing.

The sequel of our lives today contains the same offering of His grace. Because of His love, the Genesis account describes that God made garments of skin for Adam and his wife. He himself covered them from their nakedness. God's act seemed as if he was saying remove your covering; you can not hide your disobedience, immorality or sin; only through my divine act can your sin be veiled. God still works this way today because nothing has changed for man. He cannot save himself. He continuously tries to hide his immoral works from God and his neighbors by failing to acknowledge his shortfalls, unethical decisions, and earthly thoughts through prayer and communication with the Father. Man attempts to hide his or her immorality by faltering in not praying with one another and for one another, and also, by not acknowledging their sins to one another. Surely, even today, we can say Adam's children have not changed.

Chapter Four
Don't Let Dirt Get Into Your Eyes
Morals On Fighting Back And Revenge

"… where your treasure is, there your heart will be also. "The eye is the lamp of the body. If your eyes are good, your whole body will be full of light. But if your eyes are bad, your whole body will be full of darkness. If then the light within you is darkness, how great is that darkness!" Matt 6:21-23

The Battlefield of the Mind

Today the battle within the mind is still being fought. Clearly, pertaining to Genesis chapter three, many men and women have discarded the truth as methodological or fictitious. Others distinctly interpret the account as allegorical, ultimately, denying any literal or historical implications. How can we win the spiritual war if men and women do not accept the fundamental teachings that cautions humanity that sin's major strategy is to gain access into our minds by luring us into immorality and seducing us into temptation? Satan's cunning schemes cause many to succumb to biting off more than that they can chew. He enters through what we see and what we hear. Millions of people today live their lives in defeat because they have listened to the enemy. Instead of recognizing and casting untruths and immoral thoughts out of their minds, they entertain Satan's suggestions. Like Adam and Eve, they also fall into the ploy of the enemy and in the end result to biting off more than they can chew.

When discussing mankind's failures or shortcomings, how should we review morality and ethics? How can we affirm God's perspective, virtues and position concerning sin without first accepting the third chapter of Genesis as one of the greatest and convincing chapters of the Pentateuch? It is essential because for the first time, we meet Satan and confront sin. It is here for the first time that we discover that man and woman with their great freedom and dominion abused it. For the first time, it is here that we are given that mankind thought they could control sin, only to discover that immorality was uncontrollable and the question, "Could it be tamed?" It is here that man and woman found, at the most expensive cost, that disobedience is detrimental to the human health, psyche, social environment, economics and life.

The chapter's moral significance lies in the fact that it is here for the first time that humanity discovers some of the strategies of Satan's warfare on the battlefield of the mind. He will use lies, deception, temptation, and every possible tactic or weapon to cause men and women to surrender obedient thoughts and moral behaviors to disobedient conduct and imagination. As a creation of God that is made in His image, we must consider every desire, imagination, thought and impulse that is immoral and contrary to God's word. When they enter our minds and cause us to doubt the will of God and His wonderful promises, we are to reject them for our benefit, our brother's benefit and ultimately for the glory and edification of God.

The story is classified under Sin and categorized as "The Fall of Man". It is to be viewed literally, historically and allegorically. No one explanation is sufficient in effectively interpreting Genesis chapter three. To gain a clearer understanding "Don't' Let Dirt Get Into You Eyes" is to discover how men and women were seduced into letting dirt get into their eyes causing humanity to view life from a different perspective, to see and judge circumstances, situations, their environment, and people from an unclear panorama.

Stay Focused

In these last days, believers need to stay focused. They cannot afford to permit Satan with his underhanded tactics to toss dirt in their eyes causing them to lose sight and the rest to become distorted in their vision. The moment that we begin to become lackadaisical in our spiritual life by relaxing and letting down in our praying time, by becoming unenthusiastic about reading the word of God, by ceasing to be vigilant of the diverse methodologies of Satan, he will seize the opportunity to attack and toss dirt in our eyes. Today, there are Christians who fall into the trap of the enemy. They are living defeated lives. They are bound to their desires of the flesh and some are even walking under the influence of false doctrines. All of this has taken place because they lowered their defense and allowed the enemy to strike a wounding blow through access into the eye gate or ear gate.

Satan's strategy is to fill the minds of believers and non-believers completely full of temptations through the eye and ear gates that the desires of the carnal flesh will be provoked. Once the natural man is aroused, it seeks to manifest itself in our actions and reactions. The eye, I am referencing is the spiritual eye or vision. It is very vital to man and extremely detrimental to the enemy. This is why literally Samson's eyes were put out by the enemy when the Philistines captured him. Symbolically, they had distorted and stolen his spiritual vision. Samson's case reveals to readers the extreme result of the attack of the devil when he manages to get dirt in your eyes.

Let us never forget a related encounter which took place with a man that sort after God's on heart. Even he had dirt thrown in his eyes. Similar to Samson who relaxed from war, David had taken a break from the battlefield. He went up to his rooftop one day and it was there that Satan placed a temptation before his eyes. David saw Bathsheba, the daughter of Eliam, and the wife of Uriah. She was bathing, she was beautiful, and she was a citizen of his kingdom. Satan tossed dirt in David's eyes by deceiving him into permitting a fleshly enticement of pleasure to cause him to lose focus. The consequence of his affair was that he faltered in protecting the people that he pledged to God to defend while serving as their king. Also, he hurt a citizen and even had a great warrior and defender of Israel killed. He brought brokenness into a family's home. David lost sight of the plan and purpose God had ordained for him. While remembering David, let us discern that there is a higher purpose for you and others to seek above the fulfillment of individual needs.

There is another that had his share of challenges but I'd like to share with you an occasion when he did not allow dirt to get into his eyes. Unlike Samson's encounter with temptation, it did not transpire after a great triumph. Unlike David, his battle with the enemy did not occur in a great time of prosperity. It took place at a time of struggle and adversity. Often the enemy will attack by catching people off guard and unprepared directly after they have experienced some form of spiritual victory. Though he has diverse methods, Satan should not gain advantage of God fearing people: for we are not ignorant of his devices II Cor.2:8. Therefore, whether we abound in life's condition or abase in life's situations, we are to stand and be strong in the Lord and in the power of His might. Mankind should not allow dirt to get into their eyes. By resisting temptation and warring against the enemy in season and out of season and by standing against all the methods devised of the devil, believers will always emerge victorious.

Isaac encountered such an experience. There came a time when a famine had come to the land of Canaan. The omission of rain in the land caused harsh conditions to exist. Factors of the famine burdened the people and the flock. The strain of the drought forced Isaac and his family to travel to the land of the Philistines. There he had to contend with the exposure of personal trials. Because of a series of events, King Abimech sent Isaac with his family away from his people. He said, "Get from us; for you are much mightier than we." He departed and pitched his tent in the valley of Gerar. At the time, there remained a desperate need for water. So, Isaac dug again wells of his father's that were covered with dirt by the Philistines.

His servants dug in the valley of Gerar and found a well of springing water. What a wonderful and exhilarating moment; however, immediately, the herdsmen of the land quarreled with the shepherds. They claimed the water. They said we possess this water; it is ours. Isaac named the well Esek, meaning strive, because the herdsmen strove with him and his shepherds. To overcome the dissension, Isaac moved and had his servants dig another well. Yet, when water was found at the second site the herdsmen again contested him and his men. He called this well Sitnah, meaning enmity, because of the opposition encountered by his people. Finally, Isaac gathered his possessions and relocated. For the last time he searched for water. He named this well Rehoboth, meaning freedom, because at this location there were no disputes, disagreements or conflict.

The greatest characteristic regarding Isaac, during this particular trial is his ability to not allow dirt to get into his eyes or the eyes of his servants. A lot of dirt came from the ground to dig those wells but none of it got into Isaac's eyes. Isaac was a wise man. He was a man of faith and action. We should admire him because he did not let the dirt that king Abimelech dished out or the dirt that the herdsmen tossed at him effect his vision. He did not permit the actions of others to dictate his reaction. God told him not to leave the Philistine land, so he moved down into a valley. Isaac rested in God's word. He remembered the promise of God. In so many ways, didn't He say, if you would hearken to my word and be obedient by staying in the land of the Philistines I will bless you. We as a people of God must recognize who we are and whom we belong to. We must remain obedient to the Creator.

After the multiplicity of confusions, Isaac stayed put. He knew in his heart that striving was not advantageous, so he sought a location where peace would reign. This account indicates to the reader that no matter what the ungodly may say, no matter what your enemy attempts to do to you, you must not allow their efforts to cloud your vision. You must not allow them to cause you to lose focus. Always remember, regardless of whether strife reveals itself in your life, opposition prevails against you, or conflict seeks and finds you, do not lose focus, for you battle not against flesh and blood but principalities in higher places. Thus when these strategies of warfare rear-up their ugly heads against you, start digging that you may find a well of living water springing forth that shall never run dry. Let neither the dirt from others nor the dirt from your own digging get into your eyes.

Moral Application: Often dangerous temptations avail themselves to mankind in the form of objects or situations appearing to be bright, colorful, and full of beauty and optimism. Unfortunately, as situations and circumstances unfold, individuals discover that the beauty of it all was only skin deep. The greatest tool of the enemy is deception. Regardless as to whether men and women are basking in a time of plenty or experiencing a period of challenge, the enemy comes to tempt them; he aspires to place dirt in their eyes. He relentlessly seeks to cause men and women to lose focus. Stay focused! Stay vigilant! Stay alert! Keep your guard up! Never allow them to be lowered!

Chapter Five
Temptation Is Coming - It Cannot Be Deferred
Morals On Fighting Back

Matt 3:16-4:3 "As soon as Jesus was baptized, he went up out of the water. At that moment heaven was opened, and he saw the Spirit of God descending like a dove and lighting on him. And a voice from heaven said, "This is my Son, whom I love; with him I am well pleased." Then Jesus was led by the Spirit into the desert to be tempted by the devil. After fasting forty days and forty nights, he was hungry. The tempter came to him and said, "If you are the Son of God, command that these stones be made bread."

The moral of facing temptation is to first understand that trials and temptations are destined to enter into man and woman's life. The tempter, also the Great Accuser, will come against you at the most opportune time and you must be filled to the brim. For only the Holy Spirit can help you to face-up to the tempter and help you to prove your love and obedience. Only the Holy Spirit can help you to prove God's power when you are tried. There is no sin in being tempted; for Jesus "was in all points tempted like as we are" Heb 4:15. Nor does temptation necessitate sinning. Remember Jesus when tempted was found not to have sinned.

The fact that a call to service is associated with trial is often misunderstood. Notice that it was the Spirit of God that led Christ in the wilderness to be tempted only to prove Christ. Conversely it was Satan that tempted him to disprove Him. How wonderful it is to know that God has a hand in our trials. It is He that led Christ in and out of this specific challenge. It is God that must permit events to take place. Is not He and He only that is in control of all things? Most importantly, how can one prove his or her loyalty without facing trials? Is not this the question that the same tempter asked God when he said, "Job fears you for nothing. You have put a hedge around him and his household and everything he has. You have blessed his hand and caused him to prosper in all his works. You have protected him so much that even his flocks and herds are spread throughout the land. Job loves you because you bless him. He has not experienced any trial. If you would cease in blessing him and stretch out your hand and strike everything he has with trial, he will surely prove to be unfaithful and disobedient to you. If you permit him to be tried just once He will curse you to your face." To disprove the tempter's accusation and to prove Job's loyalty God said, "Very well I will remove my hedge of protection from Job and permit you to try him in all things except his life." Jesus was led into trial to prove his obedience to the Master just as Job was permitted to be tried to reveal his faithfulness. As believers we all will follow the cross and journey that Christ walked including trial; yet, like his trial, it is designed to prove us, not to disprove us. In the profound words of Joseph the Israelite, I encourage you by restating "Satan meant it for my bad, God meant it for my good."

Things That Do Not Defer The Tempter

Being Spirit Filled

Solitude

Fasting and Praying

Riches or Treasures (Living an exotic or elaborate life)

Isolation or Segregating yourself (Living in a wilderness)

<u>Being Spirit Filled</u>: Take heed of this moral truth. When Christ was baptized and straight away came out of the water the Holy Spirit of God descended appearing as a dove and landed upon Him. In our terms, Christ was filled with the Spirit. He was empowered for missions but the tempter still appeared. Neither the filling of Jesus nor the pronouncement of the Father that confirmed Christ to be His Son influenced the tempter to stay away. For believers the call to repentance literally means to change one's mind and attitude. It is a call to a proper attitude toward God, self, and sin against others and His creation. Once believers are baptized by the Spirit and filled with the Spirit we truly begin to war against Satan by serving God. Many are perplexed with the thought or wonder how life was so smooth when one was not saved and after getting saved trouble started. I once read a story that clearly explains the trials of believers.

Sam, the servant of a wealthy plantation owner, often prayed so loudly at night that others could hear him. One morning his master said, "Sam, you prayed so loud last night that you kept my wife awake. I don't see why you, who are such a good man, must pray so much." "Well," said Sam, "The devil was bothering me very much, so I prayed for the Lord to help me." "That's funny." The plantation owner said, "the devil doesn't trouble me any, and so I don't see why he should bother you." The servant explained, "You know, Master, we were duck hunting the other day." "Yes, but what has that to do with it?" "Well, when you shot, you killed some and wounded others. Then you sent me after the wounded ones. Why?" "Because I knew I had the dead ones for sure, but the wounded ones might get away." "In just the same way, Master, the devil knows he's got you for sure, and he doesn't bother you, but he is not sure about me, that's why he keeps after me all the time."

Solitude: When Jesus was on the mountain He was alone in a secluded place. Yet, even solitude did not stop the tempter from coming into his life. Many people believe if they avoid others or confine themselves from certain situations, events or experiences in life and if they steer clear of conflict or potential challenges their lives will be free of troubles. How soon we discover that isolation from others and circumstances does not defer trial in one's life.

Fasting and Praying: While Christ was in the wilderness He fasted for forty days and forty nights. He also prayed for the same duration. Often after speaking with many believers concerning fasting and praying, I leave with the impression that most believe that if they fast and pray, trials are not to enter into their lives. This gives an indication that there is a misunderstanding of the purpose of fasting and praying. Fasting and Prayer is given to believers to prepare them for warfare and to spiritually edify them with a strength that only the process of it can offer. Christ fasted and prayed for spiritual warfare against the tempter. He did not go into the wilderness blind or without a clue that he would be facing Satan. Thus, he prepared himself for war. When we fast and pray we are not deferring trial. We are preparing ourselves or ourselves and others for victory over the tempter. The example that confirms the ethical principle is Christ's response to His disciples when He said in Mark 9:29, "This kind can come forth by nothing, but by prayer and fasting." Indicating that certain trials can only be defeated by prayer and fasting.

<u>Neither An Exotic Life Nor A Life Of Wilderness</u>: Adam and Eve lived in an area known as paradise. Yet, within their perfect environment the tempter entered to try them. Men and women today are under the impression that if they rear their children in elaborate homes and become a part of certain social economic statuses they are confident their efforts will suspend trials. Far be it from the truth. It is a modern day philosophy sold to those who will buy into it. The extreme opposite thought is turned toward living a life of wilderness. People that believe a life of escape from social demands or responsibilities is the answer. Perhaps these are the same people that believe by seeking to live a rural life, one without electricity or central air and heat, and raise their own garden and livestock will relieve them from trial. Possibly, it could be those that selected to dwell in the urban wilderness and opted not to possess anything of value; whereby, allowing the government or working citizens to support them; thinking that they have made their life easy by deferring trial. It is not long that they discover that similar to Christ, wilderness and John's wilderness trial is ever present and the tempter is near.

How Does Evil Get To Us?

As we address the subtopic "Things That Do Not Defer The Tempter", a prominent inquiry that's well associated with trial and temptation is, "How does evil get to us?" If men and women cannot defer the tempter, then let us address how evil maneuvers its way through the maize of morality, through the thickets of ethics, through man's vast awareness of God's Law, through an immense legalistic society and manages to touch us, grab hold to us, and become entangled in our lives. In many cases it causes people to falter or stumble to some of the lowest states ever experienced in their lives.

First, evil gets to us because it is present or so near. When we look around our world we discover that evil exist in all arenas of life. Within all strands of mass media the communication received is universal turmoil and it is not propaganda. The scope of evil presence is national and international. The prevalence of evil is global. It extends from the war in Israel or the war on terrorism to the war on discrimination and injustice within the United States. Regardless, our efforts in building alliances and formulating various treaties, evil has established its presence in man's life. If we would agree that evil is equated to all acts, deeds, thoughts, articulations, and motives that are immoral or that all acts, deeds, thoughts, articulations, and motives that do not conform to the law of Love are immoral, then we are just to state immorality exists in Adam and Eve' environment, it found its company in the days of Noah, immorality cohabitated with the men and women, especially with the religious groups of Jesus' days, and today we continue to struggle with the tempter that entices humanity to live immorally. It is ever present in our environment. Dr. George A Buttrick said, "A man can be walking down 5th Ave. intent only on the sights – nay, he may even be uplifted in mind to think on the kindness of a friend – when suddenly, as if some demon had fallen through the air to whisper in his ear, a base treachery waylays him. The voice says ... "Brother can you spare your soul?" Evil gets to us because it is so near.

Secondly, evil gets to us because it manifests itself in subtle ways. Paul suggests in II Cor.11:14 that when evil or immorality confronts each individual it disguises itself by presenting itself as an angel of light. Evil approaches us as if it was a servant of God; however, evil is the father of lies. He disguised himself by using the serpent in the garden to deceive Eve. There are accounts that he used men and women to influence others to commit immoral acts. He will use your mother as he did Harodius to convince her daughter to behave immorally when she requested for John the Baptizer's head. He will use your father as he used Saul, Jonathan's father and king of Israel, to commit the immoral act of attempting to kill David. Evil will disguise itself through friends. Timothy informs the early church that many men and women, theirs friends, will become lovers of themselves, and live without self-control. They will become lovers of false gods. If that does not make you aware of evil's subtle ways, then be on alert that another conning disguise of evil is, it can use you if you permit it to commit immoral acts. Did not Cain listen to the immoral thought within him? His interpersonal desires caused him to kill Abel. Evil masked itself and Cain accepted it without an inward struggle. Evil gets to us because it manifests itself in subtle ways.

Thirdly, evil gets to us by appealing to our innate quest for freedom. Psychologically, there are innate characteristics of men and women that influence their behavior and emotions. When the evil one ask Eve, "Hath God, said, 'Ye shall not eat of every tree of the garden?'" his question was designed to eat at the heart of man's innate desire to be free and exercise his or her autonomy. And notice, next the tempter was shrewd enough to allege that by eating the fruit that man and woman would become as gods; thus, infringing on the innate aspiration of mankind to control, rule and dominate. Averting their attention from God and causing them to appease their innate psyche for the quest of freedom was the tempter's plan. That's how he got to us.

People have a tendency to focus on the things they will not be permitted to do as Christians. No one should evaluate their life by reviewing the things they are called by Christ to be separated from. We all should rejoice in the many things God allows us to do and the freedom Christianity offers. We ought to willfully lie down the earthly things and gladly enjoy the newness of life in Christ Jesus. Jesus said, "Take my yoke for it is easy and my burden is light." Yes, there are restrictions in the life of believers but without separation from immorality you cannot have true fellowship with God. As believers, what more honor could there be in knowing that God is in control of all things and if we allow Him to have full control of our life, all that we say and do will be pleasing to the Father.

Fourthly, evil gets to us by challenging our interpretation of God's commandments. The first aspect of the tempter's strategy was to get close to mankind. In doing so, the tempter disguised himself. Then, to influence men and women to act immorally evil preys on mankind's innate quest for freedom. Finally, it is an interesting fact that the battle in the Garden of Eden between man and woman and the tempter, and the battle in the wilderness between Christ and the tempter encompassed the moral factor. Yet, both entailed profound messages concerning a deep cry for proper interpretation of God's word. The word of God is the means by which God makes Himself known, declares His will, and brings about His purposes. The phrases such as word of God, and word of the Lord are applied to the commanding word of God that brought creation into existence and also destroyed that same world through the waters of the Flood. It declares God's commitment and promises, his blessings and particular instructions from God.

God's word is totally dependable. When heard and responded to, His word meets deep needs in the human heart and provides joy, satisfaction, and confident direction that can be achieved in no other manner. The importance of God's word and the significance of what it attributes to the life and well being of humanity distinctly determines the fact that mankind can not indulge in detrimental debates over the word of God. We must constantly seek clarity of God's word and not incline ourselves to private interpretations because evil gets to us by challenging our interpretation of God's commandments.

How To Fight Back: The Weapons Of Our Warfare Are Not Carnal

Jesus answered, "It is written: 'Man does not live on bread alone, but on every word that comes from the mouth of God.'" Then the devil took him to the holy city and had him stand on the highest point of the temple. "If you are the Son of God," he said, "throw yourself down. For it is written: "'He will command his angels concerning you, and they will lift you up in their hands, so that you will not strike your foot against a stone.'"

Jesus answered him, "It is also written: 'Do not put the Lord your God to the test.'" Again, the devil took him to a very high mountain and showed him all the kingdoms of the world and their splendor. "All this I will give you," he said, "if you will bow down and worship me." Jesus said to him, "Away from me, Satan! For it is written: 'Worship the Lord your God, and serve him only.'" Then the devil left him, and angels came and attended him. Matt 4:4-11

The greatest example of spiritual warfare is given by the victor himself. He is Jesus Christ. Where Adam and Eve lost the battle He won the war. We learn in Christ's temptation that believers can overcome trials, challenges and temptations by fighting back the tempter. We can overcome temptation by doing God's will. Most importantly, we can only overcome the tempter by using the full word of God. This is how believers fight back; by allowing the word of God to be our shield and sword. Each of the three temptations Christ faced had overtones of the decisions that He had to make throughout His entire ministry. Additionally, they represent the three categories of sin that we must stand firm against throughout our lives.

If ever the Devil transformed himself into an angel of false light he did so then and more so now. He disguised himself by presenting himself as a genius or guardian angel. He subtly joined the need of Christ's hunger with an act he labeled proper. It was concealed in his request for Christ to turn the rock into bread. He always tries to get us to do things his way or our way but never God's way.

Doubt even serves the satanic purpose more so than blatant denial or heresy. For the tempter will inquire of you, "If you are a child of God, why then are you sick. If you are a child of God, why don't you have this object or that item? If you are a child of God why does everyone appear to be better off than you? "If" is a word filled with contingencies and often used by the tempter to cause doubt. Christ taught us how to fight back with the word of God. Each time Jesus responded He said, "It is written."

What does "It is written" mean? In the general sense because it references the word of God and God is the word, then it carries a similar connotation as the name "I Am". "It is written" therefore cannot be clearly confined to a specific term or meaning. It is diverse in nature. It is what it means for each given situation or event, however, clearly the term is stated in full worship and reverence of the Creator. Within the three trials of Jesus "It is written" means that men and women are to place a priority on the word of God and live by it not solely by the desires of the flesh, or earthly ordinances and advice. It means never test God. Allow Him to lead you in all aspects of your life. Also, it means to fear God and worship Him only.

When we review the complete word of God we discover that we fight back with a wealth of knowledge or keen awareness of truth just as Jesus did. If you become ill or seriously sick, you will be able to face trials knowing that in the word of God it does not say you will not get sick but it does say that God will comfort you and He is able to heal you of all your infirmities. Paul had a thorn in his flesh that many interpret to have been a physical disorder. However, when he viewed the word of God he found that the thorn made him stronger in his focus on completing his work for Christ. Paul wrote Timothy and addressed his stomach problem. When we discover that we are confronted in trial that places us in dire need, we can fight back with an alertness that God's word does not say we will not have a need but what it assures us is God will provide all of our needs. Peter saw that there was a need among the early church so he collected land and items from believers that had possessions and distributed them among believers that had a need. Also, when the tempter comes to try us through the contingency of prosperity we can fight back in confidence that we are a rich people because we are heirs of the Kingdom of God. For the word does not say you believers will prosper more so than anyone; yet, it does say He will take from those that have and give it to those that have not. Remember Paul. He was one of the most educated Pharisees; but prosperity for himself was not his goal. His goal was the prosperity of the gospel unto the entire world. He became abase that others would abound. Yet, in all things he was content. In trial or prosperity always be conscious that God takes you down, such as Jesus was baptized first, to build up; however, Satan builds you up only to take you down. The things of Satan can look so appealing but they are transit. Not only are they temporal, they are embodied to steal, kill and destroy.

Filled With The Holy Spirit

To defeat the tempter you must be full to the brim with the Holy Spirit. Eph 6:11 say, "Put on the full armor of God so that you can take your stand against the devil's schemes." You must be filled with the Spirit because the apostle Luke informs us that the tempter is persistent in his challenge of believers. Luke says, after Christ fought back and immerged victorious, Satan left him for a short season. Though evil is not more powerful than good, because he was defeated in heaven, in the wilderness, on the cross, and at your baptism, we find out that he never quits. Satan would have us believe that if we win one battle we have won the war. The wilderness was not the last time that Satan tempted Jesus to take a detour around the cross. The temptation to bypass the cross followed Jesus even into the Garden of Gethsemane. The forms of temptation are the same for us as they were against Jesus. The way of victory over temptation is the same for us as it was for Him. To fight back we must stay filled to the brim with the Holy Spirit because the next plan of attack from the tempter is to catch you off guard or at your lowest level.

Moral Application: Though God is influential in the trials we face, we are assured that He will give us no more than we can bear and that He has provided a way of escape. That way of escape is centered in how we fight back. If we would stand against all trials and temptations by saying, "It is written", we would use the full word of God against the tempter. The way we fight back is by putting on the full armor of God that we may stand against the diverse attacks of the tempter. I remind you that diverse means physical and psychological warfare. I often reflect on Luke 4:5. During the time when Jesus was in the wilderness, which was miles away from Jerusalem or any major city, Satan took Him up into a high mountain and immediately showed Him all the kingdoms of the world. Then Satan carried Jesus from that particular place to Jerusalem and set Him on a pinnacle of the temple, and said throw yourself down. All of these adventures originated from the wilderness and journeyed to vast destinations. Yet, they concluded at the origin of the wilderness. Were they actually physically achieved or were they psychological /spiritual ventures? To properly respond to such a challenging question I bring to your memory that in areas of the Bible we read that the Spirit led, meaning that a spirit can physically lead you. In certain text such as John the revelator, we read that the Spirit caught him up. This means that spiritually or psychologically men and women can be transported, transfigured, transformed and even translated. Thus, it would behoove all believers not to let dirt get in their eyes by fighting back with the awareness that battles can be either physical, spiritual, and or psychological. Perchance, your battle could consist of these challenges.

A Cry for Ethical and Moral Strength

Chapter Six
Partiality
Morals Against Prejudices And Improper Judgments

The word of the LORD came to Jonah son of Amittai: "Go to the great city of Nineveh and preach against it, because its wickedness has come up before me." But Jonah ran away from the LORD and headed for Tarshish. He went down to Joppa, where he found a ship bound for that port. After paying the fare, he went aboard and sailed for Tarshish to flee from the LORD. Then the LORD sent a great wind on the sea, and such a violent storm arose that the ship threatened to break up. All the sailors were afraid and each cried out to his own god. And they threw the cargo into the sea to lighten the ship. But Jonah had gone below deck, where he lay down and fell into a deep sleep. The captain went to him and said, "How can you sleep? Get up and call on your god! Maybe he will take notice of us, and we will not perish." Then the sailors said to each other, "Come, let us cast lots to find out who is responsible for this calamity." They cast lots and the lot fell on Jonah. So they asked him, "Tell us, who is responsible for making all this trouble for us? What do you do? Where do you come from? What is your country? From what people are you?" He answered, "I am a Hebrew and I worship the LORD, the God of heaven, who made the sea and the land." This terrified them and they asked, "What have you done?" (They knew he was running away from the LORD, because he had already told them so.) The sea was getting rougher and rougher. So they asked him, "What should we do to you to make the sea calm down for us?" "Pick me up and throw me into the sea," he replied, "and it will become calm. I know that it is my fault that this great storm has come upon you." Instead, the men did their best to row back to land. But they could not, for the sea grew even wilder than before. Then they cried to the LORD, "O LORD, please do not let us die for taking this man's life. Do not hold us accountable for killing an innocent man, for you, O LORD, have done as you pleased." Then they took Jonah and threw him overboard, and the raging sea grew calm. At this the men greatly feared the LORD, and they offered a sacrifice to the LORD and made vows to him. But the LORD provided a great fish to swallow Jonah, and Jonah was inside the fish three days and three nights. "..."And the LORD commanded the fish, and it vomited Jonah onto dry land. Then the word of the LORD came to Jonah a second time: "Go to the great city of Nineveh and proclaim to it the message I give you." Jonah obeyed the word of the LORD and went to Nineveh. Now Nineveh was a very important city-- a visit required three days. On the first day, Jonah started into the city. He proclaimed: "Forty more days and Nineveh will be overturned." The Ninevites believed God. They declared a fast, and all of them, from the greatest to the least, put on sackcloth. When the news reached the king of Nineveh, he rose from his throne, took off his royal robes, covered himself with sackcloth and sat down in the dust. Then he issued a proclamation in Nineveh: "By the decree of the king and his nobles: Do not let any man or beast, herd or flock, taste anything; do not let them eat or drink. But let man and beast be covered with sackcloth.

Let everyone call urgently on God. Let them give up their evil ways and their violence. Who knows? God may yet relent and with compassion turn from his fierce anger so that we will not perish." When God saw what they did and how they turned from their evil ways, he had compassion and did not bring upon them the destruction he had threatened. Jonah chapters 1,3.

Sending a Person of Peace

The story of Jonah is one of the least understood and most abused books in the application of its moral significance. Some get caught-up over the questions whether the fish was a whale or whether it was possible for God to make a fish large enough to swallow a man. It is sad to note that for many people this story is nothing more than a tale of a big fish. We would be wise to turn our thoughts toward this book as a divine word centered on God's great plan and purpose for all people and communicating His message that is so desperately needed by all nations. Unfortunately, demonstrated in the story of Jonah is the profound truth that partiality toward various people has attempted to hinder the spread of the Gospel.

The name Jonah in Hebrew means *dove, peace, or pur*ity. How special is the man or woman that God selects to carry a message of peace to a person or people. Even God's word says

"Blessed are the peacemakers, for they will be called sons of God." I remind you that Jonah was the son of Amitai, which means *truth*. In translation, Jonah already was the son of God, because God is T*ruth*. A specially selected man was called to go into a foreign land to be impartial unto a foreign people. This request was uncommon of a Jew. They were nationalist. They associated little or none at all with many nations. The most prevalent factor that many either do not know or do not understand about Nineveh is it was founded by Nimrod son of Cush and grandson of Ham. Nineveh was built and inhabited by descendents of Ham that grew to a population exceeding two hundred thousand people. Much later it became the capital of Assyria and was known as one of the most ancient cities of the world. Three days journey was its measurements, which in part encroached on the territory assigned to Shem, Jonah's forefather. Nineveh was a city of bloodshed. For the Assyrians waged many wars of conquest and employed brutal methods in killing captured warriors. They stripped cities of their wealth and enslaved many.

Partiality in Missions

Because of God's request that Jonah serve as a true missionary, Jonah rose to flee the presence of God. He did so by traveling in the opposite direction that God instructed him to go. His decision to go to Tarshish which means the presence of God, revealed His bigotry. Have you stopped to really think about it? Jonah was a bigoted Jew whose prejudices caused him not to have dealings with heathens. I do not say this in a derogatory fashion; however, I do attempt to properly disclose the element of partiality within the story that is rarely conveyed.

You can't stay in the presence of God when you refuse to do his will. Why? Because God will chastise you and He will not allow you to have peace within yourself. There will exist an internal struggle. Like the city, Joppa, Jonah only saw and he desired religion too glamorous or beautiful just as it was in the temple with its well-maintained facility, eloquently orchestrated music, and adoringly attired priest. Not many seem to want a religion that requires them to get their hands dirty through the toils of missionary work. Most do not desire to struggle for the advancement of God's Kingdom. They want things in life to be handed to them on a silver platter.

Moral Application: Jonah was a son of Abraham. He discriminated against all that were not of the same heritage. He is a symbol of the pre-church and their staunch snobbish attitude that seems to have characterized Israel's religion and partial outlook on other people in his era. Bitterness, injustice, indifference, and discrimination is a malignancy of the spirit that plagues the church and deters growth. It is a sickness that does to the soul what a disease does to the body. Partiality affects the body of Christ as cancer affects our physical body.

The partial perspective that the pre-church displayed is made obvious in the church of today. Jonah was called by God to carry peace into a foreign land and to a foreign people. Today God is calling the Reformed churches, the Puritans, the Evangelicals, the Christians, the Congregationalists, the Presbyterians, the Apostolic, the Pentecostal, etc., to carry a message of peace to the lost. However, similar to Jonah's response, the Creator has to work on the present day churches' partiality. He has to chastise many believers to turn them away from their denominational prejudices that they may put away self, heritage, culture, social economic statuses, and various other psyches for the furtherance of the Gospel. Partiality is contrary to faith in Christ because He is the Creator of all, Sustainer of all, Forgiver of all, and Lover of all. Partiality is against God's promise because it is His will that all receive the awareness of His son Jesus the Christ. Partiality is not in the best interest of Christians because if believers are partial or indifferent toward certain people we have pre-judged and shown favoritism, which abandons the "Golden Rule." Do unto others, as you would have them do unto you. If it could be said any better, it would be "love your neighbor". Thus, partiality is a violation of the law of love. In the moral sense, an astute believer will be found precious in God's sight if they would act in love towards others.

Chapter Seven
The Problem With Partiality
Morals Against Prejudices And Improper Judgments

"Coming to America", starring Eddie Murphy, Arsenio Hall, James Earl Jones and John Amos was a fascinating movie. The character Akeem, played by Eddie, was an African prince. At the age of twenty-one Akeem defied the wishes of his kingdom by refusing to marry the beautiful bride chosen for him. Instead he journeyed to America disguised as a peasant to find a woman that would love him as a person, and not love him for his possessions or lofty position. Akeem knew of people's partiality and how they treated persons of riches versus their appalling treatment of those that have little. In the midst of his masquerade he gets a job working for a fast food restaurant owner, played by John Amos. Arsenio Hall who plays Akeem's servant disguised as his friend in America also is employed by the owner. For weeks, both engage in menial and manual labor but Akeem proves to be a hard worker that has taken interest in the owner's daughter; however, the owner notices his passions and does all he can do to keep them separated. He desires for his daughter to marry another young man that comes from a family with a little clout and the potential to gain much money. In an effort to deter Akeem, the owner treated him and his friend harshly and with a snobbish attitude. However, the daughter continued to gain an interest in Akeem and eventually grew to love him for his hard work, commitment, ability to listen, compassion for others, generosity, joviality, and kindness. Later, the owner discovers that his employee is a prince and begins to treat him differently; yet, his daughter continued to love him for who he was as a person.

Partiality is a snobbery and favoritism that is usually predicated on exterior conditions. Similar to prejudice it is a bias opinion either favorable or more often unfavorable. Discrimination is to make a distinction by action or words for or against a person on the basis of race, sex, religion, or socio-economic status. There are countless expressions of discriminations based on men and women's prejudices. The disciple James states that believers are to live under the law of freedom or to others the law of liberty. If we are to fully understand that Christ sets oppressed people free, that He extends mercy to all men, and without prejudice he welcomes all to his table, then we know that He loves without discrimination or respect of person and so should we. The law of freedom requests believers to speak and live by the complete word of God in vigilance that the same law shall judge them.

The Law of Freedom

James questions the presence of prejudice and discrimination in the church. He says, "My brothers and sisters, you cannot really believe that you have faith in our Glorious Lord Jesus Christ, and yet continue to have respect of person." Can a person really perceive that they are practicing true religion or are truly worshiping Christ while harboring in their heart partiality? To God, the finest worship you can offer Him is service of the poor and oppressed. It does not rest in elaborate preaching or magnificent music or carefully administered services. It is perfectly possible for a Church to be so taken up with the beauty of its building and the splendor of its liturgy or the euphoria of its service, that it has neither the time nor the money for practical Christian service. Peter stated so clearly, God is not a respecter of person and believers should grab hold to this truth and allow it to dock in their hearts. Consequently, many do not.

Suppose a man came into your worship service wearing a gold ring and fine clothes, and secondly a poor man in shabby clothes also enters. Have many believers shown special attention to the man wearing fine clothes by saying, "Here's a good seat for you," but snobbishly said to the poor man, "Stand over there" or "Sit on the floor right by me"? Then even churches have discriminated among themselves and become judges with evil thoughts. Prophesied from James 2:2-4.

The moral against partiality is that within the church there must be no distinction of rank and prestige when men or women meet in the presence of the King of Glory. There can be no merit of heritage in the presence of the supreme holiness of God. The hymnist, Reginald Heber, in 1826 expressed it so clearly through the lyrics of "Holy,

Holy, Holy." He wrote, "Casting down their golden crowns around the glassy sea;" In His presence all earthly distinctions are less than dust and all earthy righteousness as filthy rags. The church should be a place where masters come and sit next to the slave, where both rejoice and praise the Father together, where leaders enter and are led by common folks into worship. It must become a place where the gap between the rich and poor is dried up and men and women are merged, a place where lines of the have and have-nots are broken.

If Christ was Partial

Unfortunately, the church is the most segregated institution in the world. Each Sunday morning each congregation's membership is a manifestation of this profound reality. As followers of the law of freedom and believers of our Glorious Lord; believers must cease their practice of partiality. Honestly, if Christ were partial at all, evidence would lean towards the poor. Did he not choose the poor to become rich in faith and heirs to his Kingdom? Yes, 1 Cor 1:27-28 agrees by stating, "God hath chosen the foolish things of the world to confound the wise; and God hath chosen the weak things of the world to confound the things which are mighty; And base things of the world, and things which are despised, hath God chosen, yea, and things which are not, to bring to naught things that are:" And Luke 4:18 agrees by stating that the Spirit of the Lord came upon Christ, because he hath anointed Him to preach the gospel to the poor; he had sent Him to heal the brokenhearted, to preach deliverance to the captives, and recovering of sight to the blind, to set at liberty those that are bruised. Abraham Lincoln said, "God must love the common people because he made so many of them."

When considering the law of freedom concerning partiality, believers are reminded that they cannot decide to keep part of God's Law and ignore the rest. If the law is broken in the slightest form it has been violated in totality and the person is guilty. Thus, let believers that are guilty of partiality seek forgiveness and be renewed with a love for all their brothers and sisters.

Carl L. Sweat, Jr., D. Min.

Chapter Eight
I Am Glad That You Have Come
Moral Strength Against Discrimination

Have you ever attempted a task knowing that it was too difficult for an individual to accomplish? Yet, you began to work at it, only to grow weary with every effort toward productive labor. Suddenly, from the midst of no-where someone appeared to help you accomplish an impossible assignment. When the task was completed you peered over to the God sent angel and said, "I am so glad that you've come. I do not know what I would have done without your support." This is the identical scenario that occurred between man and God. Man started a task of laboring toward his salvation but he only grew weary with every effort of his labor. Then God showed-up from heaven and accomplished for us that which we could never achieve. What we could not do by ourselves, Jesus finished. Jesus Christ was the personification of the Father. He was God incarnated in the flesh. Today, we can say to God, "I am so glad that you have come. I don't know what I would have done without your help." The story of Cornelius and Peter is parallel to our example.

At Caesarea there was a man named Cornelius, a centurion in what was known as the Italian Regiment. He and all his family were devout and God-fearing; he gave generously to those in need and prayed to God regularly. One day at about three in the afternoon he had a vision. He distinctly saw an angel of God, who came to him and said, "Cornelius!" Cornelius stared at him in fear. "What is it, Lord?" he asked. The angel answered, "Your prayers and gifts to the poor have come up as a memorial offering before God. Now send men to Joppa to bring back a man named Simon who is called Peter. When the angel who spoke to him had gone, Cornelius called two of his servants and a devout soldier who was one of his attendants. He told them everything that had happened and sent them to Joppa. Prior to the servants reaching Peter, he had a vision that revealed that God is not partial, but Peter did not understand the vision. While Peter was wondering about the meaning of the vision, the men sent by Cornelius found out where Simon's house was and stopped at the gate. They called out, asking if Simon who was known as Peter was

A Cry for Ethical and Moral Strength

staying there. The men replied, "We have come from Cornelius the centurion. He is a righteous and God-fearing man, who is respected by all the Jewish people. A holy angel told him to have you come to his house so that he could hear what you have to say." Then Peter invited the men into the house to be his guests.

The next day Peter started out with them, and some of the brothers from Joppa went along. The following day he arrived in Caesarea. Cornelius was expecting them and had called together his relatives and close friends. As Peter entered the house, Cornelius met him and fell at his feet in reverence. In his action and words he conveyed that he was glad Peter had come. But Peter made him get up. "Stand up," he said, "I am only a man myself." As Peter was talking with him, he went inside and found a large gathering of people. He said to them: "You are well aware that it is against our law for a Jew to associate with a Gentile or to visit him. But God has shown me that I should not call any man impure or unclean and that I should not be partial to any man. Peter then realized how true it is that God does not show favoritism. He began to speak to them concerning the birth, life, death and resurrection of Christ. Especially how God anointed Jesus of Nazareth with the Holy Spirit and power, and how He went around doing good and healing all that were under the power of the devil, because God was with Him. Peter was an eyewitness of everything Christ did in the country of the Jews. While Peter was speaking these words, the Holy Spirit came upon all who heard the message. Everyone present was astonished that the gift of the Holy Spirit had been poured out even on the Gentiles. Acts 10.

Soon after much fellowshipping, as Peter and those that accompanied him prepared to leave, Cornelius, his kinsmen and near friends drew closer and with joy in their hearts, smiles on their faces and laughter in the air, they extended Peter their gratitude by saying to him "We are so glad that you have come to us." In return, Peter said to them, "I am so glad that I have come…"

Salvation, justice, equality, and liberty is generally assumed to be the birthright of all men and women; yet, mankind is anything but free, treated fairly, and extended the gospel without partiality. Bondage appears to be our common lot, for partiality and segregation is prominent in everyone's life. We are bound by our daily patterns of life. We are bound by social economic statuses. We are bound by language or accents. Men and women are divided by education. We are segregated by heritage, race, or color. We are separated by employment and sex. We are bound by our diverse dreams and aspirations. People are even partial to one another because of their faith. Despite man's partiality, whether it is psychologically motivated, economically generated, originated from a social parameter, or religiously inspired, Peter, with his profound insight into the need of man to unify has forever made clear that God is not a respecter of person.

Just as Christ was the personification of God the Father and the expressed image of God, similarly are all men and women made in the image of the Father. Is it not written, "God created man in His own image, in the image of God created he him; male and female created he them."? Thus, we are to reflect his likeness unto the world as we allow our light to shine. Believers are to mirror the image of God. However, problems of our Christian character and image begin to surface when we find that we are not clearly exhibiting the true image of the Father to others. When many view themselves they discover that they are identical to Peter. Similar, to Peter we are men and women that need to set aside certain prejudices, certain preconceived ideas, and remove the many differences that have caused us not to be true neighbors and worshipers of God.

Peter's response to his vision gives revelation to mankind. It acknowledges that in no case or circumstance can any reasonably suggest that another person, nation, or race, that God has created, is unfit for your help, unsuited for your compassion, unmerited for your love, or unwelcome to His gospel because, often, through you God will shine on the just and the unjust. He will rain on the just and the unjust. He is God, we are his servants, and He loves all men and women for He is the Father of all creations. Thus, in his likeness we are to be fathers and mothers to all creations.

Many are Waiting for You to Come

Notice that Cornelius waited for the man of God to come and when he arrived he immediately invited him inside. Also, he had invited his relatives, neighbors, and servants. Why? Because Cornelius knew something that we often forget. Cornelius recognized that a man and woman of God possess life-changing power. The same power that was in Christ, the same power that raised Christ, the same power that Christ used to heal and deliver people is in men and women of God.

Power that makes people whole again.	Power that gives new life and a new beginning.
Power that cast down your burdens.	Power that sets the captive free.
Power that defeats all sickness and diseases.	Power that makes all things possible.

Should we as a people deny anyone access to the power that we possess? Should we permit our partiality to prevent men and women from hearing an encouraging word from God the Father? Should we allow our prejudices to exclude the word of God from lifting other's spirits or from causing men and women to yield themselves to the Father? Should we be permitted to hinder the Holy Spirit from moving in anyone's life because of our prejudices? The answer to all these questions is No!

Moral Application: Cornelius was aware that a man of God was coming to preach deliverance to the captive, set at liberty them that were bruised, and share the Holy Spirit with those in his or her company. He was so excited that he called all that he knew so that they may receive a blessing from God. This is how believers are to make the entire world feel. The world should feel excited about the power the believers possess and excited about the great possibility of spectacular and supernatural things that can take place while they are in the presence of a believer. Christians are not to be partial. Upon Peter's arrival, Cornelius bowed to honor him but Peter told him to stand. He said to Cornelius, "I myself am nothing but a man." How wonderful it is when men and women do not pull rank on others. How magnificent it is when men and women can say that all I have and all that I am is because of Christ. How glorious it will be when people can lift one another up, look each other in the eyes with a level mind and heart, and without partiality say, we are but men and women. We all are brothers and sisters and our common bond is that we are lovers and servants of God. Peter proved to be a Good Samaritan and all believers should possess the same character because a Good Samaritan must extend love and compassion to all people that have a particular need.

Chapter Nine
Thank God, I'm Jesus' Neighbor
Moral Strengthening In Christian Duty

"A man was going down from Jerusalem to Jericho, when he fell into the hands of robbers. They stripped him of his clothes, beat him and went away, leaving him half dead. A priest happened to be going down the same road, and when he saw the man, he passed by on the other side. When a Levite came to the place and saw him, he also passed by on the other side. But a Samaritan, as he traveled, came where the man was; and when he saw him, he took pity on him.

He went to him and bandaged his wounds, pouring on oil and wine. Then he put the man on his own donkey, took him to an inn and took care of him. The next day he took out two silver coins and gave them to the innkeeper. 'Look after him,' he said, 'and when I return, I will reimburse you for any extra expense you may have.' "Which of these three do you think was a neighbor to the man who fell into the hands of robbers?" The expert in the law replied, "The one who had mercy on him." Jesus told him, "Go and do likewise."

Go and Do Likewise

To bid a man to love his neighbor as he would himself can be most difficult especially when considering the fact that many people, similar to the scribes, whose passion for the Law caused them to define man's neighbor as their fellow Jews or fellow believers. They feel that no one outside of their mold or circle is their neighbor. Thus, they refuse to assist persons that are not believers of the faith. But thanks be to God that Jesus does not see love in the same manner.

We shall find that we are all Jesus' neighbors not by works or by position, but because He possesses a love that seeks the good of all men under all circumstances. His love for us is a spontaneous overflow of a heart that sacrificed self in the presence of human need.

In separatism, the lawyer stood and facetiously inquired of Jesus to define the term neighbor. He asked Jesus, "Who is my neighbor?"

Jesus, not only defined the term neighbor, he also disclosed our responsibility to them. Thank God, that Jesus saw me as his neighbor and thank God He sees all men and women as his neighbors. Jesus defines a neighbor as a person that is in need. Coincidentally, His definition fits the condition of mankind because all have fallen short and are in need of the salvation of the Lord. Thank God He has come to our rescue and thank God that he sees all men as His neighbor that he would give all that He had not excluding his very life so we could be healed of the wound of sin. The glory about being Christ's neighbor is that Christ was the expressed image of God, He thought it not robbery to be compared equal with God, but he made himself of no reputation or supremacy, and took upon him the form of a servant and was made in the likeness of men. Though He is God He did not exert his authority over us. It is for our cause that He is not ashamed to call us brothers and sisters.

Peter saw Cornelius's need and helped him. He also picked him up when he was down. The angel picked up John the Revelator and said we both are servants of God. This is what Jesus does; he is not partial toward us because he knows our every thought, our needs, and he considers us as his brothers and sisters.

There are five characters within the parable of the "Good Samaritan." First is The Certain Man.

Take heed that it was a "A certain man that went down from Jerusalem to Jericho, and fell among thieves, which stripped him of his raiment, and wounded him, and departed leaving him for dead." The traveler obviously was a reckless and fool-hearted character, for people seldom attempted the Jerusalem to Jericho road alone if they were carrying goods or valuables. Seeking safety in numbers, Jews normally traveled in groups. We can sympathize with the "Certain Man" because more and more of our society is becoming individualized. People are proclaiming their independence of one another. Less and less true friendships are being cultivated causing persons to attempt things generally done by two or more. Today, people are placing themselves in unsafe and unsecure positions because of the environment of social, economical, and religious

A Cry for Ethical and Moral Strength

divisions that we live. Independence is a good thing but it can be detrimental at times.

This "Certain Man" has no name. That means he represents either you or me. His identity is concealed so that we can insert ourselves into this story. Each person in life is on a journey. Paul states in Philippians chapter three that life is nothing more than a journey, whereby we travel through. The roads that we travel are rocky and have their ups and downs. Often, the enemy that overcomes us at times confronts us and we find ourselves needing help. The thief will always come to steal, kill and destroy, but glory be to God that Christ comes to all men that they may have life more abundantly.

The robbers stripped the traveler of his raiment and wounded him. They departed leaving him for dead. To be stripped is to become exposed or made naked of your innocence and righteousness. The thief stripped Adam and Eve of their innocence when their eyes were opened discovering that they were naked. The thief wounded the traveler. To wound means to take away your strength and power. Exactly, what he did to Adam and Eve. He wounded them by taking away the power of dominion. Finally, the thief left the traveler for dead. Satan left man and woman in the Garden of Eden spiritually dead and physically in the process of dying. But glory be to God, because Christ is our neighbor, He saw our need and He covered us with His blood. He paid for the healing of our infirmities through His suffering. He is an adequate propitiation for all men and women. He makes no distinction between those He helps for He is no respecter of person.

The second character is the priest. It was by chance that he came down the same road. However, when he saw him, he showed partiality by crossing over to the other side of the road so as not to make direct contact with the wounded traveler. Notice the words by chance. It cautions the reader to consider that at a certain place in time of the process or work of God, when men were half dead and steadily moving toward complete darkness of death, He sent a priest to assist them. But the priest became partial and did not respond to the people that needed help. Today, believers are of the priesthood and we are called for such a time as this; yet, are we helping those in need or are we demonstrating our partiality by avoiding persons in need?

The third character is the Levite. Likewise, he journeyed to the same location of the wounded traveler but he had the common decency to at least look at him. Unfortunately, after he looked at the traveler, he also passed by on the other side. The Levite seemed to have ventured closer to the man but offered no help. With the exception of the line of Aaron, the Levites were chosen by God to assist the priest. Coincidently, believers are chosen by God to assist Christ, who is the chief priest, in Kingdom building. We are Disciples of Christ. We are His servants. We are His helpers. Thus, can we select those we will help and those that we will not help? Can we decide whom we will discriminate? No. Unlike the Levite, we can give the wounded the impression that we are interested in their welfare and not help them. We cannot go half way in the work of Christ. We must go all the way. We must not be partial to anyone. All people are important to Christ and as His helpers they are important to us.

The fourth character is the Good Samaritan. A certain Samaritan journeyed and came to the wounded traveler. When he saw him, he had compassion on him and helped him. If you were a Jew, such as the lawyer listening to this story, you would obviously expect that with the Samaritan's arrival the villain had arrived on the scene. The name Samaritan did not always directly apply to a person's culture or race. Sometimes it was given by the Jews to describe a man or woman who was a heretic and a breaker of the ceremonial law. At times, the person just didn't do things the normal way society required them to be done. It was applied to Jesus during an occasion when He had healed a person. The Jews said unto Him, we know well that you are a Samaritan and hast a devil.

In our society we use the term Good Samaritan when a citizen helps in a time of desperate need or when a person provides the armed forces, police, or any other agency with information that will assist them in apprehending a wrong doer. People use the term without a clear understanding of its origin or original meaning. It truly means anyone that goes against the norm to do what is right for a person. In our society it is normal to turn and look the other way when things are not right. In our society it has become commonplace not to help or to get involved.

> It is normal not to inform the authority when things are going wrong in our communities.

> It is normal to see people oppressed and not speak out for civil rights.

> It is normal to see injustice and proclaim justice for all.

Perhaps this man was called a Samaritan in the sense of being one whom an orthodox community, society, or group despised because he did not do things in the order the group desired them to be done, or because he did not act the way that the majority suggested he should act. The greatest problem confronting churches today is they are searching for people just like them, when they should identify with people that have different identities. They should seek persons who are different than them. Churches fail to comprehend that diversity can serve as a possible strength.

The Samaritan was Christ, who came to save a half dead and dying people; All races marked by strife and massive difficulties of life, and a world branded by increasing corruption and violence. Romans 5:17 states For if, by the trespass of the one man, death reigned through that one man, how much more will those who receive God's abundant provision of grace and of the gift of righteousness reign in life through the one man, Jesus Christ. The Samaritan went to the wounded traveler. He bound up his wounds. After, pouring oil and wine on his wound, and sitting him on his own beast, He brought him to an inn, and took care of him.

Not withstanding the fact that our Good Samaritan has come to man and woman's aid, Christ has bound up our wounds through His suffering and death. Let us never forget, unlike the Priest and the Levite, Christ also was on a journey; though He traveled the road of Jericho as symbolically portrayed within this story. He is known more so for traveling the road of "via Dolorosa". Via Dolorosa is identified as the way/path of suffering, pain, betrayal, resentment, abandonment, and crucifixion. Yet, through his suffering we are offered salvation and through salvation we are offered deliverance from hurt, harm or danger. Through via Dolorosa we are made safe and we are rescued from the enemy.

Christ has anointed believers with oil, the Holy Spirit. He has poured from the heavens the wine of a new covenant, the dispensation of grace. All men and women are Christ's neighbors because He looked down on us and saw our every need. As a good shepherd, He placed us on His shoulders and placed us in a safe position. Knowing that He had to depart, He asked the innkeeper to care for all believers until He returns. It becomes morally clear within this story that the traveler's weakness profoundly reveals the Good Samaritan's strength and power. Paul confirms this truth when he states that Christ said to him "My grace is sufficient for you, for my power is made perfect in weakness." Therefore I will boast all the more gladly about my weaknesses, so that Christ's power may rest on me." II Corinthians 12:9.

The Life Application Study Bible gives three moral principles about love concerning this parable. First, the lack of love is often easy to justify, even though it is never right. Secondly, our neighbor is anyone or any race, creed or social background who is in need. Thirdly, love means acting to meet the needs of people. Thank God that we are Christ's neighbors and He is a Good Samaritan to all that have needs. He also promised that he would return and how exciting it will be to behold him face to face and have the opportunity to thank Him for saving lowly persons like us.

You Must Have A Dream

To be a Good Samaritan you must have a dream. When evaluating the Good Samaritans of the modern world, one thing is consistent in their lives. They all have a dream. The reason why Good Samaritans rub against the norm, stand for justice, peace, and equality, or undertake persecution and ridicule for the benefit of those they accept as their neighbors can be found inside of them. They had a dream that the immorality in the world could be transformed into morality. That evil in societies could be overcome with good, and that oppression could be defeated with the prosperity of love.

A Cry for Ethical and Moral Strength

We have viewed that Joseph was a type of Christ and discovered that he had a dream that offended his brother. His belief in the dream caused his brothers to mistreat him. Christ, our Good Samaritan has a dream. His dream is that the men and women will love the Lord God and love their neighbors. His dream is that the world will be erased of all evil and that peace will reign. Christ's dream caused Him to come to earth, struggle against the ways of the world, and be mistreated by His brothers and sisters for our betterment. Paul was a Good Samaritan because he had a dream. His dream was to fulfill the command of Christ. His dream was to spread the gospel of God. The dream within him burned deeply and caused him to sacrifice all for the furtherance of God's word. His love for others and desire for all to know Christ caused him to stand against the Roman government and the Jewish leaders. Like Christ, he too was beaten and placed in prison. Martin Luther King, Jr. had a dream. He was a Good Samaritan who stood against society's social, economic and political laws. Similar to Christ and Paul, his dream was the purpose of his living and dying. Dr. King's dream was that one-day the world would be transformed into an oasis of freedom and justice for men and women, that people would love their neighbor, and they would treat others, as they would like to be treated. To be a Good Samaritan, you must have a dream that one-day earth will become a better place and know that God rules and reigns even in the new world.

Carl L. Sweat, Jr., D. Min.

Chapter Ten
You Can't Handle The Truth
Morals On Hearing And Doing

The Truth Can Hurt

Each night my wife Janice rumbles through her closets preparing her attire for the next day. Of course she wouldn't agree with me but Janice would say that she meticulously selects her clothing. But, we both agree that she is very conscious about the clothing she chooses to wears to work. I believe she has a subconscious ritual. What she does is watch the news to be informed of the type of weather she may face the next day. She goes over in her mind the schedule of tasks that she will carry out on that day. She attempts to gauge how she may feel. Perhaps, by saying, and I have heard her say this, "No I don't think I feel like I want to wear that." Often she mentions, "No, I wore that blouse or skirt last week." Then after a series of individualized calculations that I dare say I comprehend or suggest there is a rudimental formula, she has an outfit laid out to wear for the next day. Yet, when tomorrow comes, several things can take place. Either she is pleased with her selection or she goes back through the process of selection again. However, one thing remains consistent. If I am present, she never fails to ask me, "How do I look?" or "Does this look OK on me?" "Are my pants too tight or too loose?" "Does this shirt match with my shoes?" Some days, when things are not coordinated I am a little apprehensive in telling her the truth. My wife is a sensitive person just as many people are. Therefore, before I comment, I say to myself, "You can't handle the truth." I am leery in being truthful because I take into account the effort she has put into selecting her clothes, styling her hair, and putting on the make-up that matches. I am concerned that if I share the truth that the outfit doesn't coincide or look that well on her I might hurt her feelings and her day may be ruined. But, despite all her attempts to get it right, I have to be truthful with her. It's the only right thing to do. I can't dream of allowing her to believe that she has done well and look well. I can't imagine being honest when she looks great but being dishonest when she doesn't look so great. So, in compassion and in love I tell her the truth. And as usual, her beautiful eyes begin to lower along with her head. The smile she woke up with turns upside down and the joyful chatter diminishes to silence. Actually, speaking this is a subtle experience in discovering that the truth can hurt.

I am quite sure that Jesus found Himself in a similar position with the rich young ruler that approached Him and asked, "Good Master, what must I do to ensure that I gain eternal life?" Jesus knew that the young ruler had tried very hard to obey the law. Regrettably, despite his impressive efforts there was something he was lacking and it had to be fulfilled before he could inherit eternal life. Knowing Jesus, His love and compassion for men, I can't help from pondering if Jesus paused before He spoke and during his silence, if He thought to Himself "Young ruler, You can't handle the truth?" Undoubtedly, I do believe that Jesus did not want to break the young man's heart because He loved him. Yet, to help the man, Jesus told him the truth. Immediately, after hearing from Christ that he was lacking something, the young man's face fell, then he turned and walked away for his heart was rent. Jesus knew he could not handle the truth. Once again we discover that the truth can hurt.

> As Jesus started on his way, a man ran up to him and fell on his knees before him. "Good teacher," he asked, "what must I do to inherit eternal life?" "Why do you call me good?" Jesus answered. "No one is good-- except God alone. You know the commandments: 'Do not murder, do not commit adultery, do not steal, do not give false testimony, do not defraud, honor your father and mother.'" "Teacher," he declared, "all these I have kept since I was a boy." Jesus looked at him and loved him. "One thing you lack," he said. "Go, sell everything you have and give to the poor, and you will have treasure in heaven. Then come, follow me." At this the man's face fell. He went away sad, because he had great wealth. Mark 10:17-22

Good Intentions

The young man apparently had waited for Jesus to exit the house He had visited. When Jesus came out of the house the ruler ran up to him and threw himself at the mercy of Jesus. The amazement of this aristocrat falling at the feet of the penniless prophet from Nazareth is that he sincerely desired advice from one whom had come to be known as a celebrated, outstanding teacher. Somehow the ruler felt compelled to seek Jesus' great counsel of blessedness for his personal clarity and interest.

By falling to his knees, he expressed great regard for all that Jesus represented. He demonstrated that he was willing to surrender all to Christ. He was willing to yield to His teaching and direction. Unfortunately, often men and women come to Christ and say, "I surrender all." Yet, deep within there are areas of their life that they are reluctant to give up. There are areas that they will allow God to have complete control and in other areas they try to be in control. Like the young ruler, many Christians are only interested in religion or being influenced by religion. They are not willing to permit themselves to be controlled by God. I beseech you therefore, brethren, by the mercies of God, that ye present your bodies a living sacrifice, holy, acceptable unto God, which is your reasonable service. And be not conformed to this world: but be ye transformed by the renewing of your mind, that ye may prove what is that good, and acceptable, and perfect, will of God. Rom 12:1-2

Obviously, the rich young ruler did not fully understand the cost of eternal life. He assumed that living a Christ-like life or some might say a religious life primarily consisted of certain works you performed that pleased God and therefore awarded men and women the right to heaven. Like many people, he sought a true religion for all the wrong purposes: happiness, self-satisfaction, prosperity, and security with God. He did not perceive religion as the complete sacrifice of self. He did not view true religion as bearing your cross. Comprehending not, that no action or deed is adequate payment or an acceptable substitute for the penalty of sin, he asked, what must I do for eternal life. Clearly, the question cannot be, what must I do, it has to be, what must we surrender?

Persons of this modern world want salvation; yet, not at the expense of yielding their lifestyle. They want to make it into heaven but won't practice living a completely moral life. One of the basic problems of life is to obtain fellowship with God and to be at peace and in friendship with Him. Similar to the rich ruler many have tried all their life to get into the right relationship with God because they desire eternal life. They try to observe the laws and the traditions of

A Cry for Ethical and Moral Strength

the church but they soon discover that works, the law, and tradition cannot give eternal life. Jesus defined eternal life as life everlasting approved and granted by God to those whose earthly life is found pleasing. Thus, it is apparent that all people that choose to live a moral life and seek to please God will gain access into His Kingdom. The ruler asked the question of Jesus in good faith and with the best intention but only Jesus knew that the young ruler was not prepared for what He had to say. He could not handle the truth.

We all Fall Short

Just as Janice fell short of color coordinating her attire or properly preparing for the next day, all people have missed the mark or allowed uncertainty and indecisiveness at some time or another to enter their life. It is written that all have come short of pleasing God but can be justified freely by His grace. This is what Jesus meant when He said, "Why call me Good?" there is none good but one, that is God." His reply is very significant because Jesus is saying all people will error in life but God is available to forgive us and by His grace justify men and women. Every good and perfect gift comes from above. Individually, we haven't done anything to deserve the riches and earthly treasures we have acquired. We can't handle the truth. Everything we possess is given as a gift from God. We can't handle the truth. The earth and the fullness therein belong to God. This was the ruler's problem and the dilemma of many people of today. They presume their possessions belong to them and not God. The existence of such a mentality in a person's life causes them to lose focus of God's plan and eventually miss-out on eternal life.

Moral Application: All have fallen short in life and if people continue to live their lives by the process of the law, rituals, or personal traditions as they prepare for the tomorrow, which may be the future of eternity, they are not ready for the truth. Issues concerning personal or materialistic things should not hurt people so deeply. The true things that matter are our relationships with God and with our neighbor. I remind you that Jesus questioned the young ruler about the relationship he had with his parent to caution us that our relationships with others are very significant to the inheritance of eternal life. The fifth commandment is viewed as the authority and relationships commandment. It extends a blessing to those that honor it.

If mankind would review how they have attempted to follow God's law, and how they have prospered, thinking it was something of their doing; yet, review the many relationships God has given them and how they have exploited people or taken others for granted, they could not handle the truth. The truth being that people have invested plenty of time in getting and having. They have spent an abundant amount of time in debating the law and little to no time in visiting the poor, raising their children, giving of self to the community, etc. We can't handle the truth because we have earnestly indulged ourselves in worldly matters; yet, overlooked the one commandment Jesus left us with, that is, love one another, as I have loved you. Are men and women willing to give up all they have to honor this commandment in order to follow Christ?

Chapter Eleven
What Do We Give Up By Not Letting Go?
Morals On Hearing And Doing

At this the man's face fell. He went away sad, because he had great wealth. Jesus looked around and said to his disciples, "How hard it is for the rich to enter the kingdom of God!" The disciples were amazed at his words. But Jesus said again, "Children, how hard it is to enter the kingdom of God! It is easier for a camel to go through the eye of a needle than for a rich man to enter the kingdom of God." Mark 10:22-25

Don't You Want To Go?

Are men and women willing to allow their love for possessions and wealth to exceed their love for others to rob them of eternal life? If so, then let's be concerned about what we give up by not letting go. The young ruler chose to cling to his possessions. He held tight to his riches or earthly treasures. He optioned not to be as the camel that goes through the needle's eye in the parable referenced by Jesus. He could have gone through the small gate, famous for being known as the needle's eye, by first being unloaded of his baggage and then lowering himself. Just as the camel had to position itself into kneeling position in order to enter the city, people must first unload their baggage, and then prostrate themselves so that they may enter the city of eternal life. It can only be entered on your knees. However, the ruler refused to relinquish everything and his pride disallowed him to truly lower himself to Christ for the gain of eternal life. Men and Women continue not to let go. The challenging questions are, "Is it worth it?" "Is what you are holding on to worth losing the splendor of eternal life?" There is an old cliché, "I'm not going to let you or anything cause me to lose my salvation." How is it that there are some things that we can attest that God is displeased but we keep them in our lives? We know that they are no good for us, that the things are of no value to us, and that they cause more harm than good, but people like to store-up garbage and stir-up trouble. Many hold on to pride but pride comes before the fall. The baggage people carry includes anger of the past, bitterness of the present, and hostility for future encounters. The O'Jays asked a vital question in one of their songs. The question was, "Don't you want to go to heaven?" They went on to suggest that there is nothing as sweet and pleasing as "Heaven". Nowhere is nicer than "Heaven". "Don't you want to go?"

Things We Give Up:

Read Revelation chapters twenty-one and twenty-two to learn of the things that can be regained. The following are some of the things we give up by not letting go:

> We give up the paradise regained. Because Adam and Eve would not let go of their desire for knowledge of good and evil, humanity lost paradise. Yet, will Jesus restore Eden. Paradise is regained. It is offered to persons that are willing to give up all for Christ.

> We give up living in a place where there shall be no more curse, no more night, no sun because God will be the light of all paradise, no more death, neither sadness, nor crying, neither shall there be any more pain. It is a place where joy reigns.

> We give up the water of life. John saw a pure river. It was clear as crystal and it proceeded out of the throne of God. Jesus spoke to the woman at the well about this water that gives eternal life. Once you drink from it you will never thirst again.

> We give up seeing the throne of God and seeing the Father sitting on His throne and the Son on His right hand side. We give up beholding Christ face to face in all of His Glory.

> We give up the New Jerusalem. John saw the new city come down from heaven. The building appeared unto him having walls of jasper and the city was pure as gold. Each foundation of the wall of the city was garnished with all manner of precious stones, and the twelve gates were twelve pearls.

> We give up our citizenship to the kingdom. If we fail to let go the things of the earth, we forfeit the right to become heirs as children of God and the right to His kingdom. We give up our

new name that He offers to us and our crowns awarded to us for our many sacrifices made for kingdom building.

We give up the tree of life. It was taken away from man and woman at the time of the fall. A flaming sword and cherub was assigned to guard it. In "Heaven" it reappears and we can again eat of its fruits and leaves.

We give up ceaseless rejoicing, praise, and worship of God. We will praise God with the angels, with all the nations, and we will praise Him with our family and friends that have gone before us.

Glory to God, for it is written: Eyes have not seen, nor have ears heard, not even has anyone's mind conceived the things God has prepared for those who love him. But God has revealed it to believers by his Spirit. 1Cor 2:9-10

Consider these glorious things we give up by not letting go. Don't you want to go to "Heaven"?

Count All Losses as Gains

During the fall of 2003, Hurricane Isabel came and demolished ninety percent of the state of Virginia. People throughout the state contacted their insurance carriers and submitted damage claims. Insurance adjusters traveled to Virginia from all parts of the nation. Homeowners and automobile owners were irate concerning their losses and the inconveniences their lives were subject to endure. They were perturbed about the numerous sacrifices they had to make to adjust to what used to be their daily lives. Conversely, Paul reflected on his past. He reviewed his life's losses and the many sacrifices he endured. Yet, he was not a bit discouraged. He found himself encouraged. He said, "That which I thought made me an elitist in life, those thing I assumed positioned me above other men and women, possessions that I considered to be valuable and secured me in life, I willingly lost them. I personally and intentionally placed them behind me because the earthly things we presume are gain in life must be yielded for the gain of someone more precious. That someone is Christ. He is more precious than silver and gold".

Paul had many possessions not excluding a rich heritage. He was reared in the Jewish faith. Circumcised at eight days old, taught by Gamaliel, one of the most honored Pharisaic professors, and born of the tribe of Benjamin, Paul was considered a Hebrew of Hebrews. Despite his heritage, prestige, and power, he counted all these things but dung that he may win Christ. What an ultimate change of mind and heart. Truly, his statement is revealing of a converted man for only through being born again can a man or woman's mind be changed. Previously, Paul had zealously persecuted the church and was found blameless for his action because of the morality which was in the Jewish law. But, what society approved as morally sound he discovered was immoral and unacceptable to Christ. Thus, his mind was renewed and he chose to please God instead of man.

In his letter to the Philippians, Paul is not suggesting that you literally toss your acquired possessions out the window. Nor is he proposing that you literally excommunicate yourself from your heritage. In actuality, did he lose his nationality? Did he lose his inheritance? No! During several occasions of trial he proclaimed his birthright and adamantly demanded the rights of his Jewish origin and Roman citizenship. What then was Paul recommending to his readers? He was giving them moral advice not to place anything within their possession or personal background before Christ. People are to place all things behind him or her and Christ before them.

You Will Gain A Hundred Times More

Peter said to him, "We have left everything to follow you!" "I tell you the truth," Jesus replied, "no one who has left home or brothers or sisters or mother or father or children or fields for me and the gospel will fail to receive a hundred times as much in this present age (homes, brothers, sisters, mothers, children and fields-- and with them, persecutions) and in the age to come, eternal life. But many who are first will be last, and the last first." Mark 10:28-31

One of the greatest struggles that unbelievers must overcome before they submit their life and possessions to Christ is to become content with God's answer to their question, "What will I gain after I give up everything?" After Peter heard Christ's response to the young ruler's question and witnessing the man deliberately refusing Christ, he considered what Jesus said to him and all His disciples "Come and Follow Me". He must have thought back on how Jesus was walking beside the Sea of Galilee and saw two brothers, Simon, who was Peter, and his brother Andrew. They were casting their net into the lake for fish. Peter must have recalled how they left where they were and traveled until they saw two brothers, James and John. The brothers were in a boat with their father Zebedee preparing their fishing nets. "Come, follow me," said Jesus and at once the brothers left their nets and their father to follow Him. Peter reflected on Jesus' request to all His disciples and how all of them immediately surrendered all their possessions and followed Him.

Knowing Peter as the rambunctious one and the spontaneous spokesperson of the disciples, we can ethically characterize his reaction to the unpleasant experience as normative moral behavior. He said to Christ, "We have left everything to follow you!" His implication to Christ was, what shall we receive in return? Realizing the end for those that have refused Christ's invitation to discipleship and those that have chosen to cling to earthly treasures, Peter genuinely desired to know what he and his friends were to receive for forsaking everything and following Him. Christ understood Peter's inference and said to him, you will gain a hundred times more than you have sacrificed. Christ's promise to Peter and the disciples assures to all believers that the earthly riches and treasures they lay down cannot be compared to the rewards they will receive for accepting the invitation from our Creator. Thus, the interpersonal debate within unbelievers pertaining to surrendering what they have and choosing to follow Christ should be a resolved matter. Just to know that you will gain a hundred times more than what you give up in your life is exhilarating and a guarantee that selecting Christ is the best choice you can ever make.

The above truth is not only confirmed in the New Testament, it is long established within the Old Testament. Recognizing that scholars note the patriarch Joseph as a type of Christ, believers can view Joseph's life or circumstances to be somewhat comparable to the life of Christ. Joseph is presented as the beloved son of Jacob. He told his brothers that he had a dream and they would bow to him. Yet, instead of honoring him for his indisputable truth, they got angry and sold him into slavery. He was an innocent man but Potiphar's wife told a lie on him that he would be placed in prison. Though he was dead to Jacob, he would live again. He rose to power over all accept Pharaoh. In the end, his brothers bowed to him. They discovered that God sent Joseph ahead of them to prepare a way for them and all life to be saved.

Similarly, Christ is the beloved Son of the Father and Christ had a dream of uniting the people and becoming their Lord. His dream was to reign over all in the spirit of love and peace. However, His brothers envied Him, brutalized Him, and sold Him. The Pharisee(s) (the brothers of Christ) got mad when they heard that every knee shall bow and every tongue confess Jesus as Lord. God the Father sent him before us that we could be saved from the judgment to come and that we received the bread of life and prospered a hundredfold. He was innocent but they presented false witness against Him. Christ was once dead but He lives again and ascended to Power. It was Christ that prepared the way for us.

As we attempt to discover areas in our lives that we should review for the purpose of surrendering things that master, control or bind us, I turn your attention to the Old Testament. Genesis chapter forty-seven contains clear examples of three essential things believers are to relinquish in order to gain eternal life and much more than what was once possessed.

The First element is the Love of Money. During a seven-year famine, Joseph collected all the money that was to be found in Egypt and Canaan in payment for the grain they were buying, and he brought it to Pharaoh's palace. When men and women can put in proper perspective mammon or better said the love of money, then and only then can true love for God and their fellow man be properly perceived. How often must it be said, that the love of money is the root of all evil? So many people live life with money as their master. The desire to have or increase their personal wealth is the primary driving force of their existence. From this story it is revealed that there are some things money can buy. No one has enough money to buy eternity. There is no amount of money that can pay for life.

Some persons are willing to give God a portion of their money but they do so with the wrong motives. They give because they can use it as a tax write off. Some give because they have means to recuperate it. This is why the second element is that we must surrender unto Jesus as Our Means of Profit. When the money of the people of Egypt and Canaan was gone, all Egypt came to Joseph and said, "Give us food. Why should we die in your presence? Our money is used up." Joseph said to them, bring to me all your livestock. "I will sell you food in exchange for your livestock, since your money is gone." So they brought their livestock to Joseph, and he gave them food in exchange for their horses, their sheep and goats, their cattle and donkeys. Because they surrendered their livestock to him, he ensured that they survive that year with food. This was an enormous sacrifice for them to do. It's identical to a farmer giving up all his mules or tractors. It's similar to a landscaper giving up all his or her lawn mowers. Their means to make money has been relinquished. When people can cease relying on their investments, jobs, or personal connections with others as means to recover from trial or means to regenerate wealth and place their solemn trust in Jesus then and only then can they receive life. Jesus is the origin of all things. He is the resource we are to tap into at all times. If people place their safety in any other means they will be disappointed in the end.

Finally, self needs to be surrendered. Notice that as soon as that particular year was over, they came to him the following year saying, since our money is gone and our livestock is in your possession, you know there is nothing remaining for our lord except our bodies and our land? Purchase us as your slaves and buy our land in exchange for food. We will be in bondage to your lord, Pharaoh. Give us seed so that we may live and not die, and that the land may not become desolate." So Joseph bought all the land in Egypt for Pharaoh. The people had given up all their money, their cattle, livestock and all other aspects of their lives that could be used as means to generate mammon but one thing remained that is vital to life eternal. That facet was self. In order for any individual to gain life they must turn over themselves to become servants unto Jesus; thus, becoming slaves of God. For, when Joseph brought them they became the property of Pharaoh. Take heed that the land accompanied their offer of self. Why? Because man is connected with the land and if we fail to be ever mindful that from dust we have come and to dust we shall return then we will always have trouble letting go of the temporal things of life in exchange for life eternal.

After a period of time and the famine judgment appeared to be ending, Joseph gathered the people and said to them, "Now that I have bought you and your land today for Pharaoh, here is seed for you so you can plant the ground. But when the crop comes in, give a fifth of it to Pharaoh. The other four-fifths you may keep as seed for the fields and as food for yourselves, your households and your children." "You have saved our lives," they said. "May we find favor in the eyes of our lord; we will be in bondage to Pharaoh." It is here that the reader gains knowledge that you can't sow a field without having land or cattle to cultivate the land or seed. Therefore, everything they surrendered to Joseph he restored it to them and more. Such it is with Christ. When you submit mammon, means, and self to gain life eternal, Christ restores everything you have turned over to Him and He blesses you with more. All the people were assured that they would prosper. Joseph said when the crop comes give a portion to the lord, which was Pharaoh. He did not say if the crop comes. There is no apathy in Christ's word. You will prosper beyond a hundredfold when you surrender all to come follow Him.

A Cry for Ethical and Moral Strength

Chapter Twelve
Things That Last
Morals On Worship

On His way to Jerusalem, Jesus traveled along the border between Samaria and Galilee. While entering a village, ten men who had leprosy met him. They stood at a distance and called out in a loud voice, "Jesus, Master, have pity on us!" When he saw them, he said, "Go, show yourselves to the priests." They turned and began to walk towards the priest and as they went, they were cleansed. When one of lepers noticed he was healed, he immediately returned praising God in a loud voice. Throwing himself at Jesus' feet, he thanked him for having mercy and compassion on him and his friends. Above all things, this man was a Samaritan. Jesus looked down to him and asked, "Were not all ten cleansed? Where are the other nine? Why is none found to return and give praise to God and worship Him except this foreigner?" Luke 17:11-18

True Worship Begins When You Know Your Spiritual Leprosy

The human body is exposed to a number of fearful and frightening maladies. Sin has sown its seeds of decay and sorrows in every part of earth's system, and these seeds have produced a harvest of painful and distressing difficulties. However, during the Savior's sojourn on earth, He exercised His power and grace in allaying and restoring mankind from the various ills that the flesh is heir to. He went about doing good both to the bodies and souls of men. Yet, as He healed, as He saved, as He redeemed, as He forgave, as He delivered, as He blessed, as He taught, and as He proclaimed, it was the response of each person that stood in judgment. It is the individual's response to situations, events, people and God that will last. All other things such as possessions, miracles and gifts will fade away. Yet, all that men and women say, and all that men and women do in response to trials, temptations, worship, and service to God goes before them to the end of time; then we shall stand before the living God.

This passage is divided into a two-part story. The first scene involves a healing. It portrays a case of mankind's evident need. Also, it exemplifies each man or woman's cry to Jesus for help. Not considering the lepers' condition, Jesus treats them as they are already healed. By sending the lepers to the priest, it becomes obvious that compassionately Jesus intended their cleansing to take place prior to arriving at the temple. He conveys that their faith activated the power of God. The second portion entails a scene that deals with "Things That Last." It is the Samaritan who praises God and gives thanks to Jesus. It is the foreigner to whom Jesus says, "Your faith has made you whole." The salvation of the foreigner is addressed.

To the Jews, leprosy was a disease that represented judgment of mankind's sin. It was incurable by man and only God could clean it. It spread just as sin spreads. Leprosy was even forbidden by Jewish law and by custom that lepers were not to come near clean people. If believers would see this account in the light that men and women are spiritual lepers, their insight should cause them to humble themselves. Their awareness should cause them to approach Christ with thanksgiving for cleansing them of their sins, immorality and unrighteousness.

Feeling unworthy to enter into His presence because He represents all that is holy and pure and they symbolize everything that was wretched or filthy, the lepers stood afar off. The centurion who requested that Christ come and heal his soldier that lay dying did not permit Christ to come too close. He restricted Christ from entering his house. Like the lepers He asked that Christ speak healing knowing that Christ's words carried the power to heal. Because Christ is afar off in the pure and glorious heaven and believers live in this immoral and unethical earth we must call on Him from a distance knowing that He hears believers and He does not have to lay hands on people to heal them of their dilemma. His words have the power to deliver all from their sins.

True Worship Is United And Unselfish

Jewish, or Gentile, raise their voices on one accord in agreement that all people need Christ's strength, love, and help. Believers must become of the same mind that humanity faces the dilemma, which is sin and living an immoral life. Those that unite in hope and expectation for help from Christ must receive Him as their Master, for if He becomes Master in their life, He becomes Lord and Savior. If He becomes Master in their life, He becomes their Messiah.

A Cry for Ethical and Moral Strength

In unity the unclean cried a prayer to Christ seeking His mercy for all. Together they said, "Have mercy on us." Their prayer to Christ was one of impersonal self-desire. Their implication suggested, we are a group in need, help us or we are a people in the same boat with the same crisis, help us. As they were companions in suffering they were companions in collective prayer.

Their prayer may have been brief, but it was expressive and fervent. True worship causes men and women to collectively seek Christ's face on behalf of one another not in long drawn-out wordy prayers but at times in limited sincere words of prayer.

Christ knows our dilemma. They did not have to pray in detail concerning their need. They only said, "Have mercy." Verbally they did not infer to their leprosy or specify their need. And Christ assures believers that He does know all things and is willing to aid them at all times He says, "Go show yourself, to the priest." Glory to God, for it is wonderful to know that believers worship a God omniscient and omnipotent.

If believers would attempt to count their blessing they couldn't count the many ways the Lord's blessing, deliverances and cures were wrought. In this worship experience, "Go" is a command connected with obedience. Christ directed them as if they were already healed. God is a God of no time constraints so to Him you are already healed. As they went, though their healing was not immediate, it was etched in walking in faith. The lepers had recognized, acknowledged and depended on Christ's goodness and power, but Christ caused them to exercise their faith. True worship is not knowing that Christ can heal and that He cares. It is obediently exercising your faith. The principle applied in this text is, if you take one step Christ will do the rest.

Here was a cure by wholesale. A whole group was restored to health with one directive given. Christ was so powerful that all were cured with one command. We must reflect on the gravesite of Lazarus for a clearer understanding. Recall at the grave of Lazarus, Jesus did not say, "Come forth." No. What He did say was, "Lazarus come forth." Why? Because, if He had given a general command such as, "Come forth", the power of His words would have caused all to wake from their sleep and come out of their graves. Therefore, Christ's general directive given to the lepers permitted all to be cured.

When one saw he was healed, in haste he ran back and prostrated himself at Jesus' feet and glorified God. While believers are on their journey to see the most high priest, are we not to stop just a moment to worship and praise God for His many blessings? Are we not to take a little time to exalt God for extending mercy to us? However, of the many people that receive mercy and grace from God, there is but a few that return to Him thanksgiving. Once again the Good Samaritan proves not to be consistent with the norms of the world. A Samaritan gives thanks but not a Jew. How often those prove most grateful from whom it was least expected.

God Desires To Be Praised

God desires to be praised; yet, often it is received from strangers and not from professing believers. How consistent with the church of today. God does not often receive true worship from persons reared in the church or from those who have strong ties with a local church. Perhaps it is because they are steep in tradition or bound by laws. Whatever it may be, if traditional worshippers will not worship Him, untraditional men and women will worship Him in spirit and in truth. The stranger, the Samaritan, disregarded what the nine may have said when he returned to Christ. He disregarded what they may have done to him when he decided to turn back. He was determined to give thanks and worship Christ for himself.

Where is my Praise? Were there not ten cleansed? Where are the other nine? Where is my Glory?

The things that last are believers' responses toward God for His tender Mercies. The hymnist Rhomas O. Chisholm wrote "Great Is Thy Faithfulness." In the lyrics he says, "Great is your faithfulness! Great is your faithfulness! Morning by morning new mercies I see: All I have needed, your hands have provided, Great is your faithfulness, God, unto me!"

A Cry for Ethical and Moral Strength

True Worship Is Your Response To The Works of God

The things that last are also our responses toward one another. Everything each person does or says in response to God and man will be judged in the end. Miracles will fade, gifts will fade, they are only given to capture the attention of people and to draw men and women closer to God. In the end, the person who receives a blessing from God will praise and worship Him for it.

The Pharisees desired a miracle for the sake of a miracle only. Herod and Pilate desired Jesus to perform a miracle for their personal satisfaction. Today, many that receive miracles or gifts do not grow closer to God. They do not use the two for witnessing to others or testifying of God's love. Neither does most people use their gifts of blessing for edification of the Church. Thus, Christ did not perform a miracle for them because He knew their response would not be one of true worship. Believers are to respond in true worship in the good times and in the bad times because only what we do for others with last. Only our response to Christ will remain. When believers respond by praising God in times of trials, God is glorified and he or she receives an incorruptible crown. When believers worship God in times of prosperity, God is exalted and he or she receives an incorruptible crown. Who believes that your response to stimulus is what lasts because in all things God is to be glorified and He desires to be praised?

Action Speaks Louder Than Words

The disciple, James, questions faith absent of works. In his inquiry he suggest that worship of God is the practice of true religion. To him pure worship or religion is to visit the fatherless and widows in their affliction and to keep away from immorality. In a parable, Jesus confirms that God is truly worshipped when believers behave as Good Samaritans by helping those in need. In Matthew 25:35-36 Jesus says, When I was hungry you gave me something to eat, when I was thirsty you gave me something to drink, when I was a stranger you invited me in, when I needed clothes you clothed me, when I was sick you looked after me, when I was in prison you came to visit me, these are the times you responded in worship to God the

Father. These are the times you acted as Good Samaritans. These are the times I was pleased because your actions were of the image and character of the Father. Also, these are the times your actions glorified God.

<u>True Worship Is Given By Them That Owe Him</u>

One of the Pharisees invited Jesus to have dinner with him, so he went to the Pharisee's house and reclined at the table. When a woman who had lived a sinful life in that town learned that Jesus was eating at the Pharisee's house, she brought an alabaster jar of perfume. She stood behind him at his feet weeping and began to wet his feet with her tears. Then she wiped his feet with her hair, kissed them and poured perfume on them. When the Pharisee who had invited Jesus saw this, he said to himself, "If this man were a prophet, he would know who is touching him and what kind of woman she is. She is a sinner." Jesus answered him, "Simon, I have something to tell you." "Tell me, teacher," he said. "Two men owed money to a certain moneylender. One owed him five hundred denarii, and the other fifty. Neither of them had the money to pay him back, so he canceled the debts of both. Now which of them will love him more?" Simon replied, "I suppose the one who had the bigger debt canceled." "You have judged correctly," Jesus said. Then he turned toward the woman and said to Simon, "Do you see this woman? I came into your house. You did not give me any water for my feet, but she wet my feet with her tears and wiped them with her hair. You did not give me a kiss, but this woman, from the time I entered, has not stopped kissing my feet. You did not put oil on my head, but she has poured perfume on my feet.

Therefore, I tell you, her many sins have been forgiven because she has responded to my mercy with much love for me. But he who has been forgiven little responds to my mercies with little love. Luke 7:36-47

Chapter Thirteen
Mastering Your Masters
Morals On Spiritual Warfare

> Many people are mastered by their conditions. They are not masters of their conditions.

Freedom is generally assumed to be the birthright of all men; yet, man is anything but free. Bondage is more likely to be the common lot of many people. For some their bonds may be psychological, or others they may be chained by economical strains, and still for others social or political ties have shackled their lives. Realistically, we can agree that each waking day of an individual's life serves as the beginning of confronting challenges and trials that of themselves they try to gain control of that person's life or that it attempts to master them. These trials, circumstances, and parallels influence the lives of most people and in others they have power over their attitude, behavior, perspective of the situation or life. All go through life dragging their personal ball and chain, things that confine and restrain them. And the most obscure thought concerning this truth is some accept it to be a normal way of life.

If this is to be true, then life, religion, and society can conjure up an image in people's minds to accept these restraints as social, economical, and religious norms. The pre-modern definition of slavery is in need of broadening. A human being who is owned, as property by another person, one who is subject to his or her will and possess no freedom of rights is not a completed definition. Today believers realize that slavery is not only constituted by the ownership of another person, spiritual forces can institute it. For our struggle is not against flesh and blood, but against the rulers, against the authorities, against the powers of this dark world and against the spiritual forces of evil in the heavenly realms. In addition, relationships to certain people, events, and circumstances that surround individuals influence their lives. Certainly, slavery is an appropriate word to describe the intimate level of commitment and relationship God demands of believers.

For this self same reason, in Philippians, Paul is determined that every obstacle confronting each person serves as an obstruction to living a moral and ethical life. Also, they exists as an impediment in his or her path to God. The only way people can remove obstacles or impediments is by mastering them. Read the encouraging words that Paul was inspired to write.

Now I want you to know, brothers, that what has happened to me has really served to advance the gospel. As a result, it has become clear throughout the whole palace guard and to everyone else that I am in chains for Christ. Because of my chains, most of the brothers in the Lord have been encouraged to speak the word of God more courageously and fearlessly. It is true that some preach Christ out of envy and rivalry, but others out of goodwill. The latter do so in love, knowing that I am put here for the defense of the gospel. The former preach Christ out of selfish ambition, not sincerely, supposing that they can stir up trouble for me while I am in chains.

But what does it matter? The important thing is that in every way, whether from false motives or true, Christ is preached. And because of this I rejoice. Yes, and I will continue to rejoice, for I know that through your prayers and the help given by the Spirit of Jesus Christ, what has happened to me will turn out for my deliverance. I eagerly expect and hope that I will in no way be ashamed, but will have sufficient courage so that now as always Christ will be exalted in my body, whether by life or by death. Phil 1:12-20

Mastering your Master is a very challenging undertaking because God has called all believers to be more than conquerors. It is complicated because the question becomes, "How can you master something or someone that attempts to master you or already has control over you?" Do not be discouraged. Why? Because I can tell you that it happens everyday. People are maturing in their Christian walk. They are regaining control of their lives. Many believers are growing strong in God's might to the level that no one or nothing rules or dictates their behavior, emotions, and love for God and their fellow man. They are fighting back so that never again will these negative forces gain control over them or their life. As a people, they are learning more and more that they are responsible for their actions. They are responsible for their thoughts and they are accountable for everything that is done out of their physical body.

Thus, people today are taking back control from the things in life that have once controlled them. Yes, today many are learning how to

A Cry for Ethical and Moral Strength

master their master. Despite people's circumstances and situations they are learning to rejoice in all things and to praise God in the midst of the bad times and the good times, for men and women have but one Master and He is Jesus Christ. He is their joy and regardless of his or her common lots they still have joy, unspeakable joy. He is the rock of their salvation.

Paul is a great example of this truth. He was a prisoner but far removed was his imprisonment from precluding his missionary activity. The chains of imprisonment did not master Paul. He saw them as instruments that opened up doors for actually expanding the gospel. I assure you that you can master your masters. Like Paul, who was innocent, found himself shackled; yet, he did not allow the master of bondage to master him. Like the Israelite and African American slaves of old that were innocent and found themselves in chains, yet, refused to allow their task masters to master their hopes, dreams, or the promises of God. We who are innocent but find ourselves bound by the master of financial crisis, chained to the master of the thirst for a successful career, cuffed to the master of stress, and depression, tied to the master of work-holism and prosperity is better known as get- ahead-ism. Even those that have found themselves gripped by sickness or disease will no longer go through life dragging these balls and chains in fear. No! They have decided to master these masters.

Three Ways To Defeat Your Masters

There are three ways to master your masters. The first is viewing your trials as opportunities. Paul said that when he reviewed his life, the things that happened didn't just fall out of the sky in chaos. No! Rather every aspect of his life fell in order and served as opportunities for the furtherance of God's word. How many of you know when things fall out in your life, they are only falling in order for your strength and for God's sake? Rom 8:28 says, "We know that all things work together for good to them that love God, to them who are the called according to his purpose."

These trials or challenges are no more than God's opportunities to assist believers in their spiritual growth so that they can soon face and master their masters. They are opportunities that believers can witness to and strengthen others in the furtherance of the Gospel.

If we could only ask Joseph, who was unjustly placed into prison; yet, was raised by God to become the second in command in Egypt, how did you master your masters? He'd undoubtedly say to us, the devil may have meant it for my bad but God meant it for my good.

If we could only ask Daniel, who was taken a prisoner of the Babylonians; yet he too rose to reign as second in command, perhaps he would say to us the same words he uttered to the king the next day after being shut-up in the lion's den. The king arose early the next morning, and went in haste to the den of lions. He cried with a lamentable voice unto Daniel. He said, "Daniel, servant of the living God, is your God, whom you serve continually, able to deliver you from these masters, these kings of the jungle?" Daniel said unto the king, "My God has ceased this opportunity to send his angel. He has closed the mouth of these masters. They cannot hurt me."

If we could ask Shadrach, Meshach, and Abed-nego how they mastered their masters when they were bound and about to be tossed into a fiery furnace, I believe they would say, within your trials and challenges God is with you. He was that fourth person. God goes through the fire with you and if it be so He helps you to master your masters and if He chooses not to deliver you from any master, let it be known to all that He is able.

If we could ask the Negroes of old such as Medga Evers who was martyred in the struggle for equality, Addie Mae Collins, Carol Roberts, Carol D.McNair and Cynthia Wesley who were martyred in the bombing of the First Street Baptist Church, I believe they would say, principalities, forces and rulers in higher places can kill the fleshly body but they can not take your soul. Only one master can take your soul.

Maybe Muhammad Ali who was jailed for not fighting in a war he believed to be unjust might say, those so called masters stripped me of my heavy weight belts and they took from me my titles but they can't take my heavenly name nor my heavenly crowns. We could ask many others how they mastered their master during times of depression and struggle; however, they would tell us the same story. That story is, in perilous times they discovered it was a great opportunity for God to strengthen them and other people.

The Christian world was strengthened by Paul's bondage. His imprisonment made many people confident and bold. His bondage assisted believers to stand while facing persecution. Martin Luther King's, Jr. letter from the Birmingham city jail inspired the nation to stand for justice and civil rights. His bondage served as an opportunity to affirm to an African minister that Christian discipleship was at the heart of the African American Struggle. Nelson Mandela's silent plea for freedom for a nation and a people from his prison in Robben's Island profoundly strengthened a nation and the world. These Nobel Peace Prize winners saw their trials as opportunities to increase the gospel.

Secondly, to master your master, you must view trials objectively or from the big picture. Paul said while he was in prison some people preached Christ of contention and these same men did so supposing to add to his affliction but others sincerely preached Christ because of their love for Him. Not withstanding either, for when I view both from a non-bias and objective perspective, I rejoice because Christ is still being preached. Regardless, the motive of any man or woman preacher, the gospel abounds. Paul's comments assert to all readers that they are to stay focused on the big picture and that is the expansion of the gospel into the uttermost parts of the world. If believers are to ever master their masters they must take their eyes off what is happening to them and contemplate on God's will and purpose.

Finally, to master your masters you must elicit your inner strength. Paul apprehended, just as all believers should feel confident in knowing whatever you are enduring will serve as a platform for your deliverance. Believers are assured to conquer their masters due to the prayers of the saints and explicitly because of the abundant supply of the Spirit of Jesus Christ within them. Undoubtedly, with great expectations and endless hope in our glorious Lord, believers can always face any master convinced that neither death nor life, neither angels nor demons, neither the present nor the future, nor any powers, neither height nor depth, nor anything else in all creation, will be able to separate us from the love of God that is in Christ Jesus our Lord. Believers must face life knowing that they can master their masters and they must, for it is the will of God.

Chapter Fourteen
The Church Is Gone Fishing And
They Are Fishing On The Wrong Side Of The Boat
Morals On Missions

One bright morning Jesus appeared again to his disciples by the Sea of Tiberias. This is how it all happened. Peter, Thomas, Nathanael, and two other disciples were together. Peter said, to them I'm going fishing. The other disciples said you are not going fishing without us. We're going fishing with you. So they walked down to the seashore and got into the boat. They fished all night trying every technique they knew, but they caught nothing that night. Early the next morning, Jesus stood on the shore, but the disciples could not recognize him. He called out to them saying, "Friends, have you caught any fish?" "No," they answered. So, Jesus advised them that they were fishing on the wrong side of the boat and then said throw your net on the right side of the boat and you will find some fish. Immediately, they obeyed the stranger and when they did they were unable to haul their net into the boat because of the great multitude of fish. Right away the disciple whom Jesus loved said to Peter, "It is the Lord!" John 21:1-10

Where is the church in the battle against immorality? Where is the church in the war for justice and equality? Where is the church concerning its position for peace? Has it taken a firm stand for the teaching of the principles of God or has it become weary in well doing? Has the church become tolerant permitting a great river of injustice, immorality, and oppression to freely flow throughout the land? Without reservations it can be said that many churches have become more concerned about self- preservation than committing themselves to the will of God. Their voices are lifted with words void of interposition and nullification of ungodliness. Such as the disciples, when they went fishing, many churches have abandoned the Great Commission and now operate their organizations called churches as professional institutions. Similar to the church of Ephesus that left its first love and the church of Laodicea, that God was ready to spew them out of His mouth because it became lukewarm, many believers have taken their eyes off the prize and centered their efforts on organizing, planning, programming, styling and profiling more than they place emphasis on the saving of souls.

Lawrence Richards and Clyde Hoeldtke in their book titled "Church Leadership" suggest that many leaders have institutionalized the operations of the church. Based on their implication, like the disciples that were experts in fishing, many leaders today believe that the knowledge they possess is sufficient to run or rule the church. However, because they have made the church a professional career or job, most churches that function under this theory or similar doctrine will desperately employ their energies but emerge unsuccessful because they have removed Christ from being the head of the church. Regrettably, like Peter, the leader of the early church that influenced the disciples to go fishing against the will of God, many religious leaders have convinced congregations to go fishing for men under their own strength, expertise, and knowledge. These churches have gone fishing and they are fishing on the wrong side of the boat.

Jesus showed himself again to the disciples at the sea of Tiberias. This was the third time He made himself known to the disciples after the resurrection. The first appearance was on Resurrection Day in Jerusalem and His second appearance occurred in Galilee on the first day of the week but on this occasion he showed himself to some disciples while they were fishing during a weekday.

Would you believe that Christ not only will meet believers on Sunday while they are assembled together in church but He also visits leaders and members when they are at their place of employment. He visits believers while they are performing their common business or everyday activities. If knowing this to be true then churches and leaders should understand that Jesus is willing to be a part of every intrinsic aspect of the believer's lives. Why then are men and women overwhelmed with managing their lives and the lives of others? It is God that gives the increase. The selection of the disciples enlightens Christians on the subject that witnessing is now less connected with the ministrations of the church. It infuses the awareness that mission should be no longer imposed on the priest or a single leader. In this period of Grace the focus is Christ's call of the entire Christian body to save souls by witnessing to the lost. Christianizing the world must and will come through the entire Christian body witnessing during their everyday activities. This is Christ's plan for mankind.

A Cry for Ethical and Moral Strength

When The Church Plan Differs From Christ's Plan

Peter said to them "I go a fishing." They said to him, "We will go with you." Like you and I, these were believers called out and separated from the world and commissioned to be fishers of men. They were commanded in Lk.24:49 to go to Jerusalem and wait for the Holy Spirit that they could be anointed with power to perform their mission. Nonetheless, Peter acted individually and his act plus motive did influence and affect the body of Christ.

Today, without hesitation it can be stated that many believers follow leaders of various capacities within the church. So often they follow them without considering that the leaders plan, program, activity, movement, or mission may not be in the will of God. Surely, it's not a part of God's divine will for the congregation but it becomes a part of his permissive will. Whether it is introduced as a vision to build a new church; whether the mission is a new church start; whether the goal is incorporating a contemporary worship service with modern theology or music in the church, these leaders say it is being executed in the name of saving souls, but is it true in most cases. Honestly, is all the work and toil of churches God led?

We know what the disciples did and what some churches do today is not exclusively the will of God. Why do churches do things outside God's will? Peter saw that after the scandal of the cross and that persecution seemed to be at hand for the disciples; therefore, he logically presupposed that their sources of support for food, money and employment were going to be cut off and they would experience a grievously hard time in the city. Each day most church leaders look at the signs of their declining congregations, their shrinking budgets, the dwindling participation within various church programs and of their own intuition, they logically assume that they must react and devise their plan for self-support, survival and self-sufficiency. Identical to Peter's disregard of Christ's plan, most churches have instituted their plans as alternatives. Can such behavior of the present day church leadership be classified as apostasy at work? In Greek, the word apostasy means to desert or abandon. This was not the first time that Peter or the disciples had abandoned Christ. So often, believers desert Christ by not doing His will and occasionally turning to do things their way or living life as they desire. Just as the Jews often deserted God, likewise, believers tend to abandon Christ and take matters into their own hands.

Believers Have Gone Fishing

Peter was the leader of the early church and he was to assist in setting the example; yet, instantaneously readers discover that one of the greatest problems with reacting to a situation is the failure to pray. Peter didn't say to the disciples, just as Daniel said to his friends when they faced death, come let us pray to our God in heaven. He didn't seek God. He didn't say, Christ left us with the command to wait here until our change comes. He didn't say, things look pretty rough but we're going to do just as He said. No, he acted upon his own will. Peter and the disciples made that choice to go because they knew how to fish. They were professional fisherman. They did not go for food only. They went for self- preservation, self-substantiation, self- appropriation and self- identification. They chose to go fishing for the sole purpose of "Self."

Seven of the eleven disciples went fishing because it was a way of business and profit. They went fishing because it was the culture of that time. This staggering statistic shares with us that within a democratic and capitalistic society two thirds of believers are apt to lose focus in their original mission, purpose and calling. Once we have been with Christ we are to never return to the "Cultural Religion" by becoming preoccupied with survival, materialism, and success. The Cultural Religion of today is men and women becoming members of churches just to network and be a part of a social club. The Cultural Religion of today is people building immaculate mega edifices; yet, censoring it from the less fortunate, expurgating it from the downtrodden and purging it of undesirables. The Cultural Religion of today is communities of congregations developing programs and projects that accommodate the influence and activism of elite and selective groups.

Now we can see clearly, if leaders of the church have little faith then the followers of the church will have little faith and can be lead to live their lives outside of the commission of God. They can be lead to operate the church as a business by carrying out mission programs for the purpose of self-sustenance. They say it is good business because the programs profit their budgets and increase their membership rolls. Contrarily, what these churches are doing is fishing on the wrong side of the boat. They have returned to the "Cultural Religion." A culture that has misappropriated its priorities, a culture that idolizes creation and not the Creator, a culture that has romanticized immorality, and a culture that has stylized ungodliness.

When Christians are out of the will of God and they are living life through the means of their best efforts they will not be victorious. By going fishing the disciples thought that everything was going to turn out alright. They went and entered into a boat with the impression that all was assured and they would catch many fish. Yet, I remind you that Noah entered into an ark and Moses was placed in a small boat but these arks served God's purpose and plan because they were of His divine providential security of the righteous.

Perhaps various churches believe that all is well, that they are safe, and that they will be able to sustain themselves because of the arks of their investments, the arks of their affiliation, the arks of their influence, and the arks of the ability to carry out programs of administrative soundness. However, let it be known that God is not involved, and those churches and leaders have developed a false sense of security that will not last. The boats of Humanism, Individualism, Liberalism, and Administrative and Managerial soundness cannot serve as foundations that sustain the church. Jesus is the only adequate foundation for the church and its leaders. Believers must have faith in knowing that Christ is enough and His grace is sufficient. Though we need programs and are to invest, we are not to place them before God or people because works do not save souls only Christ can do that great work.

Proverbs 16:25 says, "There is a way that seems right to a man or woman, but in the end it leads to death and destruction".

Believers Aren't Catching Anything

More and more professionalism is being requested of churches. Professional people are becoming members of churches. Some are people that have their own businesses or private practices. Many members of congregations are professionally skilled people. Most are diversely skilled. Unfortunately, many are untrained formally and possess little to no knowledge of the Gospel of Jesus Christ. Often, because of their professional capabilities church leaders recruit many to serve in various capacities. Though they are to serve Him in the Great Commission of the Church, just as the disciples did, contemporary leaders have also turned to their earthly talents in carrying out the operation of the church. They have employed to their earthly expertise for the survival of the church, not men. They, themselves, have returned to business as usual for they have no faith in Christ.

The Church has gone fishing and they are fishing on the wrong side of the boat. The disciples, the professional fishers, caught no fish. They knew that the best time to go fishing was at night.

They were very familiar with the Sea of Galilee and the area in which to fish. They knew the proper equipment to use to catch fish. Indicative of today's church leaders, they know how to write programs, they know how to conduct a worship service, they know the keys to witness and they are experts in locating and identifying people that have needs. The churches employ their skills earnestly but when they pull up their nets they too discover that they have caught nothing. They emerge empty handed. Believers are living in a dark world and an evil time when the harvest is plentiful but even at the best time for fishing we are catching nothing.

The Brightest Of The Morning Star

Jesus is the believer's bright and morning star. In His presence believers find hope and joy. Christians can't do anything without Christ shedding light on their situation, condition, or circumstance. Yet, the disciples knew him not because they were not waiting on Him as they should have been in Jerusalem. When believers do not wait on the Lord or stay focused on serving and seeking Him they are apt to miss Christ when He shows on the scene. God does not have to come to churches by way of an earthquake, fire, rushing wind, or hit them on the head to give revolution. He can make himself known by a calm still voice. He can come in any form He pleases and if leaders and believers would only walk with Him and talk with Him each day they would never miss Christ when He presents Himself.

Jesus called them "Children." Believers are the children of God and God is their Father. Also children are those who are young in spiritual growth and are limited in faith. "Have you any meat?" was His question. Notice He used the words children and meat together.

In fact, though by this time you ought to be teachers, you need someone to teach you the elementary truths of God's word all over again. You need milk, not solid food! Anyone who lives on milk, being still an infant, is not acquainted with the teaching about righteousness. But solid food is for the mature, who by constant use have trained themselves to distinguish good from evil. Heb 5:12-14

It implies that this is a time in life when believers and leaders should be feeding on the meat of the word. This is a time when they should be teaching the world about God and living life by the complete word of God. Yet, they are in need of being taught again. It is also a question asked of all believers that have been working in the fields, what have you to show or offer me for all your labor?

They said, " No, we have no meat." Inadvertently, the disciples were admitting:

>No, we are not teaching the word, as we should.

>No, we are not applying the word, as we should.

>No, we are not studying the word, as we should.

>No, we have not been obedient to your command.

>Lord we are not living the word, as we should.

>We have nothing to offer you or show as proof of our faithful labor.

Fishing Not Man's Way But Christ's Way

Jesus said "Cast the net on the right side of the boat, and ye shall find". The text confirms that the church was fishing on the wrong side of the boat. They didn't even know this to be true. They thought they were correct in their efforts. They were fishing improperly and many Disciples of Christ are fishing improperly, today. They are fishing under their humanism and professionalism. Believers are to turn from their ways and the tempter's ways and be obedient to Christ. Only then will churches bring forth a bountiful harvest. So bountiful that those leaders will have to call on lay members to come and assist them in gathering the harvest. The Church must acknowledge that only what we do for Christ will last and that only He can cause us to prosper. Similar to the net of the disciples, Christ can use what we have as a resource for our increase. He used the rod of Moses, the sling-shot of David and the jaw-bone of an ass that Samson had in his hand to cause them to emerge victorious in the midst of their trial. He will do the same with your gifts and talents if you submit to Him and allow Him to use you. Never attempt to utilize human or earthly means to accomplish spiritual objectives.

Moral Application: Jesus gave the great commission, which is for the believer to teach the word throughout the world. Instead the church has gone fishing for profit, security, and self-sustenance. Today, many churches are in dire need of relinquishing their professional way of fishing. The need is to listen to Christ and fish the way He directs men and women to carry out the mission. Many believers and leaders are in desperate need of recommitment to Christ. They need to re-institute their faith and place the love of God and the love of their neighbor before the love of buildings and self-achievements. For many will say Lord, Lord I did this and that in your name; yet, the Lord will say, "Depart from me because I never knew you."

Chapter Fifteen
How To Make Your Church Great
Morals For A Growing Church

Cornell is a young man that lives in a rural county. At the age of thirty-five he possesses a keen sense of obligation to his church and community. He is very active in both areas of his life. However, regardless of his many hours of work and despite the many resources he has extended to his church and community, Cornell noticed that his contributions were not improving his church or community. He began to carry a great burden concerning the church he attends, Mt. Zion. Mt. Zion is Cornell's home church. He was born and raised within four miles of the church's location. For many personal reasons he loves the congregation, the leaders, officers and all that Mt. Zion represents. Unfortunately, over the past five years, Cornell noticed that Mt. Zion's membership was declining. In addition to the decline in membership the church was beginning to experience financial difficulties. Cornell wanted to know why his home church was not growing while certain local churches near his county were flourishing. Their membership was increasing and they were very active. Because of his love for his church, he decided to investigate what makes a church grow and what makes a church die out. He began to study various church growth and church leadership manuals. Then he interviewed the pastors of three churches that were growing rapidly within the county. In his study, he discovered within each manual that information pertaining to an effective church was consistent. He learned that there were certain patterns that the three growing churches practiced that were consistent with the Early Church. Also, to have a growing church, leaders and congregations must follow the patterns that are exhibited in the Bible. The application of his study suggested that churches use the seven characteristics of the Early Church as a model for church growth because they assure effectiveness and efficiency. Should churches not follow the God given example, they digress to become ineffective and some resolve to close their doors. The following is Cornell's report that contains the seven characteristics that the three growing churches within his county had consistent with the Early Church. The report was presented to the pastor and official board.

TO: Rev. Joseph John Johnson
      Pastor of Mt. Zion Church

From: Cornell DeWhite Sting
      Congregational Member

Re: What Makes A Church Grow?

Dear Pastor Jones:

Everyone wants to attend a great church. Everyone wants his or her church to excel. I am one of those who have prayed and sought answers to the question, "What makes a church grow? Generally, when people speak of a "Great Church," they reference the church as a great facility, or that it has an eloquent preacher and exceptional music program. It appears that this is the current evaluation of our present generation. However, I have discovered seven characteristics that God defines as the greatness of a church and assures us at Mt. Zion and any church willing to practice that the pattern of the Early Church represents unimaginable church growth.

The promise is for you and your children and for all who are far off-- for all whom the Lord our God will call." With many other words he warned them; and he pleaded with them, "Save yourselves from this corrupt generation." Those who accepted his message were baptized, and about three thousand were added to their number that day. They devoted themselves to the apostles' teaching and to the fellowship, to the breaking of bread and to prayer. Everyone was filled with awe, and many wonders and miraculous signs were done by the apostles. All the believers were together and had everything in common. Selling their possessions and goods, they gave to anyone as he had need. Every day they continued to meet together in the temple courts. They broke bread in their homes and ate together with glad and sincere hearts, praising God and enjoying the favor of all the people. And the Lord added to their number daily those who were being saved. Acts 2:39-47

After Peter preached to the people, they were deeply moved by his message and three thousand of them surrendered their lives to Christ that day. The church grew from about one hundred and twenty members to about three thousand one hundred and twenty. Seven attributes for church growth were revealed on that day. They are as follow:

> First, <u>The Early Church was a growing church because it had a great leader and was a community-oriented church.</u> Notice that within the same day men and women were added unto the church. Peter, the leader of the church seized the opportunity and shared the Word of God to unbelievers. He boldly stood before men and women of all walks of life, proclaimed the day of the Lord, and publicly asserted that all people must repent. The early church grew because all of the apostles were leaders that permitted the Holy Spirit to direct them in all things. The early church and the apostolic leaders were found within Jerusalem. They were in the right place at the right time. Because of their obedience, great things took place and the community was blessed.

The early church was community-oriented because Peter preached to all, nurtured all, assisted all to grow and mature in Christ. He preached and taught anyone that was willing to hear him, not a particular group, particular political establishment, or particular family. When churches cease to be family oriented and begin to centralize their preaching and evangelization on their community, people will gladly receive the word of God. When churches stop nurturing specific groups and begin to nurture their immediate community they will witness an increase in response to the word of God. If any church minister and congregation, like Peter and the believers at that time, would preach to the lost within their community and not for the benefit of certain groups with influence or political power, then men and women will be convicted and gladly receive the word. It is saddening to say that many churches are supplied with great theologians and seminarians but people of the community neither gladly receive their message nor come to be baptized because the pastor does not compassionately proclaim God's word's to the community. He or she preaches to the appeasement of the congregation. Christians are baptized into a community of believers and to that community all of its members are citizens of God and the community is not divided or separated by various family structures.

Secondly, <u>The Early Church was a growing church because it was a teaching church.</u> Peter and the disciples dedicated themselves to the teaching of the new converts. There were many that had been added unto them and these babes in Christ needed teaching. They didn't have the time to establish programs of outreach. They didn't bog themselves down with the tedious work of planning. They did not permit organizing and administration to take precedence over teaching believers the true word of God. The leaders of the Early Church did not allow finances to sidetrack them from teaching the word of God. They were so adamant about teaching God's word that they told the people to select deacons to help with the finances and concerns of the church because they desired to devote themselves to be about constant prayer and teaching. Their motto should have been, "Teach Them That They May Know."

Too often much is placed before teaching new converts the word of God. Leaders of churches have become so inedited with the administration of the Church that they no longer spend adequate time in prayer with God, reading His word, and teaching others the word of God. All disciples are to maintain teaching others about Christ as a top priority of their life. Why? Because, Christ commanded believers to teach others all things that He has taught them. All Disciples of Christ should continue steadfast in teaching His word.

Third, <u>The Early Church was a growing church because it continued steadfast in fellowship.</u> A growing church has a great quality of togetherness. This is important because they realized that no man or woman is of himself or herself. We need one another; the Spirit of God has come down to knit believers together in fellowship. The church becomes a real church only when it is bonded together in fellowship and love. One of the most frequently quoted verses in the Bible

A Cry for Ethical and Moral Strength

is, "May the grace of the Lord Jesus Christ and the love of God, and the sweet communion of the Holy Ghost, be with you all." Amen. Believers have heard it a thousand times or more but have they stopped to think what it really means. Communion of the Holy Ghost is God working in your heart and mine. He is fellowshipping with all believers, helping them to enjoy the things of God together.

When the one hundred and twenty gathered in the upper room in fellowship, the Holy Spirit baptized them with power. The same baptism took place at Cornelius' house when the people came together in fellowship with Peter. God's promise to believers is when they come together in His name; He is present and will give them strength. "For where two or more are gathered together there I will be also." Believers are to never forsake fellowshipping with all people, everywhere, and at all times because in the midst, Christ's presence and power is made available. Many churches of today are accused of not having good fellowship. There are infinite factors that tend to divide believers. If it is not the race, sex, or the color of a person's skin, it is his or her denominational, economical, or political affiliations. Youth are leaving churches because there is little to no fellowshipping with them. Seniors that are not able to attend church services on a regular basis feel abandoned by the church because there is little to no fellowshipping with them. Unbelievers within the community do not attend a local church because many have never been invited to the church or invited to fellowship with believers at special church programs. To regain the interest and commitment of the people, churches must not only fellowship more with one another; they must fellowship with their communities and internally within their own church body.

Fourth, <u>The Early Church was a growing church because it continued steadfast in breaking of bread.</u> Never in the Christian faith is the world to be placed before Christ. Never in the faith are buildings or administration to be placed before Christian service. Never in the Christian journey are believers to forget the pain and the suffering that Jesus endured for their freedom and the freedom for whosoever that comes unto Him.

A church becomes a growing church when it remembers and holds dear to the principle of communing with Christ. For when people come together in fellowship as often as they can they are to commune with Christ. Paul suggests that communion within fellowship promotes unity. A growing church seeks to stamp out division by fostering relationships with Christ. It constantly evaluates itself by reviewing what it has done, what it is doing, what it has not done, and what it needs to do. A growing church remains in a state of repentance of its failures and sins. It continues to seek God's forgiving power and grace. A growing church remembers Christ is in control and believers are accountable to Him.

Fifth, <u>The Early Church was a growing church because it continued steadfast in prayer.</u> Prayer is the Christian method of communicating with God. Because God is personal, all people can offer prayers and have public or private conversations with God. Before Christ ascended into the heavens, the disciples asked Him to teach them how to pray. Not only did Christ show them how to pray, He also demonstrated the power of prayer and He prayed for them. And the Early Church heavily relied on the power of prayer because as Christians they recognized their dependence upon their Creator. They recognized that they were faced with difficulties greater than their own strength. They understood that their challenges were beyond what they could comprehend and that they had every reason to express gratitude for God's blessings, strength, and protection. Yet, the Early Church did not only pray because they faced enemies or persecution, they had far more reason to respond to God in prayer. They prayed to God for His love for them, for revealing Himself through the marvelous incarnation and life of Christ, for God's atoning provision at the cross, His resurrection, as well as His continuing presence through the Holy Spirit.

A growing church continues in prayer because through prayer all things become possible. A growing church never ceases in praying for one another because the prayers to the saints avail many things. On no account does a growing church lose hope for any person. It continues to pray more fervently for the lost and the backsliders, so that one-day believers can say I did arrive at this point of my faith journey on my own accord, I am so glad that someone prayed for me. The strength of a growing church is its congregation is in constant prayer for each other, their families, their community, their nation, and the entire world.

Sixth, <u>The Early Church was a growing church because it reverenced God.</u> The Early Church feared God, meaning they lived life in awe of God. They lived life in expectance of His immediate return and they eagerly longed for His coming. A great philosopher said men and women should live life as if it was a temple. He suggested that each person live life as if it is sacred and that God demands perfection and Holiness from all people. All are to live life in reverence of God because the earth is the Lord's temple and everything in it belongs to Him. When men and women become familiar with God's presence and reverence Him, when they acknowledge that He is more than an excellent God with great power, they can begin to expect wonderful things to take course in their lives. They can look forward to supernatural things to happen on their behalf.

Somewhere many churches have lost their reverence for God. They have allowed godliness to incorporate itself in the church. Immorality exists within the ranks of the church and within many believers' lives. Churches function with no sense of urgency. Without the fear of Christ's return, to most believers everything is business as usual. Miraculous experiences have nearly ceased to take place on behalf of the church because believers lack faith, they have low expectations of their God, they fail to treat their communities and churches as temples of God, and they possess little fear of God. A growing church attempts great things because it reverences God.

Finally, <u>The Early Church was a growing church because it graciously shared.</u> All that believed were together and had all things in common. They distributed to each other as they had need. Unlike the Rich Young Ruler, these believers sold land and houses to meet the needs of poor Christians. They also contributed to the relief of churches in need. They followed Christ's teaching that it is more blessed to give than to receive. The Early Church practiced the principle of not accumulating themselves treasures upon earth where such riches perish, but they stored their treasures in heaven where they last forever. They were generous to one another because of their love for their neighbor.

It is not normal that most modern churches follow the characteristic of generosity that prevailed in the Early Church. They rarely share their resources among their community. How then can one imagine churches sharing resources with each other? However, if churches would put into practice the royal law of love their church would prosper, their communities would flourish, and they would become growing churches. Only if believers would love their neighbor as they love themselves, then all churches would do well.

We hold these moral truths within the Bible to be self-evident. Vowing that churches be willing to exemplify these seven characteristics of the Early Church and follow the God given pattern are they assured efficiency and effectiveness in their missions and Church Growth. These promises are extended to individual believers because they are the true Church of God. They shall increase and prosper as they live according to the word of God.

Cc. Official Board Members

Chapter Sixteen
Do Not Sell Your Birthright
Morals For Valuing An Inheritance.

A good man leaves an inheritance for his children's children, but a sinner's wealth is stored up for the righteous. Proverbs 13:22

Each day, like clock work, the school bus picks Chad up and delivers him safely to school. Almost daily before he could sit comfortably in his seat he could hear the snickering and the jokes. Chad did not grow up with the luxuries that other children possessed. His mother and father were migrant workers. They lived off all that they earned. People gave the family clothing for themselves and for their only son. The Tucker family was very appreciative of the gifts they received. Often when Chad was at school some children would tease him. This continued until he graduated. After graduating from high school Chad worked with his father in the fields because they could not afford for Chad to attend college. One day his mother died from a sudden illness. One year later his father became stricken with a fever and an uncontrollable cough. He called Chad to his bedside and said you know that your mother and I love you, never had much but we tried to live a moral and just life and our desire is that you do the same. Come closer to me that I may hold you. When your mother and I worked in Oklahoma in nineteen seventy-six we were given two acres of land by the owner for tending his crops. The land is located near the outskirts of the city. Here is the deed. Never sell this property. It is all we have in our name. It was our desire that you have an inheritance and that your children's children become heirs to this property. Chad's father passed that same day. Chad honored his mother and father by never selling the land. Four generations later and to this day the property remains recorded in the Tucker's family name.

The Inheritance Of Our Fathers

Some time later there was an incident involving a vineyard belonging to Naboth the Jezreelite. The vineyard was in Jezreel, close to the palace of Ahab king of Samaria. Ahab said to Naboth, "Let me have your vineyard to use for a vegetable garden, since it is close to my palace. In exchange I will give you a better vineyard or, if you prefer, I will pay you whatever it is worth." But Naboth replied, "The

LORD forbid that I should give you the inheritance of my fathers." So Ahab went home, sullen and angry because Naboth the Jezreelite had said, "I will not give you the inheritance of my fathers." He lay on his bed sulking and refused to eat. His wife Jezebel came in and asked him, "Why are you so sullen? Why won't you eat?" He answered her, "Because I said to Naboth the Jezreelite, 'Sell me your vineyard; or if you prefer, I will give you another vineyard in its place.' But he said, 'I will not give you my vineyard.'" Jezebel his wife said, "Is this how you act as king over Israel? Get up and eat! Cheer up. I'll get you the vineyard of Naboth the Jezreelite." So she wrote letters in Ahab's name, placed his seal on them, and sent them to the elders and nobles who lived in Naboth's city with him. In those letters she wrote: "Proclaim a day of fasting and seat Naboth in a prominent place among the people. But seat two scoundrels opposite him and have them testify that he has cursed both God and the king. Then take him out and stone him to death." So the elders and nobles who lived in Naboth's city did as Jezebel directed in the letters she had written to them. They proclaimed a fast and seated Naboth in a prominent place among the people. Then two scoundrels came and sat opposite him and brought charges against Naboth before the people, saying, "Naboth has cursed both God and the king." So they took him outside the city and stoned him to death. Then they sent word to Jezebel: "Naboth has been stoned and is dead." As soon as Jezebel heard that Naboth had been stoned to death, she said to Ahab, "Get up and take possession of the vineyard of Naboth the Jezreelite that he refused to sell you. He is no longer alive, but dead." When Ahab heard that Naboth was dead, he got up and went down to take possession of Naboth's vineyard. IKing 21:1-16

There are two sides to every story. I say this because within this chapter you will soon read a section titled, "Do Not Sell your Birthright"; wherein, the inheritor sells his birthright and later regrets doing so. I have entitled this section "The Inheritance Of Our Fathers" because men and women have an earthly father that leaves them inheritances and they also have a spiritual father who extends to them an inheritance. And through death they became legal heirs to their father's possessions. All that is their earthly father's or spiritual father's becomes their inheritance at the point and time of death. For believers, it is at the foot of the cross that you become sons and daughters of God. Also, at the very moment of His death on the cross believers became heirs to all of His riches and treasures. Discouragingly, so often it is discovered, what others have worked so hard to obtain or maintain their children have taken the inheritance for granted and sold their inheritance for less than what it is worth. The same applies to God's creations. Many people have taken the great inheritance offered them through the blood and death of Jesus Christ for granted and have sold their rightful inheritance for peanuts.

Fortunately, this story is different. It conveys a man that stood up for his father's inheritance. Naboth the Jezreelite had a vineyard directly adjacent to the palace of King Ahab of Samaria. Ahab was desirous of the most picturesque sight in Israel to the point that he coveted the property. The land was an immaculate piece of property because Naboth cherished his forefather's gift of inheritance. He constantly tended the land that was passed down from generation to generation. The same land that his father's father had cultivated with care was bequeathed as a most sacred possession. Without any reservations, Naboth was well aware that he was to honor, value, and protect his inheritance.

Each time people would pass by they informed Naboth that his vineyard was gorgeous and produced some of the tastiest grapes in the land. Whenever someone offered to purchase the field, Naboth declined the offer. But there was one that adored the vineyard for a long period of time. He watched it from his palace and gazed at it when he journeyed along the path. It was the king of the land. One day King Ahab told his driver to stop that He might speak to Naboth. He pulled Naboth to the side and told him how much he adored his vineyard. Naboth was honored to hear such pleasant words from the king. But the king didn't pull him to the side just to tell him how much he adored his field. His primary goal was to purchase the land. Therefore, he said to Naboth my fields near the palace connect to your field. Give me your vineyard so that I can add it with my land and use it to grow a garden. I will allow you to choose a vineyard of mine that is better than this one or I will give you whatever price you think the field is worth.

Like so many people that see the dollar signs when an open ended opportunity similar to this one comes along, the young man listened to his royal master and realized that the hand of prosperity, materialism, and fortune was knocking at his door. And I, like Satan the king was attempting to lead Naboth to believe that the transaction would benefit him more than his existing inheritance. He tried to persuade him to believe the bargain would afford or produce opportunities of increasing his personal wealth. This same spirit that used Ahab as an instrument to tempt Naboth in his garden came disguised as a serpent to tempt Eve in her garden. He also tempted Jesus by offering him many things in exchange for his passions of inheritance with God.

Nothing Is Better Than Your Inheritance

The King Ahab possessed much just as Satan possesses much. If they didn't have much they could not have offered so much in their tempting of godly men. The king and Satan owned many treasures but they did not own the gift of God's spirit, the love of the Father, or the enjoyment of the promise of the new land to come. How could the King Ahab offer Naboth something better when what he had as a gift from his father and from God? His inheritance was the greatest in value and Ahab desired what he possessed. As the reader reviews Naboth's story, the question becomes why would any person surrender the greatest inheritance anyone could receive for something of less value? That inheritance is the gift of eternal life.

When Adam was the heir of all the earth he made the horrid mistake of selling the inheritance of his father for something he perceived to be of a higher value. He sold it for the knowledge of good and evil. He sold it for moral wisdom. These are the things he received in exchange for life, liberty, and the world. He received death in exchange for eternal life. He received the knowledge of morality and immorality in exchange for spiritual blindness. He traded peace for fear. He swapped paradise for a world of sickness, disease and sin.

Unlike the first Adam, the second Adam did not sell His inheritance. He was willing to die for what originated from His Father. Christ would not barter or sell the promises and blessings of God for anything. He did not allow the words of a trickster to influence Him. He held God's word above His very life and death. All believers are to respond by saying no to principalities, powers, rulers, angels and any other creature that comes to buy, steal or take their inheritance. Committed to the cause, to his forefathers and to the word, Naboth rejected Ahab's proposal. He said to him the written word of the Lord forbids me to relinquish my inheritance. As an heir, Naboth knew that no man or woman was in any way ever to alienate himself or herself from any part of a birthright. These gifted treasures are what identify believers as family and as a people. They are pieces of the whole that shape the believers' character. They give believers their identity by connecting them with the rich heritage; a history strongly linked with God, the greatest Father. Believers have no right to sell their identity. They have no right to sell their history. They have no right to exchange their inheritance, whether they became heirs by their earthly father or by the Heavenly Father.

Perhaps Naboth recalled there was a time when the Israelites had no land or possessions but God took them out of Egypt and gave them a land flowing with milk and honey. God reminded the Jews that the land belonged to Him and that they were only tenants. He also established inheritance laws that ensured that the land would remain in the possession of all families. To ensure that the land would remain in the possession of its designated family, God created the day of Jubilee. It was a celebration that took place every fifty years. During the celebration all land owned by Jews that was bought or sold was to return back to its original owner and if Jews sold themselves into servitude they were to be released from all debt. The truth is Naboth could not sell the land even if he desired to do so because it did not belong to him. It belonged to God.

There was a time that many believers' forefathers and mothers had nothing but God heard their prayers and extended His grace and mercy to them. He gave them all that they acquired in life. It was a gift from Him to the people He loved. Yet, believers have bartered, sold, and exchanged the gifts of the Father for things of the world at a lesser value. They have sold land and houses of their earthly father's in exchange for drugs, money, and material gain. They have exchanged salvation for fame, prestige, and earthly gratification. They have no right to do so because even salvation is offered as a gift to every man and woman. It is not theirs to give away. Jesus paid the price for man's salvation. God-fearing men and women should always take a stand for the inheritance of our earthly fathers and our spiritual Father.

Moral Application: Believers must stand for the inheritance of their Father, God, for they know that He gives all good things and all things belong to Him. The earth is the Lord's and all things within it. Even humans' bodies are not theirs. They too belong to Christ. He made them and later bought them with His life because of the enormous price of sin. Like Naboth, mankind is only a steward of all they have of this world and of God's word. They are to care for these gifts, protect these gifts, and be willing to die as heir of the Father's gifts.

The world is inundated with selling, buying, collecting, and exchanging so much that it has created mega-marketing enterprises to promote the concept of getting and having the better or finer things of life. This system of the world is only a decoy that causes people to settle for less. It is the prince of this world that desires your inheritance; something that he does not have and is of greater value than anything he can offer you. He doesn't come to take it by force but by trickery and he is willing to offer you many things in exchange for your inheritance.

In the world of vast trade and international exchange, know that the inheritance of your Father is more than just land such as a vineyard and material possessions. It is your peace of mind, your friends, your family, your freedom of prayer, worship, and praise, your ability to commune with Christ, the revealing of the word by the Holy Spirit, the reality of eternal life, your power to do all things, and love for humanity. None of these things are yours to trade, sell or give away. They are gifts of immeasurable value.

The Child That Despised His Birthright: A True story

When Isaac was forty years old he prayed to the Lord on behalf of his wife Rebekah, because she was barren and they had no children. The Lord heard Isaac's prayer and answered his request. Without delay, his wife Rebekah became pregnant. Something miraculous, but strange was taking place within her. She felt a lot of movement in her belly. Her belly was at constant unrest. There was much activity of tossing and turning. Rebekah wanted to know why this was happening to her. She went to a private place and asked the

A Cry for Ethical and Moral Strength

Lord. The Lord informed her that she was having twins and the babies wrestled each other while in the womb. He said to her, "Two nations are in your womb, and two peoples from within you will be separated; one people will be stronger than the other, and the older will serve the younger." When she gave birth the first child to be born was named Esau because his color was red and hair covered his entire body. They called Esau's brother Jacob because he was born with his hand grasping Esau's heel. Isaac was sixty years old when Rebekah gave birth to the twins.

As the boys grew up, Esau became a skillful hunter. He developed into a man that had a great knowledge of the open country. On the other hand, Jacob was raised to be a quiet man. He spent most of his time among the tents. The father, Isaac loved Esau because of his fondness for wild game, but Rebekah loved Jacob because he was a homebody. Once when Jacob was cooking some stew, Esau came in from a strenuous and extensive time of scouting and hunting. He was extremely hungry. So, he said to Jacob, "Quick, let me have some of that bean stew! I'm famished!" Jacob's response was, "I will share my bean soup with you but first you must sell me your birthright." Esau said, "Look, I am about to die, I have no time for playing around. What good is the birthright to me if I starve to death?" Then Jacob said, "Swear to me before I give you some of my bean stew that you will give me your birthright." So Jacob took an oath and swore to sell his birthright to Jacob. With a slight sigh then a bright grin; Jacob gave Esau some bread and some lentil stew. Esau ate and drank, and then he left.

Though Esau despised his birthright when his temporary relief from hunger was gone, he blamed his brother for taking his inheritance and later threatened to harm him causing Jacob to flee for his life. After many years passed in the life of the twins, they reconciled their friendship and love for one another. However, one thing never changed. The day Esau sold his birthright was the day his inheritance changed hands and it was never regained. To this day, the birthright remains in Jacob's family's possession. His sons and daughters are heir to the birthright that was despised by Esau and exchanged for a bowl of bean soup.

Chapter Seventeen
The Power Of Promises
Moral Of The Cost Of A Promise

Somewhere today a person is saying I would like to give up this marriage and start over with someone who knows how to love me; only God knows what I am going through with this person. But then he or she remembers the promises that were made when they took their vows of holy matrimony. After reflecting on the promises the couple committed to at the time of their marriage, the person decided to stick with his or her marriage and try to make it last for ever. The power of the promise overcame personal challenges.

Some place today in someone's home a mother and a father are saying, our child has become impossible, he or she has not turned out the way we raised him or her. We do not know our child any more. He or she acts as an imposter. We wish our child would leave and not be a part of our life at all, God knows she or he has taken us to our limits. Suddenly, one of the parents reflects on the day that the child was born and how both of them had great hopes, dreams and expectations. Then they remembered their promise to make their family the best and together as a family they would overcome all things. The parents remember the promise of Christ when He said if you obey my laws and statutes I will bless you and your children. One parent looks at the other and says remember Christ's promise that if we do not give up and have faith - all thing are possible. In that moment the power of promise gave hope and strength to a family.

On this day a minister is thinking, " I am going to give up my calling and find a line of work that pays more and offers more appreciation for my efforts. Only God knows that I am burned out from this congregation giving me the challenge of my life. But he remembers a promise he made to God when he was ordained, that he or she would minister God's word when times are good and when times are not so good. Then the minister decides to renew his or her spirit and stick with his commitment. Again the power of promises prevailed over apathy and indecisiveness.

Believe it or not, somewhere people still make and keep their promises. They choose not to quit when the going gets rough because they promised to see it through. They stick to what some may call a lost cause. They hold to a love grown cold. Yes, they dare to make promises and care enough to keep the promise they make. If your ship appears to be sinking but you have vowed not to abandon it, if you have pledged to forsake no man that has a need, or if you have a cause you are willing to die for and one you will not desert when the heat is turned up, then the power of promise is anchored within your spirit and will assist you to overcome life's every changing phenomena.

The Cost of Promises

Jesus said, "Estimate the cost to see if you can pay the price before you commit yourself by making a promise because a promise is marvelous thing." When a person makes a promise, she or he reaches out into an unpredictable future and makes one thing predictable; that they will be there even when being there costs them more than they want to pay. When the person makes a promise, he or she stretches himself or herself out into circumstances that no one can control or predict but controls at least one thing. The one thing is that the person will be there no matter what the circumstances are or what the demands of the individual turns out to be.

In the Garden of Eden, after the fall of man, God promised that He would send a savior. The power of His promise inspired men and women of all cultures, race, and ethnical origin to endure. However, the most encouraging promise ever made unto man came with a price. The price Christ had to pay to redeem man and extend salvation to humanity was more than any one in this world and the heaven above could pay. Salvation's cost was very expensive.

Somewhere in the heaven, some place within the Holy of Holies and at some point in time Christ considered His marriage with a people and how unhappy they have made Him, He considered how He has to be a great Father to all His children; yet, they have rebelled and not followed His teaching. He thought of His ministry as shepherd of the flock and how unappreciative the flock is for His work of salvation.

However, Christ placed His love and His promises above mankind's immoral behaviors and lack of love. Despite the ungodliness of men and women, the power of Christ's love and promise exceeds all of their misfortunes. God is the friend that made a promise. He stretched himself out and shielded man from the circumstances that no human could control or predict. He controls all the chaos and assures any believer that regardless of the demands of Him or what the situation may be He will be there to help them.

The writer of the book of Hebrews says that the power of God's promise cost Him the price of incarnating Himself and coming to earth to surrender His life. That same Jesus, who was made a little lower than the angels, is now crowned with glory and honor because He was willing to pay the price for a promise made by God unto mankind. He suffered death so that by the grace of God He might taste death for everyone. The power of promise cost, its price is listed as follows:

1.) God was made a little lower than the angels. To keep His promise to mankind God had to leave his riches and treasure and come to live on earth. Emanuel, God with us. John 6:38 " For I came down from heaven not to do my will but the will of him that sent me."

2.) God was incarnated in the flesh. This same pre-existing eternal Son became flesh, took upon Him a human body and dwelt among men. John says " And the Word became flesh and dwelt among us." God emptied himself into a fleshly body in the likeness of men and became a servant of all people. There was a necessity of the incarnation. First, it was necessary that He have a body that He might be "in all points tempted like as we are." Second, God had prepared Himself a body so that Christ could endure bodily suffering and become man's substitute. Christ paid the price in keeping His promise.

The Cost of a Promise can be your Freedom.

The freedom men and women demonstrate in making commitments is the same freedom that simultaneously limits their freedom. When a person makes a promise he or she limits their freedom. The liberty that offers the person the ability to be there for someone or others who trust the individual to keep a promise, limits the person from doing other things because he or she has obligated himself or herself.

When believers commit themselves to the cause of Christ, their promise to follow Him restricts their free will. When Christians promise their life to Christ to be there for Him regardless of the cost, they relinquish their freedom by surrendering it to the control of the Holy Spirit. Their promise limits their freedom. After choosing Christ, you separate yourself from the ways of the natural man and the ways of the world in order to be there for Christ and to do His will. Believers will use their freedom to become Christ's servant. To serve Him you chose not to walk the wide road. You promised that you would praise Him. You promised that you would worship Him. You promised that you would obey His word. You promised that you would stand for justice and equality. Christ trusts that believers will keep their promise by being there for Him.

The Future of the Human Race is sealed with a Promise.

There is a happy ending to all of the chaos. That happy ending rests within believers and their promise to evangelize the world. The glory is to know that many men and women have freely submitted their freedom for the salvation of all mankind. Humanity's end is etched in the Christians' promise to Christ and Christ's promises to man. The promises of God assures men and women that one day the world will finally be without sin and evil and that the Human family will discover peace, love, justice, and freedom together.

Many say that the promises were confirmed when a common Chaldean named Abraham burned his bridges and relied on a promise from God. God said to Abraham leave your country and I will give you a land and cause your people to become a great nation. He promised a son to Abraham whose wife was an old woman and he was an old man but by faith Abraham was justified. Another person confirms the promises of God. Moses needed to know whether he could depend on the voice that came from the burning bush. He needed to know if he could trust the God whose name is I Am that I Am, the God that made promises and kept each promise He made.

For he said I am the God of your Father, I am the God of Isaac, Jacob, and the God of Abraham. God has kept His promises throughout all generations.

Today, God makes the same promises with all people who believe. He says I am the God that will never leave you nor forsake you. I am the God whom you can trust and lean on. I am the God that healed your body. I am the God who was there all the time. I am the God that comforted you in your time of need. I am the God that bled and died for you. I am the God that forgives your sins and blots out all of your transgressions. Also, I am the God that keeps all of my promises.

Jesus sat down with his disciples and said, "I am the way, the truth and the life." He confirmed that He's the I Am that believers can trust. The incarnated "I AM" promised if you "Would confess with your mouth the Lord Jesus and believe in your heart that God raised him from the dead you will be saved. He promised "If we confess our sins, He is faithful and just to forgive us our sins, and to cleanse us from all unrighteousness

Moral Application: God's promises have sustaining power. They give believers strength in perilous times. Also, they give believers the power to endure all obstacles in life. Unlike men, Christ considered the cost for the purchase of man's salvation. Despite the price, He promised to mankind that He would be there to help them at all times. All they had to do was call on the name of Jesus. The assurance of His promises gives believers hope, trust and faith in Him. They are confident that regardless of the change in their circumstances, God never changes.

Chapter Eighteen
A New Beginning
Moral Of Forgiving

So often in life people attempt to hold your past before you and your feet to the fire. They try to hold your past or some fault of yours over your head. But at any juncture of life you don't want to constantly hear "Why didn't you do this or that, or why did you do this or that?" No! What all people desire to hear are words of forgiveness. The world can transform a hopeless and challenged human being into a person that sees life worth living. Only if people would forgive as Christ forgives and extends the opportunity of a new start to all, then the day of promise will be practiced in mankind's life.

Few things sound as good to most human beings as the chance to begin again. The offer of a new opportunity to make a better start in life, to wipe out tragic or blighted moments of the past, has always been alluring. Whether it has been an offer made in a fairy tale that ends with the hope of people being reunited or a soap opera that ended with a couple reconciling by firmly embracing one another and passionately sealing their reunion with a kiss; the Christian faith offers people a similar newness of reunion and hope; however, the vast difference is it is not a false hope. It is non-fiction and it is not an act. What the Christian faith offers to anyone who believes is the reality that God will give you a new life and a new beginning. The old things will be forgiven and forgotten and all things become new. The thought of newness touches a spot in every human's heart because it is a new covenant that only God can offer. It is the Creator himself that promises believers that despite the failures and misfortunes of the past, notwithstanding the numerous broken promises accumulated in life, and regardless of the shambles of life and relationships with Him and others, He extends to everyone the gifts of forgiveness and renewal.

Out of the shambles of mankind's relationships, God wants to restore people to a state of wholeness and to unite them with Him and mankind again. Throughout the generations many have attempted to suppress God's invitation; yet, His presence can never be denied and He emerges with forgiveness in his hands and in His voice. God always steps forward into the lives of men and women telling them that He is ready to give a new chance in life. He simply offers "New Life" to all people as a gift because He loves them. If there is any side of God's character that people desperately need to know more personally, it is this dimension of his forgiving compassion.

<u>A Promise Of Newness</u>

Behold, look around and notice what you see. Already, I am doing a new thing and the daytime will soon come when I will make a new covenant with two separate kingdoms that are destined to unite because of my joint favor bestowed upon each of them. This new thing will not be like the promise I made with their forefathers when they became immoral. Similar to leading the blind, I took them by the hand and guided them out of a land of darkness and sin. Though I was faithful to them like an excellent husband, they were defiant of My will.

However, regardless of their misbehavior this is the new covenant I plan to make with both nations, declares the Lord. No longer will my law be written on stone tablets. Very soon, I will place my law in their minds and write it on their stony hearts. I will be their God, and they will be my people. No longer will a person require an earthly priest or teacher to educate him or her in the way of the Lord, because when I am finished doing a new thing all people will know me, from the least of men and women to the greatest. I will give them a second chance and forgive their immorality and will remember their sins no more. Reference Jeremiah 31:31-34.

Moral Application: I will make a new covenant. I will forgive them. I will not remember their sins. These words were not spoken as promises to perfect people then or now. They were spoken to people that had lived an immoral and broken life. God's promise was written for those that recognize they are not perfect but are in need of the Savior's forgiveness. The truth is many communities are in need of a new beginning, religious institutions are in need of a new start, many families and friendships are in need of mending. Forgiveness is something that can't be bought, nor earned. It is given by the grace of God for a New Beginning. The greatest hope and assurance to a Christian is knowing that you and all willing to believe are forgiven, renewed and restored in a new life and relationship with God through Christ.

Chapter Nineteen
Will God Forgive Me?
Moral Of Forgiving

The entire day was misty with periodic brief showers. Around 8:30pm the Suffolk Police Department received a call from a homeowner that he heard shots fired from next door. The dispatcher relayed the call to all officers within the vicinity of 5th and Crystal Avenue stating there is a report of shots fired at the location for 5609 Crystal Avenue, the residence was of James Blake Jenkins. Cruising nearby were officers Smith and Dailey. They were the first to respond to the dispatcher and arrived immediately on the scene. With precision, they searched the house and suddenly Officer Smith heard some sobbing outside the home in the alleyway. Both officers left the scene to investigate the sound. They exited the back door and slowly went down the porch steps. Dailey motioned to Smith to take the lead and as Smith nodded in agreement both officers simultaneously turned the corner and stepped in the middle of the alley with their guns ready to fire. They witnessed a man standing over a body, he was weeping with his head slumped downward. He was loosely holding a revolver in his hand. It appeared as if it was being pulled from the man's hand by its on weight. Officer Dailey yielded to the man to drop the weapon and to put his hands up. Spontaneously, to the voice, he dropped his weapon, fell to his knees and raised his hands in the air.

One year later, on the first day of September within the year of nineteen ninety-eight, Jordan P. Brakersfield was convicted of manslaughter and sentenced to capital punishment. After twelve years of appeals and many letters written to the governor requesting a pardon, only seven hours remained before Brakersfield's execution would commence. He withdrew himself to the center of the cell that detained him. Secluded from everyone except the posted federal prison guard that stood directly outside of the bars of his chambers, Brakersfield knelt down and grasped his hands together as if he was preparing to pray. This position of prayer had not been visited since the death of his sister Sherry that occurred fifteen years earlier. James Blake Jenkins murdered Brakersfield's only sister. She was eighteen years old and pregnant by her husband James. James escaped from serving time for his crime because of a technicality. The court ruled that the police had illegally searched and seized evidence from Mr. Jenkins' house. The judge found James Blake Jenkins innocent by reason of insufficient evidence. From that day forth Jordan P. Brakersfield was upset with God and the police system for letting him down. However, on this day he reflected back on his entire life and looked up to heaven and said with a loud cry, "God, please forgive me."

When considering the life of Christ, without reservations many can say He was and still is the greatest advocate of forgiveness. He taught all who were willing to hear that they must forgive their neighbor an infinite number of times. One of the supreme characteristics of Christ other than His love and compassion was forgiveness. God came into this world not only to restore eternal life but also to defeat the guilt associated with sin. Believers ought to know that each person who has wrestled with the guilt of sin and has sought Jesus for forgiveness was not rejected or turned away.

The Way To Forgiveness Is Penitence

David reveals to readers the way he found the blessedness of forgiveness and how the guilt of sin was removed from his heart. He instructs all people who seek relief from the burden of sin and grace of forgiveness that they can find it through penitent prayer. David declares to all men and women that God deals with sin, sorrow, and the guidance of believers. He is a God that is always ready to extend forgiveness to all that come to Him, He is ever present with power to deliver mankind from their sins, and He is always willing to guide men and women back to the path of righteousness. Acceptance of David's declaration assures a change for the heavy laden and broken hearted. The words propose that regardless of how deep in sin a person may be, despite how far an individual is engrossed in the business or pleasure of worldly pursuit, and though a person's head is bowed under the suffering, pain, and distresses of this world, the loving presence of Christ is at all times with people. He constantly waits to offer forgiveness.

In Palms 32:1-6 David says, "Blessed is the person whose transgressions are forgiven, whose sins are covered. Blessed is the person whose sin the Lord does not count against him or her and in whose spirit there is no deceit. When I kept silent, my bones wasted away through my groaning all day long. Day and night my strength was sapped and I became weak as a person in the heat of a hot summer. My guilt and weakness existed because the Lord's hand was heavy upon me and it convicted me of my evilness. Then I acknowledged my sin to Him and did not cover up my iniquity. I said, I will confess my transgressions to the Lord. After I penitently prayed to the Lord, He forgave me and removed the guilt of my sin. Therefore let everyone who is godly pray to Him while He may be found."

Within his affirmation, David suggests four general ways people sin and require the Lord's forgiveness. So often people transgress against God. They go beyond the boundaries of God's words, ordinances, status, and commandments to do what they are aware is forbidden. To break the law is to transgress. Perhaps, Jordan P. Brakersfield's guilt and sin originated when he decided to take the law into his own hands; for the Lord said, "vengeance is mine. I will repay all those that commit immoral acts in due time and their day of disaster is near. Doom will rush upon them." No one is to take matters into their own hands. When doing so, they transgress the law. People are to leave room for God's wrath. They are to be patient and trust that the Lord judges all immorality. On the contrary, if your enemy is hungry, you are to feed him. If he or she is thirsty, you are to give him or her something to drink. In doing this, your good deeds may cause them to see the Christ in you and convert them into true Christians. Never transgress the law and become overtaken by evil, but overcome evil with good.

Secondly, All people sin. They miss the mark or fail to reach the standard that the Lord requires of the life of all believers. In some way I would like to think that it was never Jordan's goal to murder James Blake Jenkins. The mere fact that he had never been involved in a crime prior to this case or any previous violation demonstrated that he was not a person searching for trouble. During the trial the defending attorney asked several people to testify concerning the character of Mr. Jordan P. Brakersfield and all stated that he was a soft spoken and caring person.

At some point Jordan lost focus. He began to lose sight of the original goal and he became short sighted. Like Cain, Jordan became troubled or upset. Sin had grabbed him and caused him not to see things clearly. With sin eating at his spirit, his countenance fell because he lost hope and faith in the Lord. But just as the Lord said unto Cain, Why art thou upset? And why has your countenance fallen? For Jordan the Lord also inquired of his sadness and depression. His words to Jordan are similar words to all people that experience sin knocking at their door seeking to cause them to lose focus and miss the mark. Those words are if you do well I will accept your deeds and personal intent. However, if you act immorally you have opened the door and allowed giving it access to rule over you.

Thirdly, when a person turns from the proper course of moral and ethical conduct their immoralities are considered iniquities. A writer once wrote that all men are born in sin and shaped in iniquity. The implication was based on Adam and the fall of man. Since disobedience, all humans are born of what is now known as a sinful nature. The world that mankind is born in shapes children to the laws, precepts and traditions of there individualized cultures or nation. The world teaches people to become self-centered, to be takers instead of being givers. The world shapes and fashions people to a mold of godlessness. People are shaped to take on the image of the world not the image of God. But Paul cautioned men and women not to be conformed to the ways of the world but to be in the world but not of the world.

Fourthly, evil is the act of deceiving. Having guile is to be a person of fraud and deception. Anyone that is to love life and see good days is to refrain his or her tongue from evil and his or her lips from speaking guile. In no way are people's motives or intents to be deceitful. They are not to be hypocritical or misleading. Throughout Jordan's trial he remained honest. He admitted to the murder of Mr. Jenkins. He never intended to mislead the panel of adjudicators. His appeals to the court were not to be acquitted of the crime but to request a lesser sentencing than capital punishment. Nevertheless, no reprieve was extended to him. I often think, what would have happened if Adam and Eve had responded to God in truth and honesty? What would have taken place if they had not spoken with guile? Would the greatest judge of the universe have shown compassion and offered to the culprit reprieve from their punishment of death or would the judge, that holds all the evidence and knows everything because nothing can be hidden from Him, have extended them a lesser sentence?

Moral Application: In essence, David was saying in his prayer of penitence to God, forgive me Lord for I have crossed the line. You slowly bent down and drew lines in the sand but I knowingly and willingly went beyond the boundaries of your law. I repent of my transgression. Sin grabbed hold of me and instead of keeping the gates to my heart shut by resisting it, I opened the gates and like a flood, sin came rushing in. When it entered I lost focus of your plan and your purpose for my life. Short sightedness caused me to seek self-fulfillment. Sin is my reason for missing the mark. Remember me O Lord and have compassion upon me for you know that I was born a sinful man. My nature always attempts to take control of me and this world has not taught me the godly way. It has only shown me immoral things. My iniquities are not of my own responsibility. In part they are the accountability of this world's system. Forgive me Lord because I ask of you without guile. I pray to you sincerely acknowledging that all men need your forgiveness.

Three Types Of Forgiveness Counters Sin

Jordan P. Brakersfield's prayer of penitence was similar to David's. The guard's report read, while Mr. Brakersfield was on his knees, in the center of his cell, and looking towards heaven, he said with a loud cry, "God please forgive me" and he begins to pray. It appeared as if the heavens opened and immediately the heavy load of sin he carried was lifted. Mr. Brakersfield said, Father this burden is too much for me to bear any longer. Only your forgiveness can lift this weight off of me. Secondly, he said cover me with your blood because the Father cannot look upon sin. Finally, he said Lord have mercy on me and cancel all my debts. After he finished praying he fell over on his side as if he was unconscious. He stayed in that position for a time and when he came to consciousness he did not appear to be the same man. He seemed pleasant instead of bitter. He appeared content and complacent. Though Mr. Brakersfield was executed that night, he accepted death as if God had heard his prayer and answered it by forgiving Him.

Chapter Twenty
Can Men And Women Live A Perfect Life?
Moral Of Salvation

The United States gymnastics team needed a score of 9.7 to defeat the opposition and win the Olympics. Their final athlete, April Sweat performed her gymnastic routine with what appeared to be precision. The judges briefly critiqued her overall performance and then individually revealed their score. The first judge scored her at 9.6. The second judge gave her a score of 9.9. The third reported a score of 9.7. The fourth judge's score was 10. The fifth and the sixth judges gave April a score of 9.8.

What is perfection? Is it evaluated from each individuals personal value system? Is it a particular judgment based on a pervious act, behavior, or pattern performed that designates a certain standard? Is it what others define it to be? Is good, better or best perfect? Though April's routine appeared perfect to the audience; obviously, the judges' scores conveyed that universally perfection comprises a general concept. In fact, if someone uses the term perfect, it must be qualified to create a sense of unity toward understanding and assessment.

People must be cautious when evaluating and applying the term "Perfect" because an act or behavior may be perfectly sound in a particular case today; yet, unacceptable, inappropriate, and immoral in another instance tomorrow. Also, often the results of an individual's action may appear to be unsuccessful or a failure in accordance to man's standards but in the eyes of God the person's action may be perfect and pleasing to Him. Therefore, man's standards for perfection should at all times be evaluated and continuously compared to God's principles.

When a person, group, and even God qualifies perfection certain measurements are then offered for a more specific and uniform evaluation of an act, deed, thought, motive, or articulation; however, certain disparities will exist. Take heed that each Olympic judge had before them a score sheet designed to offer a method and standard for critiquing an athlete's performance. Though they used an identical scoring sheet, their evaluation of perfection ended with varying results.

For and Against

In our evaluation of "Living the good life" or "Living a perfect life", perfection must be qualified because among the masses of common folks, many scholars, theorist and philosophers have pondered the question "Can a man or woman live a perfect life?" Some have said, yes a man or woman can live a perfect life. While others have said no. It is not possible. For those that say no one can live a perfect life, certain scripture qualifies his or her decision. The following text are references that some consider validates their position:

This righteousness from God comes through faith in Jesus Christ to all who believe. There is no difference, for all have sinned and fallen short of the glory of God, and are justified freely by his grace through the redemption that came by Christ Jesus. Rom 3:22-24

Therefore, just as sin entered the world through one man, and death through sin, and in this way death came to all men, because all sinned--. Rom 5:12

The Lord looks down from heaven on the sons of men to see if there are any who understand, any who seek God. All have turned aside, they have together become corrupt; there is no one who does good, not even one. Ps 14:2-3

As it is written: "There is no one righteous, not even one; there is no one who understands, no one who seeks God. All have turned away, they have together become worthless; there is no one who does good, not even one." Rom 3:10-12

Behold, I was born in sin and shaped in iniquity. Ps 51:5

The pragmatism of his or her belief is that no person exists without sin accounted unto him or her. Yet, others that believe it is possible for men and women to live a perfect life also qualify their decision on text within the same Bible. Some of the scripture they use to support their position are as follow:

There was a man in the land of Uz, whose name was Job; and that man was perfect and upright, and one that feared God, and eschewed evil. Job 1:1

These are the generations of Noah: Noah was a just man and perfect in his generations, and Noah walked with God. Gen 6:9

And when Abram was ninety years old and nine, the LORD appeared to Abram, and said unto him, I am the Almighty God; walk before me, and be thou perfect. Gen 17:1

By faith Enoch was taken from this life, so that he did not experience death; he could not be found, because God had taken him away. For before he was taken, he was commended as one who pleased God. And without faith it is impossible to please God, because anyone who comes to him must believe that he exists and that he rewards those who earnestly seek him. Heb 11:5-6

These believers suggest that others lived and were found to be perfect by God. In so doing, men and women today can be found perfect in God's sight, for what He has done for others He surely can do for you.

Merging Perfect Qualifications

Is God a liar? Is His word designed to cause confusion among believers? Is the nature of His teaching divisive? By all means God's nature is to create harmony among men and women. And He is a God that cannot tell a lie. Therefore, what is truth and what is the answer to the question? Both responses to the inquiry are not incorrect. However, both parties have chosen to advocate only half of the total truth of God's word. If God taught both sides of the story, they must not be maintained separately. They must be combined for a greater and more complete understanding. Believers are not too confused. They must comprehensively equate perfection as a life challenged by sin, and a life consisting of sin knowingly or unknowingly, but also as a life that consist of the mercies of God. For where the law abides grace abides more. "Perfection" cannot be constituted only by the standard of living a life without error. Nor can "Imperfection" only be comprised of lives consisting of sin. Both must entail the qualification and the abundant quantity of grace. Neither Enoch, Job, Noah, or Abraham's lives been considered perfect because they were without error or sinless nor were their lives attributed to imperfection because they experienced sin or had faltered. God measured their lives perfect because they walked by the measure of their faith. They lived by what they knew to be moral, true and godly. They attempted to follow God's leading by what they perceived to be His will. They did not know or comprehend all things, only God possesses the attribute of omniscience (absolute truth) but what they knew they delighted in, diligently built upon and lived by daily. What more does God ask of each man or woman other than they live each by the measure of light and revelation He has placed within him or her? One of the greatest perils in addressing the present topic is the fact that many people seek to be, quote or unquote, too perfect. There is a great difference between perfectionist and godliness. There is a great division between a perfectionist and a person that strives to living a moral and ethical life. If men and women were perfect, why would they need God? Would they not need a God because they were perfect? Would they not need to bow down in humbleness because they made no mistakes? What would they aspire to achieve?

In evaluating the question "Can men and women live a perfect life?" the term "Perfection" will be qualified by the following standard. A person's moral, ethical, spiritual, literal, or figurative perfection is distinguished by her or his thoughts and actions based on the character's intentions or motives concerning following Christ's teaching, seeking the moral goodness of all men and women, walking justly in the path of righteousness, and enthusiastically seeking to add to his or her faith and growing in maturity.

A Holistic View of Salvation

To accurately evaluate the perfect life there not only must be a qualification to the term perfection there also must be a holistic understanding of salvation. There are three characteristics of salvation and there is a past salvation, a present salvation and an eternal salvation. Past salvation identifies that a believer is regenerated and redeemed at the very moment when the person confessed with his mouth and believed in their heart that Jesus is Lord and that God raised Him from the dead at that moment in time. Christ saved the believer from the penalty of sin and washed the individual as pure as snow. When these acts passed away, Christ held the believer blameless and they were righteous in God's sight.

Present salvation designates that perfection is working out your own salvation. Within present salvation people must remember that believers are presently justified. Whereby, a weak and imperfect human being is made acceptable to a Holy God because Christ has restored his or her relationship and charges any past sin, present sin or future sin of the individual's relationship to Christ. The same deliverer that paid the price for all of man's sins accredits the righteousness of Christ to the believer. Because of present salvation, now believers are perfectly positioned in right standing and fellowship with God and should He return at this present time believers could be gathered together to be with Him because they would be found perfect and pleasing to Him. This is why believers are to be growing, maturing and reaching higher heights in Christ Jesus. The writer of the book of Hebrews says believers are not to leave the principles of the teaching of Christ. They are to build upon them by moving towards perfection. They are to never lay again the foundation of repentance from dead works and of faith towards God.

Eternal salvation connotes the fact that Christ is coming back for a prepared people; for a bride that has made herself ready, those who have sought to live a perfect life, those that sought to increase their faith. He is coming for persons who are regenerated from the old man to a new creation and those that sought justice for all and lived morally in peace. Eternal salvation is a future state of perfection that men and women will need to live with Christ in paradise forever.

Perfection itself is triune. Christ wants to make men and women perfect for three reasons. Because of the past sin of Adam and Eve, God offers perfection through salvation. Secondly, because mankind needs perfect strength to be able to take a stand against immorality and war against evil, and to fulfill the mission He has predestined for each person, God offers present salvation. Finally, because Christ is coming back to judge all sin and immorality, God offers eternal salvation that believers will escape the judgment and live with Him forever in the regenerated world.

Moral Application: While many have said yes, men and women can live a perfect life, others have said, no, it is impossible. Clearly the dilemma with properly answering the question exists in the areas relative to mankind's perception of perfection, the qualification of perfection and the lack of understanding relative to a holistic view of salvation. If people would evaluate "Perfection" on the qualification of mankind's acts and thoughts based on their moral and godly motives or intents and their desire to live by the will of God and grow in strength and virtue, the answer to the question "Can men and women live a perfect life?" would be undoubtedly, yes they can. The answer is not based on mankind's sinless-ness or sinfulness. It is sealed and secured in God's grace.

Chapter Twenty-One
Why Did God Give The Law?
Moral Application Of The Law

The Lord looked down upon the earth and viewed how immoral everyone within the world was becoming. Mankind's thoughts, imaginations and heart's desires were ungodly and unethical. God became sorrowful on humanities behalf because He also saw their future and it did not consist of an increase in moral behavior. Once again men and women had arrived at a heightened state of immorality and once again the Creator had to make a decision concerning the evilness of mankind. Instead of instituting the same judgment that He did in the days of Noah; whereby, He said I will wipe out these people I have created along with the animals and birds. On this occasion He said I will write my commandments of love, morality, worship, and relationship so that they can see them for themselves and obey them. He continued by saying they had the opportunity to behave morally through innocence, their conscience, human representation, oral communication, covenant, and the Law but they did not follow the path of righteousness. This time I will write my commandments down on stone tablets so that no one will have an excuse why they behave immorally and unethically. The written law will serve to inform men and women when they have behaved godly or ungodly, sinful or virtuously, morally or immorally. I will give them a second chance because I am a forgiving God.

Psalms 19:7-9

"The law of the LORD is perfect, converting the soul: the testimony of the LORD is sure, making wise the simple .The statutes of the LORD are right, rejoicing the heart: the commandment of the LORD is pure, enlightening the eyes. The fear of the LORD is clean, enduring forever: the judgments of the LORD are true and righteous altogether."

To understand the law is to know sin. No man is conscious of sin until an unveiling of error has taken place in his life. The Law of God was given to man to reveal sin and assist him in his daily walk by providing and emphasizing sanctification, service, and obedience.

Let us be reminded of the fact that holiness implies being set apart because it is affixed to God. Holiness is a quality that, strictly speaking, belongs to God alone; it is that essential purity that separates Him from all things; however, that which belongs, connected or is affected or dedicated to God is Holy. The Law confesses that we should be Holy because He is Holy. We must forgive because God forgives. We must be kind because God is kind. We must be merciful because He is merciful. We must bless others because God blesses all men. We must Love God and our neighbor because Christ loves the Father and mankind. We must war against sin because Christ wars against sin. Undoubtedly, man was created in the image of holiness because he was made differently, separated from other creatures and expected to live by the pattern made in the likeness of God. Therefore, the law set apart all creations that are committed through love and obedience from His creations that have chosen to separate themselves from righteousness.

Knowing from the beginning God has revealed himself to us through the gifts of this world, His life giving power, His gift of salvation, His endless blessings, His deliverance, His guidance, and His protection, He soon teaches what He expects of His creation. As a people of faith called to the highest level of social order, we are to walk with God, talk with God, worship God, live according to His will, and exist harmoniously with His decree. Thus, the Law is the pattern for our body, our mind, our spirit, and in general our conduct. Just as the Mosaic tabernacle had a pattern by which it was built and a pattern by which Israel was to conduct worship, so is our temple (body) made by a pattern and there is a pattern that our temple is to follow for the rendering of worship and service.

Yes, you have read correctly, our bodies, our moral, social, civil, and ceremonial life has a pattern, whereby God finds acceptable for His dwelling, abiding and presence to exist; yet, the question remains "Why did God Give the Law". Allow me to further address some of the more specific qualifying deductions that ascertain God's purpose for giving the law to man. I begin with the Ten Commandments.

The Ten Commandments

"I *am* the LORD thy God, which have brought thee out of the land of Egypt, out of the house of bondage. Thou shalt have no other gods before me. Thou shalt not make unto thee any graven image, or any likeness *of anything* that *is* in heaven above, or that *is* in the earth beneath, or that *is* in the water under the earth: Thou shalt not bow down thyself to them, nor serve them: for I the LORD thy God *am* a jealous God, visiting the iniquity of the fathers upon the children unto the third and fourth *generation* of them that hate me; And showing mercy unto thousands of them that love me, and keep my commandments. Thou shalt not take the name of the LORD thy God in vain; for the LORD will not hold him guiltless that taketh His name in vain. Remember the sabbath day, to keep it holy. Six days shalt thou labour, and do all thy work: But the seventh day *is* the sabbath of the LORD thy God; *in it* thou shalt not do any work, thou nor thy son, nor thy daughter, thy manservant, nor thy maidservant, nor thy cattle, nor thy stranger that *is* within thy gates: For *in* six days the LORD made heaven and earth, the sea, and all that in them *is*, and rested the seventh day: wherefore the LORD blessed the sabbath day, and hallowed it. Honour thy father and thy mother: that thy days may be long upon the land which the LORD thy God giveth thee. Thou shalt not kill. Thou shalt not commit adultery. Thou shalt not steal. Thou shalt not bear false witness against thy neighbour. Thou shalt not covet thy neighbour's house, thou shalt not covet thy neighbour's wife, nor his manservant, nor his maidservant, nor his ox, nor his ass, nor any thing that *is* thy neighbour's." Exodus 20:2-17

The Law Identifies Sin

The Law of God identifies sin. Over ninety percent of the law begins with the statement "Thou shalt not..." The term divulges boundaries that have been established. To proceed beyond the affirmed law would constitute the transgression of God's will, John 3:4. The term also confines the in-exhaustible freedom that would reign if the law did not exist. Therefore, we can contest that without the law there would be no sin and sin gets it's strength from the law (1 Cor. 15:56). Whether it be written on our hearts, in our conscious, or written on tablets, "man would never become conscious of sin but for the law."

It becomes apparent that the law not only identifies sin, it also gives way to the occurrence of sin. Romans 7:8 states "But sin, taking occasion by the commandment, wrought in me all manner of concupiscence. For without the law sin *was* dead." Paul is saying that by means of the law sin was given the opportunity to embellish all manner of lustful desires that exist within him.

The Law Condemns Sins

Once God identifies sin that man has committed, God declares the individual guilty. God judges him for transgressing the law. Condemn means to judge, find guilty and to be sentenced. Hence, the law condemns man to a life of eternal death. Praise be to God that He gave man the covenant of the law, which opened the window for the covenant of Grace and provided a narrow avenue for escaping the penalty of sin. John 3:17 "For God sent not his Son into the world to condemn the world; but the world through him might be saved". Thank God we are extended mercy and not justice.

The Law Expresses God's Attributes

It would be a mistake to conceive of the essence of God as existing by itself prior to the attributes, and of the attributes as additive and accidental characteristics of the Divine Being. They are essential qualities of God, which infer to His very Being and are co-existent with it. These qualities cannot be altered without altering the essential Being of God. And since they are essential qualities, each one of them reveals to us some aspects of the Being of God.

Jehovah is holy, he is pure, and he is a Sanctified God. As believers, we must worship the Lord in holiness and truth. We must live a holy life that we can be presented to Jehovah as an unblemished consecrated sacrifice through our Lord and Savior Jesus Christ. Believers must be presented holy before God because he has called us into the order of the priesthood and he requires perfection in our service to him, just as he required perfection from the priest of the Old Testament.

I have submitted to you that the law was given to express the attributes of God, yet as I elaborated on the subject further we found that the law was given because Jehovah required perfection in Man's service to him. You may say there is no perfect man or no perfect service. In turn, I would agree by saying that as long as we are housed within our fleshy body we are susceptible to sin. However, I whole-heartedly confess to you the word of God: II Corinthians 13:9 "For we are glad, when we are weak, and ye are strong: and this also we wish, even your perfection". It is only through the blood of Jesus and the leading of His spirit that the believer is accepted as perfect as he or she strives to work out their own salvation.

The book of Leviticus demonstrates the perfection in which the priest was required to serve Jehovah. The priestly attire consisted of the Mitre or Turban, the Robe of the Ephod, a Girdle, the Ephod, The Breast Plate of Judgment, Short-legged trousers and an under tunic coat. When the priest entered into the presence of God and if a piece of clothing was missing, or not in order even if the priest performed something incorrect during his service to God, the priest would instantaneously die (Leviticus 10:2-3). Priest outside of the holy room had to pull the dead man out of the presence of God, by utilizing a rope which was tied to the dead priest's waist, only because no other could enter the Holy Place or Holy of Holies. Jehovah is adamant about the perfection by which we are to serve him.

Today the believer's priestly attire is the complete armor of God, (Ephesians 6:14-17). You are to take on the shield of Faith, the helmet of salvation, the Sword of the Spirit, your feet are to be shod with the preparation of the Gospel of peace, your loins are to be girded with truth, and you are to place on the breast plate of righteousness. If a believer is not fully clothed in the complete armor of God, he is in error, some portion of his attire is either missing or out of line, he is dead in Christ. I say this because without the complete armor of God, you will not be able to stand against Satan, you will fall. You will not be able to serve God in true worship nor will you be capable of warring against sin.

The priest's tasks were to offer burnt incense to God on behalf of the believers, offer up burnt sacrifices to God whether meat or fruit and then they prayed for the sins of the people. Today, the Priest's (the believer) tasks are to walk by the leading of the Holy Spirit and utilize the gifts of the Holy Spirit. Still, we are to fast and pray fervently for our neighbors so that yokes can be broken (Isaiah 58:6). The believer is to present himself a living sacrifice holy and acceptable to God, this is your reasonable service (Romans 12:1). No more are we to offer burnt offerings because Christ was the fulfillment of the law and now we only have to give of ourselves to God.

The Levitical Priest had to approach God knowing that Jehovah is holy and men are unclean in the sight of God. Their approach was a consciousness that God judges sin and his word must be obeyed in a perfection that meets his standards. Today, believers approach to God is an approach that also recognizes God's sovereignty. They are to humble themselves in the presence of Christ. We are to approach God knowing that he requires complete obedience to his word.

Though men are weak, when we choose Christ and place him as the head of our lives, his perfection abides in us, we become united into the perfect body of Christ and are equipped with the power of the Holy Spirit that enables believers to live a holy life. Remember, it is not by our might, nor by our power, but by the spirit of the Lord that we are able to live holy (Zechariah 6:4). The certainty of the Law is that no man can uphold the law through the flesh, Romans 8:3 "For what the Law could not do, in that it was weak through the flesh, God sending his own son in the likeness of flesh, and for sin condemned sin in the flesh", but, Jesus is the only man that lived a perfect or sinless life. It was because of the vicarious suffering of Jesus Christ, whereby the believers have been redeemed from the power of sin and death. We must live under the guidance of grace, for only the power of grace and mercy can cast our sins into the Sea of Forgiveness, never to be remembered. Daniel 9:9 "To the Lord our God belongs mercies and forgiveness, though we have rebelled against Him".

GOD's Anointed Does Not Live A Life Without Error

Yet they live a life free from the power of sin. (See Romans: Chapter 6-7) (Romans: Chapter 8:1,2)

When we study the life of Moses, we find that even the life of God's anointed people is not lived without error. A believer lives a life without condemnation; however, their life is not lived without judgment. Moses was judged for his error; yet, he was not condemned from eternal life. This is revealed in Jude 9 "Yet, Michael the arch angel, when contending with the devil, he disputed about the body of Moses." It is also revealed in the transfiguration, Matthew 17:1-13, whereas Peter, James, and John witnessed the transfiguration of Jesus and appeared with him on the mount was Moses and Elijah. We can say that Michael represents Christ standing for the believers and the transfiguration represents the old patriots or dispensations that preached, prophesied and provided the way toward Christ. Elijah is an illustration for the prophets of age that proclaimed the coming of the Messiah. Moses is a more than adequate depiction of the dispensation of the Law and the period of Judges. Jesus Christ fulfilled prophecy and the Law. Not only is Jesus greater than Moses and Elijah, He also established a greater covenant with Man. That covenant is the covenant of Grace.

In light of the presented information, Moses was judged but he was not condemned. We are given in the text that Moses is with God and he is highly exalted; therefore, the judgment of God which prohibited Moses from entering the promised land can not nor should be translated that Moses was not allowed to enter into heaven or eternal life, because such translation is a misinterpretation of the text, for God's Children are judged but they are not condemned. Believers will error in life be it sin of commission or sin by omission. We are rooted in the depth of Grace, Mercy and Forgiveness through the soul act of repentance.

Moses had a special relationship with God, as revealed when he was chosen by God to lead his people out of Egypt, when he was appointed administrator of the plagues that came upon Egypt, when he parted the Red Sea, and when he was selected as spokesman and judge of God (Exodus, 3:11-12). Yet, in spite of Moses relationship with God, he committed sin. The scripture unfolds that Moses sinned by rebelling against God. Numbers 27:14 "You have rebelled against my commandment in the desert of Zin, in strife of my congregation for you refuse to sanctify me."

The strife of the people caused Moses to get upset and lash out irrationally. God said in Ephesians 4:26-27; "Be ye angry, and sin not: let not the sun go down upon your wrath: Neither give place to the devil."

Moses allowed the rebellion of his people to cause him to sin against God. We must admit that when people come against us, when they persecute believers, and when they war against God, at times their conduct can affect our behavior. Moses was only human. He was no more divine or different than any believer, other than his special anointing as judge of Israel, he was not above the law (See Romans 7:13-24).

<u>Moses Sin</u>

"Take the rod, and gather thou the assembly together, thou, and Aaron thy brother, and speak ye unto the rock before their eyes; and it shall give forth his water, and thou shalt bring forth his water, and thou shalt bring forth to them water out of the rock: so thou shalt give the congregation and their beasts drink." Numbers 20:8

God asked Moses to speak to the rock before the congregation of people so that he could be sanctified, instead Moses smote the rock twice. "In this case the rebels in verse 10 would be Moses and Aaron, instead of the people, as the verse reads now." The primary ground for God Judging Moses is that he acted out of disobedience. Undoubtedly, when we search for a greater meaning we find that a deeper revelation of God's word lies beneath the surface. We are to be lead by the Holy Spirit in whatsoever we do in life. Our thoughts and actions are to be a reflection of God. God told Moses to speak to the rock and it would bring forth water for the people. God's request is the same to believers today. God said to man "And whatsoever ye shalt ask in my name, that will I do, that the Father may be glorified" John 14:13. Know that whatever you ask must be according to the will of God. We know that what Moses was to ask of the rock was according to God's will, because God directed him to speak to the rock.

The rock represents Jesus Christ. The believer has to only follow the will of God and speak to Jesus. Christ will begin to pour out his blessing upon his people. Unfortunately like so many believers, Moses crucified Christ in the presence of the Congregation. Moses smote the rock. Recognizing that Christ is the rock, we understand that without a solid foundation everything around us is as sinking sand. We also can equate the scripture to the principle that Christ is the living water that never runs dry. He is the life giver. For without water all the creation would wither and die. John 4:14 "But whosoever drinketh of the water that I shall give him shall never thirst; but the water that I shall give him shall be in him a well of water springing up into everlasting life." Though Christ is the substance of all life, we find that men war against Him daily. When Moses smote the rocks his action indicated the crucifixion of Christ.

Isaiah 53:5 "But he *was* wounded for our transgressions, *he was* bruised for our iniquities: the chastisement of our peace *was* upon him; and with his stripes we are healed." Being that Christ was the perfect, unblemished and final sacrifice, he needs not to be bruised again for the redemption of our sins. Moses smote the rock twice signifying that men crucify Christ daily, for men continuously commit sin. Moses was judged for his disobedient conduct but the act itself was very significant when adjoined to the coming of the covenant of Grace.

The Law Set The Stage For The Coming Of The Covenant Of Grace

Un-categorically, we can attest that Moses sinned, but we also can agree that within the midst of error or transgression God's grace was extended to Moses and the people of Israel. In spite of Moses disobedience water came out abundantly, and the congregation drank and their beast also, Numbers 20:11. The gift of water symbolizes the coming of a greater and better covenant, The Covenant of Grace. Hebrews 7:19 "For the law made nothing perfect, but the bringing in of a better hope *did;* by the which we draw nigh unto God." We all have fallen short of the glory of God, but today we do not have to sacrifice bulls or limbs. Isn't it wonderful to know that believers are baptized by the Holy Spirit and cleansed by the purifying fire of God? It is also joyous to apprehend that through Christ the believers are more than conquerors and in his excellent name we can offer prayer, worship, and praise to Jehovah.

The Law Offers Blessings

The Law was given because *It offers Blessings.* Deuteronomy 28:1 "And it shall come to pass, if thou shalt hearken diligently unto the voice of the LORD thy God, to observe *and* to do all his commandments which I command thee this day, that the LORD thy God will set thee on high above all nations of the earth." God has said if we would hearken to his word and be obedient, he would bless us. What more can we ask of God? How much clearer can he present the fundamental of blessings to men? Knowledge or the lack thereof, is the fact of a condition of being or not being aware of something. It pertains to having information and understanding. On the other hand, wisdom is the use of a wise attitude or course of action. More simply put, wisdom is the application of knowledge. It does men a great disservice to have knowledge of the word of God, but for personal reasons they do not apply the word of God in their life; therefore, the unbeliever knows but continues to live in sin and walk by the leading of their flesh (Romans 1: 21, 22). By reason of their disobedience of the word, God will not bless them. Yet, a person who is informed of God's word and applies it to his life experiences will reap the manifestation of God's promises. Whereas, the individual who does not apply his knowledge will only reap the curses of God (Deuteronomy 28:15). It is only reasonable to say that obedience to God's word constitutes blessings but disobedience brings about curses or the judgment of God. "This passage is applied to Christians in 1Peter 2:9,10, showing how a believer's obedience will benefit him (see also Is.43:20, 21)."

The Law Was Given Because It Establishes Order In A World Of Chaos

Every government requires legislation to maintain the order of its people. The law provides guidelines, regulation or policies and procedures for the people to abide by or follow throughout their daily activities. The Kingdom of God is no different than a government. The Law was given to the Hebrews for the establishment of a unique government in the land of Israel. The people were to reflect a Godly life to unbelievers, through their adherence to God's legislative plan.

God would have demonstrated that only his government or his law is perfect and without error. Though men are to recognize the existing authorities because God ordains them, we are the demonstrators that the kingdom of God within the believers is the most perfect and orderly government men can ever experience and submit their lives to. The greatest king and ruler we can know is Jehovah, the God that anointed His son, Jesus Christ, over all the creations, the same Son that spoke the world into existence. He created order out of chaos for the earth was without form and it was void. Darkness was upon the face of the deep; however, God made the earth, divided the heavens and commanded the light to enter and divided itself from the darkness (Genesis 1:1-10).

The Law Magnifies God's Standards

The Law of God is founded in His standard. Let it be known to all that his standard is Holiness. It is perfection and it began with Him. All aspects of holiness emanate from the Glory of God and they are bound to him in matrimony.

Holiness or God's standard was first conveyed through creation, for all of the creations were created within his divine realm of perfection, for prior to creations all was silent. Soon after silence, the heavenly hosts were created perfect. The heavens and the earth were found pleasing to him in accordance with his standard. We must agree that man and all creations of the earth were acceptable in his sight.

However, to be acceptable to God, you must be connected with his holiness.

Secondly, believers have to recognize that the laws have always been and always will be communicated. Whether God speaks to man such as he did with Adam or whether he chooses to write the law as he did for Moses, the law will forever emanate through communication. This statement is suggested even in music and songs. For we will praise and worship him in song as the heavenly host praise and worship him in song. His holiness will be praised forever. He is a God worthy to be praised and we are created to worship Him.

There are so many forms in which God can manifest Himself to communicate His standard, His will and His love. Holiness may be revealed to man in a vision, in signs, in wonders/miracles, in song, in dreams, in an oral conversation with a friend or very rarely orally with God, it can and has been given in the written word, which is the law written on tablets, and the holy script given in the Old and New Testaments. Profoundly, all of these forms of communication extend knowledge to the recipient. Knowing that in actuality, knowledge, which is truly increased by the grace of God binds us, man is judged by the measure of knowledge that has been communicated or increased within by God. Can we say then that all formalities of communication including the written Law is given to promote an awareness of God and his standard, perhaps to magnify God's holiness?

It may be best said in the following arrangement: The Word of God magnifies the Father, Jehovah. All forms of communication should be spoken or written to edify God. It should glorify the Creator and Lord, and it should witness or evangelize His holiness and deity. Forms of communication, even the written law was given to exalt Him. Why, because the standard of God has always been conveyed to his creations and he demands that his subject recognize and be obedient to his standard of holiness. This is what he commands forever.

Even Jesus edified the Father. He came to give us a living example or model of holiness that we may pattern our daily lives. He demonstrated to man how to live a life that is pleasing to God. He increased our knowledge through his teaching, and once a man is made aware of God's requirements, the knowledge he has graciously been given will become the measure of the judgment of God for that individual. Therefore, God's standard is a yoke applied through knowledge. We can apply this contemporary theory to Adam, for we agreed that Adam walked and talked with God. Can we say that God shared communication with Adam, whereby it increased Adam's knowledge? The more Adam was increased in knowledge; a greater measure of God's standard was applied to Adam's life. Now, know that God's standard is his Law because it is an instrument used to measure holiness. We can say let us all magnify the Lord by being obedient to the measure of knowledge God so graciously awarded us. He has given us the revelation of Him and illuminated our minds in accordance to His word and will.

Finally, Jesus emulated and emanated the holiness of God through the flesh. For He was God in the flesh, henceforth, He was and is the equal divine perfection of God's standard demonstrated through the flesh. The standard of measure applicable to all men's lives and the expected standard of measure we are to pattern ourselves after is Jesus' holiness in this life and to reign in holiness throughout eternity.

Communicated law and written law is given to make men aware that no one or nothing can measure up to God's standard of holiness by their own power. All things were created by God and must remain connected to him that they may be linked to holiness and considered holy. Yet, if any one distances himself from Christ, he will not measure up to God's standard nor his law, because the distance is indicative of the separate life an unbeliever lives John 3:36, John 5:23.

The Law Separates

The law was given because it separates the believer from the world. God has called the believers to separate themselves from the things of this world. In order for the believers to escape the wrath of God, they must separate themselves from the whoredom, adultery, fornication, and harlotry of this world. God has called the believer out of the darkness into his marvelous light, I Peter 2:9 "But ye are a chosen generation, a royal priesthood, a holy nation, a peculiar people; that ye should show forth the praises of him who hath called you out of darkness into the marvelous light."

"Neo-evangelicals have tended to ignore the teachings of scripture on the issue of separation. The Bible has much to say on the subject (cf. Rom.12:2, II Cor.6:14-18; Titus 3:10; James 4:4; John 9-11). Although the application of these passages is not always easy, it does have many serious ramifications. At the very least, the Christian should ask if it is possible to cooperate in any way, religiously, with those who deny fundamental doctrines such as the deity of Christ or His substitutionary atonement."

The Law Is Not New

When I began to meditate on the reason why God wrote the law on two tablets, I said to myself that many unbelievers and believers are under the presumption that the origin of the law occurred during the advent of God giving Moses the ten commandments on the top of Mount Sinai. My contention is that the law existed prior to the episode of God writing the Ten Commandments. If you accept the fact that there is nothing new under the sun and that the law identifies sin and condemns all ungodly conducts, you will embrace the cogitation that the law existed before the beginning of time and foremost it was revealed to all of God's creation in an explicit subtle extent prior to the giving of the Ten Commandments.

Editions of Divine Law

Up to this point I have primarily referred to the ten commandments that birthed the many statutes and regulations that have governed the majority of our nations throughout the ages; however, it is now time for us to pick-up the pace and dig a little deeper in reviewing the full extent of the law of God.

Excluding the era prior to the creation of man, we are provided with the divine method of gradual revelation and publication of God's law in accordance with its application to His creation. There are seven editions of divine law known to man; the Mosaic Law is only one of the editions.

Revelation of Divine Law

```
                                              Outward
                                              Life
                                       The
                                       Heart
                               Illustration
                       Scripture
               Table of
               Stone
       Conscience
Nature
```

Written on Nature

Psalms 19:1-6 "The Heavens declare the glory of God; and the firmament showeth his handiwork..." Nature is the basic state that man can begin to see there is a God. Man can witness through nature that the God of Creation is a God of love because He created the earth for man. He is a God of order and majesty. He is a God of peace because the earth was created with all life living in harmony. Jehovah is not a God of chaos or hatred. We know this to be true for the first dispensation was Innocence. God first revealed himself through nature and He communicated with Adam. God continues to communicate through nature to modern man. "Through Plato we knew the celestial harmony of the spheres, probably of oriental origin. The heavens are uttering a marvelous melody. The heavens declare better, the heavens keep recounting and the firmament keeps revealing the participles that suggest continuous action."

Written on Man's Conscience

Romans 2:15 "Which shews the work of the Law written in their hearts, their conscience also bearing witness, and their thoughts the mean while accusing or else excusing one another." The second edition of the revealed law accrued during the second dispensation was Conscience. Within this era man conducted himself according to the measure of law that he allowed to govern him from a state of consciousness. He was governed by what he believed to be correct.

The era existed after the fall of man and during the days of Noah whereby all men were destroyed except for Noah and his family. Mankind was destroyed because they allowed their conduct to become wicked through the corruption of their state of consciousness (Gen. 6:5). The dispensation of Human Government followed and was also impacted by the edition of Conscience.

Written on Tables of Stone

Exodus 24:12 The Lord said to Moses, "Come up to the mountain to me, and while you are here, I will give you two stone tablets which contain all the laws that I have written for the instruction of the people." The third stage of gradual revelation of the law was the edition of the Ten Commandments, known as the dispensation of the Law. The fundamental principles of the law were written on two tablets of stone. The Jews attached thousands of regulations and status that promulgated the principles of the Law.

Written in the Scripture

Romans 15:4 "Everything written in the Scripture was written to teach us in order that we might have hope through the patience and encouragement which the Scripture gives us." The fourth edition of the law came through the writing of the Scripture. The Scripture began to unfold the full intent of God speaking through nature, through the consciousness of man, and through the law. It was the beginning of a greater and more mature revelation of God.

Christ the Illustrated Edition

John 11:14 The Word was made flesh, full of grace and truth, lived among us. We saw his glory. The glory which he revealed as the Father's only Son. Jesus appeared on earth as the perfect embodiment of truth. He demonstrated through His teaching and His sinless life how men are to walk in the light of Jehovah, for Christ is the way, the truth and the life. This edition marked the beginning of the Church and the beginning of the covenant or dispensation of Grace.

Written on the Heart

Hebrews 8:10 "Now this is the covenant I will make with the people of Israel in the days to come, says the Lord: I will put my laws in their minds and write them on their hearts. I will be their God and they will be my people." Within the sixth edition of the revealed law the entire Scripture was completed. The final written edition of the Word was provided to man. It is God's purpose that the written Word be read by man and the precepts of the Scripture would be understood and applied in their life, for the law is written in the believer's heart. It is no longer applied from tablets or from paper because the day has come whereas God wants man to worship him from an internal love, from the heart, and not an external source. We are to obey the Lord out of a love generated from the depths of our heart.

Outward Christian Life

Living Epistles 2 Corinthians 3:2-3 "²..³Forasmuch as ye are manifestly declared to be the epistle of Christ ministered by us, written not with ink, but with the Spirit of the living God; not in tables of stone, but in fleshly tables of the heart." Seven means complete; therefore, we will be complete in our righteousness when we are born again and led by the Holy Spirit that indwells within each Child of God. Though we are complete in righteousness, we strive for perfection in our walk and growth of salvation.

Though man is now living in the seventh edition of the revelation of the law, we can soberly confess that there is much more to learn when we review the law holistically. The complexity of the law is beyond the comprehension of man and it is not captured within the generalization of the law, the Ten Commandments. Truly, the law continues to be revealed to man through God's continued unveiling of the scripture, through man's desire to worship the Lord in spirit and in truth, also through daily prayer, supplication and by being led by the Holy Spirit. <u>The Law is not new it is gradually being revealed to man.</u>

The Fall of Adam

It is a known certainty that during the occurrence of Adam and Eve's fall, the couple comprehended their sin and hid themselves from God because they had transgressed the law, Genesis 3:8. Though they were in the dispensation of innocence, God had given specific commandments. "In the garden of Eden, Adam and Eve were commanded by God concerning their duties (1) to fill the earth, (2) to subdue it, and (3) to have in subjection all living creations of the earth, sea, and the air. (Ge.1:28) They were given laws as to their deity, granting them the seed-bearing vegetation and fruit as food. (Ge.1:29; 2:16) However, Adam was given a command that prohibited eating of the tree of the knowledge of good and evil (Ge.2:17); this command was transmitted of Eve. (Ge.3:2,3) Adam is referred to as a transgressor and trespasser because he violated a stated law – Rom. 5:14,17; 4:15."

During the course of the fall of man we are given that the serpent was cursed; Adam was cursed, Eve was cursed and the entire earth was cursed because of the sin they committed against God. I submit to you, if there was no law there could be no sin, because sin gets its strength from the law. The text tells us that God talked to Adam and commanded of him a certain conduct, see Genesis 1:28 and Genesis 2:16-17. Therefore, in His word God identified sin, advertently He exposed law unto man and woman. In doing so, the uncovered mystery is that God is able to rule, judge and to maintain order because he has standards, rules, and regulations that are imposed on his creation.

The murder of Abel also validates that law was present in the lives of men prior to the Ten Commandments. Cain rose up against Abel his brother and slew him after he talked with him in the field Genesis 4:8. I have previously stated that the law promotes curses to those who are disobedient. Cain was disobedient to God's word. He committed the first murder, therefore, he was severely condemned Genesis 4:11-12. He even admits that his punishment was greater than he could bear Genesis 4:13. I would be the first to say that the punishment for sin or transgressing God's law is greater than anyone can bear. Can you begin to imagine burning forever in an eternal lake of fire? Revelation 20:15, "And whosoever was not found written in the Book of Life was cast into the lake of fire."

Finally, I would like to review eternity past in an effort to help you conceive that the law existed in the beginning. It was in the heavens when the originator of sin converted from righteousness to a life of corruption, Ezekiel 28:15-18. He is known as the Father of Lies and The Great Deceiver. He is Satan. Lucifer decided that he wanted to be like the most high. He wanted to receive praise and he wanted to be worshipped just as God is to be praised and worshipped. Unfortunately, he deceived one third of the nations causing him and all that accepted his false teaching to be cast out of heaven (Ezekiel 14:12).

I suggest to you that the law is not new. For if there was no law within eternity past, Satan's act could not have been judged as sin. As we all now know, where there is no law there is no judgment (Romans 4:15, 5:13). The law has always existed because it is the Word of God and the Word of God condemns because it cuts like a two edged sword. The Revealed Law has always existed and will remain throughout eternity because it is the Alpha and Omega, it is the first and the last. The Mosaic Law is a Type of the Word, the Word is Jesus and Jesus is Lord, for He filled all types that pointed toward holiness and directed man's attention to His coming. What we must comprehend is that Christ is more than the revealed Law which includes the ten commandments. John 1:17 The Law came by Moses, but grace and truth came by Jesus Christ. Therefore, Christ is the Law, grace and truth. He is beyond comprehension. No one can fathom Christ, the infinite one. John 1:1-2 "In the beginning was the Word (Jesus) and the Word (Jesus) was with God (Jehovah), and the Word (Jesus) was God (Jehovah). The same was in the beginning with God."

The second verse of John establishes if you reverse the second person within the Godhead with the first person of the Godhead, the meaning would remain identical to verse one. The Father also existed prior to creation. In the beginning was Jehovah, and Jehovah was with Jesus and Jehovah was Jesus. Be aware that the aforesaid statement does not suggest nor support the doctrine of Jesus Only,

A Cry for Ethical and Moral Strength

for we know that God the Father sent his only begotten Son, that whosoever believeth would have everlasting life.

There is no better way I know that I can simplify any further the fact that the law is the Word of God and the Word is God, but I must include that though the Law is God, God the Father is more than just the written Law and The Word. He is more than anyone can understand or comprehend. Therefore, accept that the law is God, know that the law is holy, just, righteous, and it will always and has always existed. Understand that the Law is interwoven with the Word of God for it is originated of God. God has a standard. His standard has no beginning. The requirement is that we be holy for He is holy. When reviewing the word *standard*, we find that the term expresses a measure by which individuals or phenomena are compared or judged. Though standards of public morality have clearly changed, God has not changed. He is ever constant. No, the law is not new, for God is not new. He is the ageless one. He is above and beyond man's imagination, yet He grants to man by grace, knowledge and understanding that leads him toward salvation.

Now that you understand the principles of God's Law, it is appropriate for me to say that you also comprehend the basic will of God. The parallelism of the will of God and the law is insurmountably consistent. Profoundly, the two serves to guide men toward and into a life of holiness.

Many say that man does not live by the law today. They say believers are saved by grace. I appeal to your intellect by stating that the law is in operation and completely affects the lives of men today. Truly, we live in a world of knowledge, and a world in which men demand and thirst for information. People of today are more informed of the law, of the word of God, and of the name of Jesus. Men are conscious of sin, yet they pervert the law daily. Obviously, we do not live in the dispensation of the covenant of the law. If we did, a multitude of sinners would not exist today. God would have condemned them for their deeds. The interim we live in is the dispensation of grace. However, the law continues to identify sin. It is because of the Grace and Mercy of God that men have not been condemned for their sin. Romans 5:20. "Moreover the law entered, that the offense might abound. But where sin abounded, grace did much more abound:"

The Law is a Type

Remember this, there are many types of Laws within the confinement of these categories spiritual law, moral law, and physical law. These laws are communicated by usage of various methods that are established to direct man's attention to God. The many types of Laws were given to cause men to zoom in or focus in on only one standard, and that is Holiness. The written Law is no more than a type of communication that points to the Lamb of God and his fulfillment of all types that were revealed in the Old Testament. Christ fulfilled the law which pointed to holiness and to the coming of the Messiah, because man could not work out his own salvation for his flesh was weak. Jesus our Deliverer had to come and give us his life. Henceforth and forever more we are to seek Christ's face. For in the beginning there was a direct relationship with God and today there is a direct relationship with God. I say to you the written Law was a type and believers need no types today. It is a summarized form of communication in which the purpose is to point to the way of holiness.

Even the Ten Commandments were abridged more when Christ addressed a Pharisee's question in Matthew 22:37. The Pharisee was well versed in the Law; therefore, he tested Christ. He said Teacher, which is the greatest commandment? Jesus said, "You must love Jehovah your God with your whole heart and with your whole soul and with your whole mind. Secondly, you must love your neighbors as yourself." Prophesy and the Revelation of Divine Law hinges on these two commandments.

Chapter Twenty-Two
It's Time To Come In For Your Curfew
Moral Strength For Living A Sanctified Life

This chapter focuses on God's call for men and women to separate themselves from the world. Man is not to be captured by what the world has to offer profoundly because earthly things are temporary and God wants men to focus on the eternal aspects of life. We are to focus on the kingdom of God, by virtue of its eternal representation. I am convinced that the lack of self-denial in the lives of Christians is the primary factor hindering the progress of the Church today. The surrendering of will is the death of self. We must recognize that consecration of self is a continual process. The cares and pressures of life have caused men and women of today to become weakened and sidetracked from the will of God. Personal goals are now man's principle objective and the building of God's Kingdom has been placed on the back burner. God's will has been labeled low priority. The church has become materialistically preoccupied.

Satan tries to hinder the unsaved and God's people from totally surrendering to God's will by making it hard for them to detect areas that they have not surrendered to Christ. However, the believer has the Holy Spirit to reveal to him the sin committed in his daily walk with God. Therefore, the believer that has not totally surrendered is similar to the unbeliever in many areas of their life. He refuses to adhere to the directions of the Holy Spirit. Many have not surrendered their will to the will of God. Personalities, personal desires etc., which pertain to an individual's will need to be presented before the altar of God. Let us be cautious in evaluating ourselves because it is often easier to detect problems and stumbling blocks in the lives of other people than it is to acknowledge and confess hindrances in our own lives.

Total commitment is required of those within the Army of God. Our decision to work the works of God is a serious commitment. We must not allow any earthly temptation to impede us from going forth in the demonstration of *God's Holy Power.* When you open your heart in rededication, you recommit yourself to God's services.

Being separated for the works of God requires time to commune with Him. It will require purification of your motives and desires by the Holy Spirit. You must yield to the Spirit of God while obstacles are being removed from your life. Finally, you have to be determined not to look back. Your mind must be made up to serve God and Him only.

God will reveal Himself just as He did when He called a slave people out of Egypt and made them a nation for His purpose of redemption in the world. God publicly makes Himself known as Lord and Redeemer of those who call upon Him. Exodus means "departure," and gives reference to the most important event in man's life, which is the departure from a land of sin. A place where he was once enslaved and being set free he journeyed to a city which has a foundation, that is the kingdom of God.

The Book of Exodus reveals the battle of the Gods. Jehovah (The Great I Am) proves that He is the only true God. The ten plagues constitute the judgment of God on Satan, his seeds, or preferably said the unbelievers. The plagues also document the outcome of man's disobedience to God's word. Jehovah reveals His power and His conquest over Satan, as exemplified by Moses' triumph over Pharaoh.

When visiting the last plague, we find that God had persistently and consistently attempted to prove to Pharaoh and his subjects that He is the God of the Most High. It is acceptable to say that before death arrives God has allowed various plagues or trials to come in our lives in an effort to gain our attention that we may depart from a life of unbelief and enter into the acceptance of Jehovah as The Great I Am. The above is very true but I find it difficult to accept because of the perception concerning the magnitude of the lost. The statement is, despite Christ's efforts, after witnessing Divine grace and human freedom many are like Pharaoh. They hard-heartedly denied God.

The Curfew

This Chapter contains the message that Jehovah has called mankind to exit a life of sin, bondage, a world of corruption, evil, and

A Cry for Ethical and Moral Strength

darkness. Upon exiting, we will become covered by His protection. His protection is the new covenant, the blood of the Lamb. John 3:16 says, "For God so loved the world, that he gave his only begotten son, that whosoever believeth in him should not perish but have everlasting life". When we accept Jesus Christ in our life and become obedient to his word, we are not touched by the judgment of sin. We enter into a new life. A life of the heavenly, where believers become of a new mind and a new walk. That walk journeys to a place of perfection, a destiny we will reach because of the guidance of the Holy Spirit. Because of Christ's blood, all men can escape death and inherit eternal life. You will find that the curfew has already been given and it is time for you to come into God's protection.

In Exodus 11:4-10 Moses said, "Thus saith the LORD, About midnight will I go out into the midst of Egypt: And all the first-born in the land of Egypt shall die, from the first-born of Pharaoh that sitteth upon his throne, even unto the first born of the maidservant that *is* behind the mill; and all the first-born of beasts. And there shall be a great cry throughout all the land of Egypt, such as there was none like it, nor shall be like it any more. But against any of the children of Israel shall not a dog move his tongue, against man or beast: that ye may know how that the LORD doth put a difference between the Egyptians and Israel. And all these thy servants shall come down unto me, and bow down themselves unto me, saying, Get thee out, and all the people that follow thee: and after that I will go out. And he went out from Pharaoh in a great anger. And the LORD said unto Moses, Pharaoh shall not hearken unto you; that my wonders may be multiplied in the land of Egypt. And Moses and Aaron did all these wonders before Pharaoh: and the LORD hardened Pharaoh's heart, so that he would not let the children of Israel go out of his land."

Defined by Webster's New Collegiate Dictionary, a curfew is a regulation enjoining the withdrawal of usual specified persons from the streets or the closing of business establishments or places of assembly at a stated hour. The definition also includes the period during which a curfew is in effect. God has called believers to separate themselves from the things of this world. There is an existing curfew given for all God's children to abide. When viewing the Old Testament, we find in the Book of Exodus, God called a curfew to separate believers from non-believers. In doing so, the believers escape the judgment of God. After viewing the scripture, it becomes obvious that the final judgment upon Egypt is death and God has revealed that when you obey him and follow the word of God, we will be led out of a life of bondage into an eternal promise, the kingdom of God.

Egypt is known as a type of sin. The Jews were in captivity, in slavery and bondage in a land that exemplified worldliness or sin. Just as all men are slaves to sin, we all must depart from a life of bondage and journey to a promised land. Man must seek a city that has a foundation. Hebrews 11:8-11 "By faith Abraham, when he was called to go out into a place which he should after receive for an inheritance, obeyed; and he went out, not knowing whither he went. By faith he sojourned in the land of promise, as *in* a strange country, dwelling in tabernacles with Isaac and Jacob, the heirs with him of the same promise.   For he looked for a city which hath foundations, whose builder and maker is God. Through faith also Sarah herself received strength to conceive seed, and was delivered of a child when she was past age, because she judged him faithful who had promised."

In an effort to hinder the believer's service to Jehovah, Satan tempts unbelievers to commit acts that are designed to entrap the believer. God has promised that the penalty would be death to the seeds of Satan for the evil temptation and deceitful lies he has set before mankind. Be assured that the seed, that is to be judged is the first born son of Satan; which are all people that have chosen to war against Christ by teaching false doctrine; persecuting Saints, and being led or succumbing to the will of an arch enemy. These people will not become heirs to the kingdom of Satan. Why? Because, unlike the kingdom of God, Satan's kingdom (the earth) is temporary and is destined to fall… Satan is the prince of the world. His reign is short lived, for this world and the heavens shall pass away, never to exist again.

It is understood that during the patriot period the first son would inherit or become the heir to the estate and possessions of the father. A student of God's word would know that a spiritual blessing is also associated with the transfer of the birthrights to the elder son or first born. In the lives of Abraham, Isaac and Jacob, we are given a detailed account of a birthright blessing. The first seed became the heir of the majority of all that the father owned and whatever he had authority over.

When comparing their ship with Satan's first seed, we must initially review the Blood Covenant that God entered into with Abram. It was years after God made a covenant with Abram that He appeared unto Abraham, at the age of ninety-nine, to confirm the covenant. God said, "I am God Almighty; walk before me and be blameless. I will confirm my covenant between you and me and will greatly increase your numbers" (Gen. 17:1,2). Abram was to become the father of many nations. God promised to multiply his seed as the stars in the sky, and as sands of the sea. He promised to give Abram and his seed the land of Canaan as an everlasting possession. Indeed the promises of God were decreed with Abram and his seed or heir. The heir of Abraham is Jesus Christ, the Messiah. If you have accepted Christ (the seed of Abraham - through the line of David) as your Lord and Savior, then you are also of the seed of Abraham. Why? You have died and are now reborn in Christ. Also, because you are of the same faith of Abraham. The incorruptible seed lives inside of you and you are adopted into the body of Christ. Believers have inherited all the promises made to Abraham through the faith they have in Christ Jesus. We have access to the power of Christ and victory, as displayed in the covenant blessing through the washing of the Blood of Jesus.

God promised the believer (the seeds of Abraham) that they would endure and be victorious in the war against the evil one. He promised that believers would inherit eternal life and reign with Christ throughout eternity. It becomes more and more obvious that the heirs of Satan will inherit nothing but damnation. The kingdom of satan will fall unto the power of Christ, who has been positioned above all the creations in heaven, in the earth and under the earth.

The unbeliever, the heirs of Satan, will only inherit the eternal lake of fire as the final result of God's judgment on sin.

As believers, professing to trust in Christ Jesus, we have exited a life of serving Satan and departed from committing willful sin. 1 Peter 2:9, But ye are a chosen generation a royal priesthood, a holy nation, a peculiar people; that ye should show forth the praises of him who hath called you out of darkness into the marvelous light. Whosoever believeth that Jesus is the Christ, becomes a specific people that Peter refers as called out of the darkness into the marvelous light.

Throughout the Bible, God informed men that he has made a definite distinction between believers and non-believers. The final plague, Death of the first-born, demonstrates how the Lord doth put a difference between the Egyptians and Israelites. That is to say how GOD places distinction between a nation of sin and a nation of chosen believers. The primary component for the separateness is that God requests obedience in our service. Men and women can choose to obey God and receive the promises He set forth in His blood covenant. Else, they can inherit the curses of God for disobeying his word.

Satan's strategy is to deceive and lead Christians into disobedience by conveying untruths to them concerning the consequences of disobedience. Some men think they will not be punished for their disobedience. The Holy Scripture makes it clear, that DISOBEDIENCE is living under the wrath of God and men and women will be punished for disobedience when Christ returns for His saints. God made it perfectly clear to Adam that the penalty for disobedience is death (Genesis 2:16-17). Satan deceived Eve into believing that she and Adam would not die for their act of disobedience, but would become as wise as God, knowing good and evil (Genesis 3:4-5).

Adam was not deceived (I Timothy 2:14); he knew the penalty, yet he listened to Eve instead of listening to the voice of God ... he willfully chose to disobey God. He yielded his will and took of the fruit and ate it. As a result of Adam and Eve's act of DISOBEDIENCE, they reaped the penalty and lived under the curse of disobedience:

A Cry for Ethical and Moral Strength

Sin and death entered the world (Romans 5:12).

All men become slaves to sin under Satan's dominion (Romans 6:16-17).

The ground was cursed (Genesis 3:17-19).

They forfeited the blessings and provision God had given them in the Garden of Eden Genesis3:23).

The beautiful, intimate fellowship they had enjoyed with God in the Garden of Eden was broken (Genesis 3:24).

There was enmity between God and man (Ephesians 2:16).

God still requires obedience. He has not changed. Every act of disobedience that has not been repented and forsaken carries with it a penalty. It will not only hinder and eventually destroy your personal relationship with God, it will also hinder you from taking possession of your spiritual inheritance and enjoying the fullness of the blessings He has provided for you. It will cut you off from the life-giving flow of the spirit of God in your life. It was because of their disobedience that the children of Israel failed to take possession of their inheritance in the Promised Land, and they died in the wilderness.

After God delivered them out of Egyptian bondage, He entered into a blood covenant with them on Mount Sinai that was based upon their obedience to Him. God told Moses to tell the people, "Now therefore, if you will obey My voice in truth and keep My covenant, then you shall be My own peculiar possession and treasure from among and above all peoples..." (Exodus 19:5, TAB). The Israelites, in turn, pledged themselves to be His people. They said, "all that the LORD hath said will we do, and be obedient" (Exodus 24:7). But, even before Moses came down from Mount Sinai with the tablets containing the Ten Commandments, the children of Israel had broken the covenant they had made with Him and had begun worshipping a golden calf. God commanded the Levites to take a sword and go through the camp slaying "every man his brother, and every man his companion, and every man his neighbor" (Exodus 32:27). Three thousand men died that day because of disobedience! Due to their disobedience, God was ready to destroy the entire nation of Israel Deuteronomy 9:13-14). Moses fasted and interceded 40 days and nights for the children of Israel. Because of His loving kindness, God responded to Moses' plea for mercy and forgave the children of Israel. Over and over the children of Israel disobeyed and tested God (Numbers 14:11-12, 20-23). As a result of their disobedience, the children of Israel forfeited their spiritual inheritance. They were not allowed to enter the Promised Land (Numbers 14:30). They suffered for their iniquities, wandering in the wilderness one year for each of the 40 days they spied out the land of Canaan. God told them, You will suffer for your sins and know what it is like to have me against you (Numbers 14:34.) God is loving, long suffering, patient, slow to anger, and willing to forgive all those who will repent of their sin and turn to Him with their whole heart. However, He will not overlook sin. He will not hide His eyes from the sins of His people.

Regulation

God's curfew is an authoritative regulation, which consists of essential details and vital procedures. God governs and directs all aspects according to his Law. Because GOD is the highest authority, He enforces all mandates of the curfew. He also implements judgment associated with violation of his commands. Whether you accept it or not, Jesus Christ has been exalted to the right hand of God. The scripture tells us in Philippians 2:10-11 "That at the name of Jesus every knee should bow, of things in heaven, and things in earth, and things under the earth; And that every tongue shall confess that Jesus Christ is Lord..."

Found in Exodus. Ch. 12, God's regulations are that they:

- Partake of the Lamb. Feast and celebrate in remembrance of how God brought you through.

- Partake of no leaven. Do not engage in any unclean acts or meditate on thoughts that are an abomination to God.

- All men are to come in from a life of darkness. One must come into the house of God, into God's protection.

- The time of the curfew is now, because we are living in a world where people love the darkness and the hour is near midnight. The hour is near the peak of evil deeds and evildoers.

- Accept Jesus in your life. Mark yourself with the blood of the Lamb.

- Abide with Christ. No believer shall go out of his house until the morning, which is a plea to stay away from sin until the day when Jesus returns.

- Be ye ready, be a prepared people, be dressed and clothed with the full armor of God because Christ can come for you at any moment to demonstrate faithfulness to His promises.

Time Of The Curfew

In the case of the final plague that came upon Egypt, God does not give a specific time for the implementation of death of the first-born. The Lord said to Moses "thus saith the Lord, About midnight will I go out into the midst of Egypt and all the first-born in the land of Egypt shall die."

Midnight represents darkness at its highest peak. In many cultures, day and night are divided into twelve hours. One of the primary reasons for this is that the settings represent opposite polars. Good and evil conflict with one another and they differ 180 degrees on a scale of 360°. This suggests a symbolism that midnight clearly refers to a sphere of time, today's time. We are living in the last and evil days. A time that brings condemnation because the light came into the world, yet men love darkness rather than the light. Man's deeds are evil (John 3:9). Since the Fall of Adam and Eve, man lives in a world of sin, a world in which man needs redemption. *The prophet John sheds light on the time "mid-night". Midnight reflects a state of darkness, meaning people of this time are walking in a position of blindness. They have allowed their wickedness to lead them, instead of being guided by the light of God.*

About midnight infers to the account that Israel knew that the plague was going to occur because God said He was going to cause it to take place. It infers that the plague would take place prior to midnight, meaning judgment will occur before sin reaches it's peak. Oh yes, sin has a climax that it can reach, but Christ will rapture the believers and soon after judge men prior to allowing sin to tower to it's pinnacle. Israel did not know how much time before mid-night in which the angel of death would come, but they knew that the judgment of God would take place about or near the time of midnight. A time when it appears that things just can't get any worst.

Man's curfew today is similar to Israel's. When Christ was about to leave this world his disciples came to him in private. They asked him "and what will happen to show that it is that time for your coming and the end of the age." Israel's knowledge pertaining to the coming judgment of God is indicative to the question the disciples asked Christ concerning the end of time. The disciples were aware that the judgment of God was near but they did not know the signs that would indicate that the day was at hand.

Matthew 24:3-14 states: "And as Jesus sat on the Mount of Olives, the disciples came to him in private and inquired, "Tell us when all this will be," they asked, "and what will happen to show that it is the time for your coming and the end of the age." Jesus answered, "Watch out, and do not let anyone fool you. Many men, claiming to speak for me, will come and say, 'I am the Messiah!' and they will fool many people. You are going to hear the noise of battles close by and the news of battles far away; but do not be troubled. Such things must happen, but they do not mean that the end has come. Countries will fight each other; kingdoms will attack one another. There will be famines and earthquakes everywhere. All these are the beginning of sorrows. Then you will be arrested and handed over to be punished and put to death. All mankind will hate you because of me. Many will give up their faith at that time; they will betray one another and hate one another. Then many false prophets will appear and fool many people. Such will be the spread of evil that many people's love will grow cold. But whoever holds out to the end will be saved. And this Gospel about the kingdom will be preached through all the world for a witness to all mankind; and then the end will come." It is obvious that we are living in the hour that is near to Christ's return. The events of the world testify that time nears the hour of midnight. Though no man knows the day nor the hour of Christ's return, we are to stay on watch and on guard as the Word states. Believers would then know from the circumstances, and situations around the world that the return of Christ is near. War, civil unrest, and terrorism are throughout the world. Famine in third world countries and profound degrees of poverty existing within prominent nations are true indications of Christ immanent return. Just as God gave no specific time to Israel for the coming plague, He does not give to us today a precise time for his return; a return that brings deliverance and judgment.

Implementing The Curfew

Exodus 12:21-23 "Then Moses called for all the elders of Israel, and said unto them, draw out and take you a lamb according to your families, and kill the Passover. And ye shall take a bunch of hyssop, and dip *it* in the blood that *is* in the basin, and strike the lintel and the two side posts with the blood that *is* in the basin: and none of you shall go out at the door of his house until the morning. For the LORD will pass through to smite the Egyptians; and when he seeth the blood upon the lintel, and on the two side posts, the LORD will pass over the door, and will not suffer the destroyer to come in unto your houses to smite *you.*"

There are procedures, ordinances or regulations we have to follow when we choose Christ as our Lord and Savior. Believers must follow God's requirements in demonstration of their obedience to His word. By following his example and being obedient to his will, you are ensuring your eternal position with God.

1. Moses informs the elder of Israel to kill the Passover lamb:

2. Strike the lintel and the two side posts with the blood of the lamb: None are to go out at the door until morning:

3. These procedures are to be carried out because the Lord is going to pass through to smite the Egyptian unbelievers.

Kill The Passover Lamb

Israel had to kill a Passover lamb. This procedure is a foreshadowing of Christ's sacrificial offering of His Body. God, Himself came down, made Himself a fleshly Body and willingly laid it upon the altar to make atonement for your soul (Leviticus 17:11). *It was not only the Romans or the Jews that killed Jesus of Nazareth. It was also you and I that killed the lamb of God. Because of the sin of Adam, all men are in need of a Savior. That Savior is Christ. T he perfect, unblemished and holy One. Jesus is the only lamb that could redeem mankind from the judgment of sin.* Now that Christ suffered for our sins, the just for the unjust, that He might bring us to God, being put to death in the flesh, but quickened by the Spirit, we need not kill the lamb but only accept Him in our life. For when Israel sacrificed the lamb, it exemplified a confession of their belief in God. Therefore, Christ awaits your confession and repentance. Surrender to GOD, that you may be united with Him.

The act of killing the Passover lamb demonstrates a beginning process of surrender to the will of God, for no one will see the Father except they receive the Son. All the following procedures are in accordance to the will of God, that men may submit in order to convey a surrounding of their will. Then and only then can man become subject to God's will. Although God gave each man a free will, Christ purchased man with the highest payment, His own life. We have been bought and paid for by God. Man's life does not belong to himself. When we become born again Christians, we have come to realize that we are slaves to Christ Jesus. We cannot repay him for what he has done for us. The old man was buried with Christ and you have been raised to life with Christ. As Paul stated, though I have died, yet I also live in Christ (Gal. 2:20). Paul indicates that believers will continuously be kept in line with the Word of God. God's desire must become your desire. His will must become your will. His purpose must become the motive of your objective. You must possess the same mind of God. I am not suggesting that you have no will. I am merely suggesting that you have surrendered in your war against Christ, for to act out your will is to wrestle against the will of God. To wrestle against the will of God is not the character of an individual that has become a conformed believer. I am not saying that Satan will not tempt or attempt to deceive the believer while he walks with God. Nevertheless, when the time involves you making a decision against that which is wrong or for that which is right, the will of God prevails as a result to your submission to God.

Not Dressed For The Occasion

To believers that have not completely accepted the word of God, which resulted in you walking backwards or sideways of the light, means only that you are not walking in the path of God. You veered from the path of light. Your own emotions and intellect rules in many areas that demand the Faith of Christ. This weakness conveys that Satan's temptation yields sin in your life. God said *"And thus shall ye eat it; with your loins girded, your shoes on your feet, and your staff in your hand; and ye shall eat it in haste: it is the Lord's Passover."* Exodus 12:11 God is saying to the believer; you are to eat the word of God in haste, because his return is upon this world. We are living in the last and evil days. We are living in a phase when God can return as a thief in the night to the man that is not prepared. Believers are to be a prepared people. They are to be on watch for Christ and clothed in righteousness. Pre-arrangements for his coming are to be made now, as we feed on the Word of God.

As we feed on the Word of God, the believer must be suited with the complete armor of God. If a man desires to be with the Creator, he cannot only feed from the Word of God, he must also be dressed with the Full Armor or clothed with the complete Word of God.

Howbeit that some believers study God's word, live among the saints of God and are surrounded by the word, partake of God's word, but have not put on the complete armor of God? Can they not conceive that they're exposed to the fiery darts of the wicked one? (Ephesians 6:16) For Paul said *"There is therefore now no condemnation to them which are in Christ Jesus, who walk not after the flesh, but after the Spirit."*

Professing Christians that yield themselves to the lusts of their flesh or are being led and controlled by their fleshly desire are condemned. They are rebelling against the Word of God and standing guilty before His Majesty. Unless they repent and turn from their sins, they will receive the eternal judgment of destruction. These professing Christians have deceived themselves because they are not applying the complete word of God to their life. They live their lives according to the dictates of their fleshly desires. True believers realize that God has given us Dynamos Power needed to overcome the evil one.

I have expressed Jehovah's discomfort with certain professing believers. Now I must also indicate a prevalence of believers that battle against Satan with the wrong weapons, carnal weapons, and how God is uneasy with their conduct. Though I will not specifically address the issue in this particular subheading, I do address the use of cardinal weapons in this chapter, under the subtopic "The Appropriate Attire". It would behoove you to maintain the notion that some believers have not placed on the full armor of God as you continue to read this chapter. For saints that have not put on the full armor of God are referred to as weak saints or even hypocrites.

Certain unbelievers are very particular about the conduct they exhibit. Many say that they know God. They say that they serve God. They even desire not to war against Christ and consciously they believe that they do not war against Him. But because these particular persons have not accepted Christ in their lives, God wars against them. Therefore, if you are an unbeliever, God wars against you. I have provided you with the basic facts concerning this matter. The war truly exists between God and Satan. If you have not joined God on the battlefield, you are a captain of the army of Satan. Your life is a ministry that conveys a doctrine that conflicts with the Word of God. I would have you to know that God wages war against you. You are a seed of the Deceiver. Your fruit and offspring are corrupt. You cannot bear anything that is good or acceptable in the sight of God. My interjection is that you may not be conscious of your war against God only because you have been swindled by an impostor, Satan. You have not perceived the fraudulence of your state of consciousness, due to the darkness in which you walk. Christ is the only one that can shed light on the darkness. Not by chance or by luck can the darkness understand the light (John 1:5)? Yet, the light knows the darkness and the light. It is imperative that you confess your sins and ask Christ to come into your life. In doing so the Word of God will take root within your heart and the Holy Spirit will begin to reveal the word of God to you, as a born again believer.

In the scripture of Ezekiel we find that all men that war against Christ are dead. We also are informed of the fact that if any man would hear the word of God, God will give him abundant life. Let us review the natural man's battle against Christ as it is revealed in the book of Ezekiel 37:1-14, 26-28 "The hand of the Lord was upon me, and carried me out in the spirit of the Lord, and set me down in the midst of the valley which was full of bones, And caused me to pass by them round about: and, behold, there were very many in the open valley; and lo, they were very dry. And he said unto me, Son of man, can these bones live? And I answered, O Lord God, thou knowest. Again he said unto me, Prophesy upon these bones, and say unto them, O ye dry bones, hear the word of the LORD. Thus saith the Lord God unto these bones; Behold, I will cause breath to enter in you, and ye shall live: And I will lay sinews upon you, and will bring up flesh upon you, and cover you with skin, and put breath in you, and ye shall live; and ye shall know that I am the LORD. So I prophesied as I was commanded: and as I prophesied, there was a noise, and behold a shaking, and the bones came together, bone to his bone. And when I beheld, lo, the sinews and the flesh came up upon them, and the skin covered them above but there was no breath in them. Then said he unto me, Prophesy unto the wind, prophesy, son of man, and say to the wind, thus saith the Lord God; Come from the four winds, O breath, and breathe upon these slain, that they may live. So I prophesied as he commanded me, and the breath came into them, and they lived, and stood up upon their feet, an exceeding great army. Then he said unto me, Son of man, these bones are the whole house of Israel: behold, they say, Our bones are dried, and our hope is lost, we are cut off for our parts. Therefore prophesy and say unto them, Thus saith the Lord God; Behold, O my people, I will open your graves, and cause you to come up out of your graves, and bring you into the land of Israel. And ye shall know that I am the LORD, when I have opened your graves, O my people, and brought you up out of your graves, and shall put my spirit in you, and ye shall live, and I shall place you in your own land: then shall ye know that I the LORD have spoken it, and performed it, saith the LORD. Moreover I will make a covenant of peace with them; it shall be an everlasting covenant with them: and I will place them, and multiply them, and will set my sanctuary in the midst of them for evermore. My tabernacle also shall be with them: yea, I will be their God, and they shall be my people. And the heathen shall know that I the LORD do sanctify Israel, when my sanctuary shall be in the midst of them for evermore."

Similar to the dead bones (Israel), we all have warred against God. We were fully equipped with the weapons of Satan. Our efforts were in vain. We, in our carnal state, are defeated. If we would only harken to God's word, He will give whomsoever life. Our soldierhood would be converted over to the victorious side of God. We will be given our spiritual weapon "the Full Armor of God". All men are considered to be dead by God unless they allow him to breathe life into them through his word. Have you received God's complete Word that you may be resurrected from the dead?

It is worthwhile to note that all men are dead in sin, for they are born in sin and shaped in iniquity (Psalm 51:5). We are also dead because of our current position in Christ. Man's separation from God connotes that we have been severed from the vine. God is the vine, for only he can give life. John 15:5 "I am the vine, ye are the branches: He that abide in me, and I in him, the same bringeth forth much fruit: for without me ye can do nothing." Jesus has come to give men life. All we have to do is harken to the complete word of God. When we are obedient in accepting God's word, we are given the gift of Life. The word will be planted within our hearts and it will grow and generate an abundant life.

The Appropriate Attire

When I speak of putting on the complete armor of God, you must understand that I am speaking to the weak believers as if the word would relate to the unbeliever. I do know that you must first be a believer prior to conversing on being dressed and clothed with the word of God. The misunderstanding exists when we do not consider that some believers are included with the Christians that have not put on the complete Armor of God. Though they attempt to face Satan and war against him, they are weak and have no power because they battle the evil one using carnal weapons in many areas of their life. Weapons of mortal men cannot be used when war is waged in the spiritual rim. II Corinthians 10:4-6 states, "For the weapons of our warfare *are* not carnal, but mighty through God to the pulling down of strongholds; Casting down imaginations, and every high thing that exalteth itself against the knowledge of God, and bringing into captivity every thought to the obedience of Christ. And having in a readiness to revenge all disobedience, when your obedience is fulfilled."

Believers must know the type of weapons Christ has presented to His children. We must also learn how to use them in combat. When talking about the weapons of our warfare, believers are not talking about some mystical phenomena that cannot be acquired. It is not an old methodological cliché when we talk about picking up our weapons. Believers are not just using a figure of speech. Spiritual weapons of God are very real and effective in their use against the principalities in higher places. Though the weapons are not visible and cannot be felt unless manifested by Christ, they are far from being non-existing. With the weapons of God, believers can wage an offensive and defensive war. The armor of God serves as defensive weapons, which protect and shield us from the attacks of the enemy. It also serves as offensive weapons, which confront and take power and authority over Satan. The armor allows the believer to be bold and aggressive in the war against sin and in the war to lead men to Christ.

In writing to the Ephesians, Paul described a spiritual "armor" they were required to wear. The armor would make them completely invulnerable to the attacks of the enemy. The Ephesian was instructed to put on God's armor. The armor is given to each believer. We know that we are fighting and wrestling unseen forces, and that our weapons are not fleshly, carnal weapons. Our enemies are of the spirit world. How is it possible for us to face the attacks of the enemy in the natural realm? Pain, sickness, financial issues, social challenges, problems in our relationships, not to exclude many more factors we face in the normal course of life, can not be fought with weapons that are not effective in ridding these issues. Can we defeat sickness, disease, financial problems, domestic problems, or any other relationship problems by using carnal weapons? No! We must pray, fast, edify God, stand on the word of God and keep the faith. The faith is with God all things are possible Matthew 19:26.

The problem that many Christians face is, when they are confronted by the enemy and are attacked in the natural realm, they pick up carnal, fleshly weapons in trying to face the enemy. They blame themselves, another man, or even God for the existing problem. Instead of picking up the powerful invisible weapons that God has afforded the believer, they attempt to condemn anyone or everybody except the true culprit, Satan. They are using the wrong weapons. They don't have on the full armor of God. They face Satan and unseen forces of evil using weapons based upon man's wisdom and understanding, man's limited strength, psychology, man-made doctrines, the power of positive thinking, and an unlimited river of self help seminars or theory.

On the surface these carnal weapons appear to be effective and produce temporary results. However, these carnal weapons are not capable of penetrating into the realm of the spirit world. They are not capable of locating the unseen forces that are the root of the problem. We must get to the heart of the problem by the discerning of that which is good and that which is evil. Once we have identified the enemy, we must lay an ax to the root of the tree (Matthew 3:10). The only weapons capable of doing this are those that God has created and provided for us to use.

God has fashioned for us a powerful armor that will protect and seal us from the attacks of Satan. Not only does God's armor enable believers to be perfect, it makes the believer invulnerable and fully equipped to become victorious in battle. The following are individual components of the complete Armor of God. They allow the believer to be strong in the Lord and in the power of God's might. Before I list them and provide scripture for the comparison or supporting text, I present Ephesians 6:13-16 as the fundamental scripture used to substantiate my argument. "Wherefore take unto you the whole armor of God, that ye may be able to withstand in the evil day, and having done all, to stand; Stand therefore, having your lions girt about with truth, and having on the breastplate of righteousness; And your feet shod with the preparation of the gospel of peace; Above all, taking the shield of faith wherewith ye shall be able to quench all the fiery darts of the wicked."

THE GIRDLE OF TRUTH: Jesus said, "I am the way, the truth, and the life: (John 14:6).

THE BREASTPLATE OF RIGHTEOUSNESS: He is righteous; He has on the breastplate of righteousness (Isaiah 59:17); He has become our righteousness (I Corinthians 1:30); and we are righteous in Him (II Corinthians 5:21).

THE PREPARATION (the readiness to proclaim) *OF THE GOSPEL OF PEACE*: Jesus ushered in the kingdom by preaching, "Repent: for the kingdom of heaven is at hand" (Matthew 4:17). No longer are we under the Law, we are currently under grace.

THE SHIELD OF FAITH: Jesus is the "Author and finisher of our faith" (Hebrews 12:2).

THE HELMET OF SALVATION: As the promised Messiah, He has on the helmet of salvation (Isaiah 59:17). There is no other Name under heaven whereby we must be saved (Acts 4:12).

THE SWORD OF THE SPIRIT - THE WORD OF GOD: Jesus is the Living Word. "In the beginning was the Word, and the Word was with God, and the Word was God...And the Word was made flesh, and dwelt among us..." (John 1:1,14).

Strike The Lintel And Post

The Israelites were informed by Moses to strike the lintel and the two side posts with the blood of the Lamb. As mentioned prior, to kill the lamb is to become a believer. For it reveals that a man must accept the sacrifice of the Lamb of God as the atonement of his sins. The killing of the lamb also reveal that these men were believers because God said it is better to be obedient than to sacrifice. The striking of the lintel and two posts today announces that believers are marked by God through the protection offered by the blood of Jesus. Throughout the Bible, God has demonstrated that marking a man either on the forehead or his hand, which includes the wrist, designates an individual has been chosen for their service to God. The marking could also distinguish a particular service a person or group is anointed to participate in the case of Israel, the marking of the lintel and the two post reflects a complete identification of a people who was chosen by GOD for his works. Today, men are chosen for the service of God. The Godly man witnesses by his service and the peace that he exhibits in his disposition that he is a believer or a chosen one of God. His Words, thoughts, and hands are marked for God's service. Men receive the promises of God and the protection of God through the Blood of Christ.

Allow me to clarify that the house of the Israelites represents the temple of man and his body. Hence, the marking of the lintel is equivalent to the marking of your forehead. The marking of the two posts could only represent the marking of your hands for they are part of your arms. An example is given by using:

> A. Rev. 7:3 - The angel said "Do not harm the earth, the sea, or the trees, until we mark the servants of our God with a seal on their forehead."
>
> Here we find that the marking is given to distinguish a particular group of people, the 144,000 servants of God selected from the twelve tribes of Israel. They are marked or sealed that they may be protected from the coming judgment upon the earth. The 144,000 are marked with

A Cry for Ethical and Moral Strength

the name of the Son and the Father to identify they are for a special ministry for God.

B. Rev. 13 - The beast forced all the people, small and great, rich and poor, slave and free, to have a marked placed on their right hands or on their foreheads.

It is in this particular scripture that we find that the hands are also used in identification. The people that are forced to receive the mark instantly become the Beast servants. The mark identifies an individual as a worshipper of the beast. In turn, allow him to buy or sell within Satan's government system.

Through the blood of Jesus every covenant promise has been put into effect. The covenant promises are not dependent upon whether or not we have enough faith to believe. The covenant promises of God are true and just as powerful as the day God spoke them into existence. They are dependent upon the power of the blood Jesus shed for us. They are dependent upon the perfect sacrifice of a life that was lived in 100 percent obedience to God.

Many Christians today are not enjoying the covenant blessings God has provided for them because they feel they must have great faith to receive healing, to receive a financial blessing, or to partake of all of the riches God has prepared for them to enjoy. As a result, they spend the majority of their time striving to build their faith up enough to receive what they need.

God's covenant promises are not dependent upon us, but upon God's faithfulness concerning the power of Jesus' blood. To fully understand the strength of the covenant promises, you must first understand the significance and the power of the blood that seals and makes the covenant promises effective. Let us review God's Holy Scripture that focuses on the wonder working power in the Blood of the Lamb.

The everlasting covenant God has entered into with man is not just an ordinary covenant or agreement; it is the closest and most sacred form of covenant ever known. It is a blood covenant. The blood covenant in the primitive world was whereby two persons covenanted to become one as "covenant friends" through being partakers of the same blood. There is life in the blood. God told Moses: "For the life of the flesh is in the blood: and I have given it to you upon the altar to make an atonement for your souls: for it is the blood that maketh an atonement for the soul" (Leviticus 17:11). Since the blood is life itself, the giving of blood represented the giving of life; the receiving of blood represented the receiving of life. When two people entered into a blood covenant where their blood was co-mingled, it represented a union or co-mingling of their lives. The blood represented a commitment unto death and "sealed" the covenant. It signified that the covenant would never be broken.

In the blood covenant God entered into with Abraham, the covenant between them was sealed and made effective by the sacrificial blood. God told Abraham to take three animals, cut them down the spine and lay each half opposite one another, creating a walkway of blood. After the sun had gone down, God manifested Himself in the form of a smoking furnace and a burning lamp and passed through the walkway of blood. The same blood that was sprinkled upon the altar was sprinkled upon the Book of the Covenant and upon the people. But, it was not until the blood had been first presented and accepted at the altar. The sprinkling of the blood upon the people signified the cleansing of their sins and their consecration and separation to God as a holy people. The people and God were bound together by the blood of the sacrifice.

It was not the death of the sacrifice, or the broken body of the animal, but the blood, which purified and cleansed the people and forever sealed the covenant...the agreement between God and Israel. "(In fact), under the Law almost everything is purified by means of blood, and without the shedding of blood there is no remission of sins" Hebrews 9:22. God required the sacrifice and sprinkling of the blood upon the altar because they spoke of a better sacrifice to come. All of the blood sacrifices under the Old Covenant were necessary to show the people the impossibility of the blood of bulls and goats to take away their sins, and were a foreshadowing of the ONE perfect Sacrifice...the Messiah...their redeemer that was to come.

When Under Curfew Do Not Go Out

When you obey GOD by coming in from a life of sin, you are not to leave God's protection to return to treasures of this world. You are to never turn back. God said, *"Let no man deceive you by any means: for that day shall not come, except there comes a falling away first, and that man of sin be revealed, the son of prediction."* Lot's wife turned back toward a previous life/city of sin. In doing so, her disobedience brought the judgment of death upon her. When some believers come in for their curfew, some disobey God by violating his regulations. They willfully committed sin against Him. Consequently, they separate themselves from his promises and His protection. In accordance to His word, they have violated God's covenant whereby subjecting themselves to the harsh judgment of sin.

So many Christians have co-mingled sin with their spiritual walk. It is devastating to know that the majority of them believe Christ has overlooked their sins. The falseness that sin is acceptable in God's sight has taken precedence over the word. Some of these Christians sneak out, some go out thinking nothing will happen and some go out and stay out. All are of the family of backsliders. The church has a multitude of professing believers that indulge in:

1. Practicing Adultery
2. Drinking Alcohol until intoxicated
3. Physical abuse of wife, children or self
4. Pornographic Laudation
5. Homosexuality
6. Bi-sexuality
7. Numerous sexual perversions that do not warrant mentioning.
8. Smoking
9. Use of Profanity

10. Lying to their brother or self

11. Stealing

12. Gossiping

13. Discrimination

14. Cheating their brother or improper business ethics

15. Drugs

I must stop here or this list would include every sin conceived in the heart of men. It is un- comforting to consider the great magnitude that some Christians are committing sin. The professing believer is committing sin as if he or she was an unbeliever. In God's eyes, the man is an unbeliever. To ponder the thought that some Christians are partaking in murder or suicide is practically inconceivable. In all cases a curfew breaker rarely admits to their violation. They normally put forth an ultimate effort to conceal their sin, just as teens deny going out or breaking their curfew. How is it that the believer committing sin has abandoned the promises of GOD? GOD promised that when you accept Christ as your personal Savior you receive confirmation of the following:

- With men numerous things are impossible; but with God all things are possible (Matthew 19:26). You cannot move your mountain alone; you need the power of God. Then and only then will you be able to speak to the mountains, better yet your problems, and they shall be moved.

- All things are possible to him that believeth (Mark 9:23). You say that you are a believer, then why have you succumbed to temptation.

- God said, "Ask and it shall be given to you: seek, and you shall find; knock, and it shall be opened unto you" (Matt. 7:7). Ask God to remove whatever deviation you have or are committing and he will remove it for you. Seek the Lord's strength and wisdom and you will discover that it is Christ living inside of the believer. Did you know

A Cry for Ethical and Moral Strength

that when dealing with issues of the darkness man must stay focused on the light? The light guides you through battles of life into a state of victory. Jesus is the light that directs his people. You have lost sight of Christ. Now that you are lying wounded on the battlefield, look to the hill which cometh your help. Knock means come to meet Christ at the door of your life. It takes an effort on your part to call on the Lord. When someone knocks at the door, you must make an effort to permit him of her to come into your house. For example, if you would turn and take a step toward Christ, He will meet you and give to you the gift of life.

- No weapon formed against a true believer shall prosper (Isaiah 53:17). No one or nothing can cause a believer to break the covenant of God. God is Almighty. There is no weapon that can penetrate the armor of God. A sinner is not clothed with the armor of God. He is vulnerable to the fiery dots of the devil.

Therefore, who are you? Are you an impostor? Are you a counterfeit or a deceiver? If so, God's eyes are like fire. He sees right through your cover. All your deeds are transparent to God. He knows you personally and you will not escape his judgment. Your armor is carnal and it's no match for God. Romans 8:37-39 "Nay, in all these things we are more than conquerors through him that loved us. For I am persuaded, that neither death, nor life, nor angels, nor principalities, nor powers, nor things present, nor things to come. Nor height, nor depth, nor any other creature, shall be able to separate us from the love of God, which is in Christ Jesus our Lord."

Who are you? Are you a child of God? If so, you should be aware that man does not earn the promises of God. They are gifts of his covenant. The promises are your inheritance. Claim Them! These promises ensure a victorious present life and a victorious eternal life. God knows that the flesh is weak. This is why he sent his only begotten son that he may live inside of your temple, whereby, providing strength beyond measure because greater is He that is in you, than he that is in the world. "For in him dwelleth all the fullness of the God head bodily. And ye are complete in him, which is the head of all principality and power." Colossians 2:9-10.

Death Of The First-Born Issued

Exodus 4:22-23 "And thou shalt say unto Pharaoh, Thus saith the Lord, Israel *is* my son, *even* my first-born: And I say unto thee, Let my son go, that he may serve me: and if thou refuse to let him go, behold, I will slay thy son, *even* thy first born."

When you accepted Christ (the seed of Abraham - through the line of David) as your Lord and Savior, you became of the first-born of God; you also became the seed of Abraham. Why? Because you have died and are now reborn in union with Christ. The incorruptible seed lives inside of you and you are adopted into the body of Christ. Believers have inherited all the promises made to Abraham through the faith they have in Christ Jesus. We have access to the power of Christ and victory as displayed in the covenant blessing through the washing of the Blood of Jesus.

God promised the believer (seeds of Abraham, and heir to the Kingdom of God) that they would endure and be victorious in the war against the Great Deceiver. He promised that believers would inherit eternal life and reign with Christ throughout eternity. It becomes more and more obvious that the heirs of Satan will inherit nothing but damnation. It is also apparent that the heirs of Satan are termed as Satan's first-born in verse 23. The Kingdom of Satan will fall unto the power of Christ, who has been positioned above all the creations in heaven, in the earth and under the earth. The unbeliever, the heirs of Satan, will only inherit the eternal lake of fire as the final result of God's judgment on sin.

It is especially clear that each detail of the existing battle between Moses and Pharaoh were truly in the hands of a higher power. Let's compare scripture I Samuel 17:47 "And all this assembly shall know that the Lord saveth not with sword and spear: for the battle is the Lord's and He will give you into our hands." We find that all things pattern themselves in such a way that God may display His magnificent power. Nothing in this world occurs apart from the will of God.

Know That You Are A Child Of God

Just as Jesus, the Son of God, was conceived in Mary's womb by the Holy Spirit the very life of Christ was conceived in you by the Holy Spirit!

According to the "good pleasure of His will," God sent forth the Spirit of His Son to dwell in your heart. God has birthed Christ's life in your spirit, which was once dead by reason of Adam's sin. Your spirit is alive, but it is not your life. It is a new life. It is Christ's life. "Therefore if any man be in Christ, he is a new creature: old things are passed away; behold, all things are become new." II Corinthians 5:17.

As a result of this new life within you, your old man is dead...you are dead to sin and alive to God. "Knowing this, that our old man is crucified with him, that the body of sin might be destroyed, that henceforth we should not serve sin"(Romans 6:6). With His blood Jesus has redeemed you, He has cleansed you of every sin. You are righteous in God's eyes. You belong to Christ. You no longer are bound by sin and the desires of the flesh. You are set free by the life that now lives in you.

The Father did not call you by His Spirit, cleanse you of your sins, and leave you on your own to live your life and serve Him as best you could. God has placed His life and the very life of the holy, all-powerful, eternal Son of God within you. And, just as Jesus lived His life on earth by the Father Who sent Him Who lived and dwelt in Him; you must live your life by Christ Who now lives and dwells in you.

Just as your physical body cannot live without food and nourishment, neither can your spirit live unless you "feed" it, drawing life and nourishment from Christ. There must be a continual dependence upon Christ, a continual drawing of strength, a continual "abiding" in Him and His Word. And, it is in this union in Him that His life will be lived in you.

Jesus lived His life on earth by the Father Who sent Him. He said, "And he that sent me is with me: the Father hath not left me alone..." John 8:29 "I am in the Father, and the Father in me" John 14:10. Jesus' words, His action, His works were all a result of the Father living in Him. He said, "The words that I speak unto you I speak not of myself: but the Father that dwelleth in me, he doeth the works." John 14:10. Because God has made you one of His sons or daughters, you are now able to live your life through Christ Who dwells in you. And because the Father dwells in Christ, He also dwells in you! Jesus said, "If a man love me, he will keep my words: and my Father will love him, and we will come unto him, and make our abode with him" (John 14:23).

When considering all things mentioned in this chapter, it is wise to say to the unbeliever and many professing Christians, "<u>It's time to come in for your Curfew</u>."

Chapter Twenty-Three
You Want The Body, Bruise The Head
Morals In Placing Christ Head Of Your Life.

And he is the head of the body, the church; He is the beginning and the firstborn from among the dead, so that in everything he might have the supremacy. Col 1:18

No battle or war is fought without a strategy. Even the enemy's techniques are well designed and plotted for the maximum affect of capturing souls. The enemy wars against the word of God by the use of false teaching, temptation, and deception in an effort to separate Christ from the lives of men and women. The enemy wars against the Son of God because He is the head of the body of Christ.

Why does Satan war against the head? Does he desire to position himself as head so that he can distort the thoughts of mankind and lead them into immorality? Ezekiel 28:15 reveals that Satan was once perfect. He was created perfect and his name was Lucifer. He was found perfect in the eyes of God until iniquity was found in him. Satan became proud of being beautiful and his wisdom caused his head to swell. "In this way the Adamic metaphor supplies a constellation of relationship very suggestive for what Ezekiel wishes to imply about Tyre's past and present situation and its coming fate." Isaiah 14:14 tells us that the iniquity found in Satan was the desire to ascend above the heights of the clouds.

He wanted to be like the Most High. Satan sought to be praised like God; he sought to be glorified. He wanted to be worshipped like God. Satan wants to be similar to God. He said like God, he did not say above or over GOD. He said above the stars of God, he knew that he could not ascend above God. Satan said he wanted to be similar to God. That is not possible - only God can be praised, only God has all power and knowledge and only God is worthy to be worshipped. The desire of evil exists within Satan because he seeks to be in control. He seeks to have dominion over all creations. Satan seeks to have authority over mankind. The evil one left his natural state of perfection by deciding to be disobedient to God's command. He was the first to choose not to give God the honor that belongs to

Him. Instead, his thoughts and deeds became immoral and darkness consumed his spirit. Because of his sin God gave Lucifer over to a reprobate mind, and to committing the ungodly things of his heart. The enemy says he is wise but he is foolish. He wars against God because of his reprobate state; a state of no return for him or the fallen angels.

When we review the fact that Satan seeks to control mankind, we must go back to the Garden of Eden. Satan deceived Adam and Eve. In so doing he gained control over the entire world. Sin was levied upon the heads of Adam and Eve. The defeat of the first Adam required God to place himself in a fleshly body so that a man would be raised victorious over sin and Satan. The Final Adam defeated Satan and reclaimed that which was originally man's. He entered into the strong man's house and then took all his possessions. Jesus has been given a name above all the creations, above all the earth and within the earth. He is the headship of all men. Every human being is to subject himself to God and every man is to submit to the word of God. They are to place God as the center of their life. They are to be led by Christ. Romans 13:1 says, "Let every soul be subject unto the higher powers. For there is no power but of God: the powers that be are ordained of God." The next text reveals that men are to respect the authority of people that have been placed as rulers over them, yet everyone gets their authority from God. Therefore, submit to God's Authority. Every man has the opportunity to become a member of Christ's body, but not all have taken the opportunity or advantage of salvation.

When we accept Christ as our personal Savior and believe on him, we are adopted into the body of Christ and we are given strength to live morally and ethically. Romans 12:5 says "So we, being many, are one body in Christ and everyone members one of another." Therefore, the enemy desires each person that has an opportunity to become adopted into the body of Christ and those who are presently of the body of Christ. Jesus died for mankind that they all may have an opportunity to live morally and ethically and that they all have the opportunity to renew a relationship with God, the Father.

How does Satan plan to gain control of the body?

According to the Gap Theory, a theory that suggests that the earth and the heavens were created perfect (Gen.1:1) but some thing drastic happened within time and space that caused a great disturbance in the existing peace and perfection (Gen.1:2), Satan attempted to gain control in the heavens and the earth. The result of his sinful conduct constituted his downfall and the destruction of the heavens and the earth. Presently, he seeks to gain control of mankind. His plan is to bruise the head. To bruise the head implies to destroy the unadulterated word of God, therefore imposing the elimination of Christ. Christ is the word and He is the head of all life. First Corinthians 11:3 states "I would have you to know that the head of man is Christ and the head of every women is the man and the head of Christ is God."

A believer must have confidence that the word can never be destroyed or severed from them because nothing can separate them from the love of God. Christ said that heaven and earth shall pass away but the word will always remain. He stated that He would neither leave the believer nor forsake them. God promised in Genesis, Chapter 3:15 "I will put enmity between thee and the woman, and between thy seed and her seed; it shall bruise thy head, and thou shalt bruise his heel." This scripture tells us that Satan's target is to bruise the word of God. He will not succeed. He will miss the mark. Instead, he will bruise Christ's heel. This statement was a reflection on the crucifixion. The attempt to kill Christ only promoted the awareness that no one can bruise the head of all creation. Christ stated that he laid down his own life and picked it up; no one has the authority to take his life. In the crucifixion, Christ laid down his life, he allowed himself to be bruised for you and He picked-up His life again. He now reigns at the right hand of God in heaven.

Satan seeks to destroy the word within the believers by weakening their prayer life, by weakening their relationship with God and by diluting the word with false conception. His tactics are designed to drive the weak believers into a state of immorality and apostasy. As for the unbeliever, Satan attempts to keep them from receiving the true word of God. He attempts to keep them from accepting the word of God as being true. He deceives them through false teachings. He deceives you through a liberal or modernized conceptual belief. Whereas, believers are targeted to abandon the word of God and unbelievers are targeted to refute the word of God. Both are targeted to follow immorality and their own lust.

Beat It Out Of Them

When two boxers compete, the goal is to win. We know that the primary target that ensures success in their goal is the head. If the athlete is successful in connecting a blow to the head, the body loses its strength. It loses its equilibrium. The mind or thoughts become distorted. Ultimately, the body falls because of the severity of the wound. Perhaps this illustration is a bit graphic, but it can be a reflection of all men and women's lives. Many have been wounded severely by the enemy. Christ no longer is the head of their life or the center of their life. How far do they think that they will travel before their lives become consumed by immoral morals and unethical thoughts and decisions? Unfortunately, many people think they can live without Christ as head of their life.

Similar to the head of the body, Christ is the head of believers. Obviously, none has the knowledge that He possesses. None have the power he possesses. He is man and woman's defense. None have greater insight of the future and none knows all things, like He does. He is victorious and only He can offer victory. Why would anyone refuse Him as his or her head or leader? Christ tells believers when to tarry and when to advance. He guides believers ensuring that they will be successful and that they will remain in the will of God.

No one should think they would be successful or prosper without Christ. If a man or a woman seeks only the riches and treasures of the heavens and earth they have failed in achieving the ultimate goal of man. If a person aspires only to live the good life, he or she has failed miserably. Without Christ no one can be prosperous because their thoughts will be distorted and they will fall because Christ is not at the head of their life. Without Christ, without his power, without his strength, without his knowledge, man and woman are lost. Just as the Israelites wandered in the desert for forty years, so will they wander in life because they will not have Christ as their guide? When He returns all they have acquired will perish in the presence of His glory and they would have enjoyed the riches of the present heavens and earth but will be denied the riches and treasures of the eternal enjoyment that is to come in the future heavens and earth.

Moral Application It is unique to clearly find that the evil the enemy's plans results in his demise. The enemy's theory is "If you want the Body (mankind and all creations), Bruise the Head (take Christ away from men, weaken his position of authority over their life)." He attempted to sit on high but fell to the lowest part of the heavens. Satan once again missed the mark. The heel was a temporary bruising of Christ. The crucifixion of our Lord and Savior was temporal because Christ in His infinite power rose from the dead and defeated death and sin. Christ will bruise Satan's head! Giving unto whomsoever believeth, the victory over sin and death. There is victory in the name of Jesus! There's only death and defeat associated with the enemy. Join the true body of Christ, and allow Christ to be the head of your life. He will lead you, guide you, and protect you.

Bruise Satan's head, become a part of the body of Christ. Choose Christ and commit yourself completely to His service.

I will put enmity between you and the woman, and between your offspring and hers; he will crush your head, and you will strike his heel." Gen 3:15

Chapter Twenty-Four
Take It To The Limit, And Don't Back Down
Moral Strength In Knowing Christ Is Ultimate

The 3rd Heaven   4th Domain -   3rd Dominion (God)

God's Throne, The Holy Place

Genesis 1:1

I Kings 8:30

Psalms 20:6

Isaiah 66:1, 14:14

II Corinthians 12:2

The second Heaven   3nd Domain - No Dominion

The Universe

Genesis 1:1

Genesis 1:15

II Peter 3:10

The 1st Heaven   2nd Domain – second Dominion (Satan & **Fallen Angels)**

The Atmosphere

Genesis 1:1

Genesis 1:8

Matthew 16:19

John 1:1

Ephesians 6:12

And The Earth   1st Domain – 1st Dominion (Mankind)

Earth

Genesis 1.1

Genesis 1:26

John 1:1

"And God made the firmament, and divided the waters which were under the firmament from the water which were above the firmament: and it was so. He called the firmament heaven." This process reveals to the readers the pre-existence of the first heaven. God bellowed the majestic words Let the waters under the heaven be gathered together unto one place, and let the dry land appear: and it was so. He called the dry land Earth. In so doing, God acknowledges that the earth was not created in this phase. It too previously existed. Again God speaks to say let there be light in the firmament of the heaven to divide day from the night. We are to interpret this as the solar space for it identifies the second heaven.

God has ordained that men view the first tabernacle as a prototype of His decree concerning the entire creation. The tabernacle serves as a model for the three realms of dominion and the three heavenly Kingdoms. The first tabernacle design was identical to the domains of creations. "The structure had compartments known as the Outer court, the Inner court, and the Holy of the holy place. In some cases the three chambers are referred to as the Outer court, the holy place and the most holy place (Exodus 26:33-34)." The similitude of the creation is that it consists of the earth and a first heaven, which is the atmosphere, a second heaven, which is outer space, the heavenly bodies or universes, and a third heaven which is the holy place, which is God's dwelling place (see Gen 1:1-18).

Certain laws that are termed as the law of dominion govern each domain. For example, though man has dominion over the earth, the law of physics is established within the earth. These laws that apply to the physical aspect of the earth have an impact on man's authority. However, within the first heaven, Satan is not bound by physics. His dominion circles the earth and is contained within the earth's atmosphere. Therefore, Satan has a higher dominion and a higher power than mankind. Paul once said that men battle not against flesh and blood but against principalities and rulers in higher places. Only a believer is excluded from Paul's confirmation. Why, because he or she is no longer of this world. The person has become a part of the third heaven, the Kingdom of God, and highest of all dominions.

When referring to the second heaven, God is not silent concerning its existence, yet He does not expose much information that addresses the second heaven's particulars. To men it remains a mystery. Dominion is not ascribed in the second heaven. Meaning it is evident that life does not exist within the massiveness of this universe. In light of this writer's various findings and reflecting on the term dominion that connotes forums of existing intelligent life, life is not referenced within the universe. For example: on earth, man has dominion in the atmosphere or in the first heaven fallen angels have dominion and in the Holy place or third heaven God has dominion over all creations.

Being that God has dominion over all realms and inhabitants, it is not contradictory, nor is it contrary to say the only life in the second heaven is God because His presence is everywhere; however, He gave dominion to the sun and the moon for the sole purpose of light to rule over the darkness of the earth and universe. No dominion is ascribed to a form of species. It is only granted to two elements. Thus, when applying the law of dominion, there is no account of alien life in the creation of the universe (second Heaven). It appears to be a neutral domain, whereby angels travel in route to deliver messages to man and to return to the third heaven. If illumination would be applied it becomes visible to us that this heaven serves as a type of barrier in that it separates the third heaven from the first heaven and the earth by a great distance. Though the previous statements are suggestive based on findings; what we do know about the second heaven is it will be destroyed along with the first heaven and earth (II Peter 3:10).

The Third Heaven is the throne of God. It truly is the most holy place. God sits in the highest of places and with an eagle's eye view He looks downward upon all the creation. There are no boundaries to his dominion. God controls all events of life. He has appointed a time and a season for all of life's affairs. He must allow every episode prior to their inceptions. God is sovereign. He created all things and has authority over His creation. Within the third heaven exists God the Father, God the Son, the Holy Spirit, and the heavenly host.

Take It To The Limit, And Don't Back Down pertains to issues regarding how believers choose Christ, yet the influence of the world causes many believers to lose hope and faith, or cause them to incorporate immorality with the true word of God. Worldly iniquity causes weak believers not to put on the complete armor of God. Many believers have attempted to worship God, but they have submitted to the immorality of man or Satan's temptation. Many Christians want to claim the glory of God and all of His righteousness, but they do not want to bear the cross that comes with the spiritual walk of upholding His principles and standard of life. I agree that when you accept Christ in your life, persecution can come through many overt forms. However, believers will endure and must endure the complete warfare of spiritual forces when they accept Christ completely and stand for Him. Do not back down, not one step. The enemy's attacks are attempts to destroy the relationship and the worship that believers have with Christ. Therefore, Take It To The Limit And Don't Back Down.

Each person in life wants to be successful. They strive to reach their greatest capabilities by developing the gifts of potential within them. They seek prosperity in their lives. Many desire to surpass all challenges or hindrances that stand before them in their efforts to succeed in their endeavors of life and they say nothing is going to stop them from reaching their goal. What about Christians? Why have many professing believers permitted oppression, persecution, and treasures of this world to weaken or defile their relationship with God? Their minds should be made up and they should say nothing could stop them or hinder their relationship with God. In Romans 8:37-39 "Nay, in all these things we are more than conquerors through him that loved us. For I am persuaded, that neither death, nor life, nor angels, nor principalities, nor powers, nor things present, nor things to come, nor height, nor depth, nor any other creature, shall be able to separate us from the love of God, which is in Christ Jesus our Lord".

Carl L. Sweat, Jr., D. Min.

The Sky Is The Limit

There is a saying that the sky is the limit. Regrettably, the sky is not the limit. There is a dominion beyond the sky, beyond the universe, and that dominion or realm is where God the Father abides. He sits in the highest of all positions. His authority transcends all imagination and all creations. His position and name is known as Jehovah the God of the Most High. His son is Jesus Christ. Theologians and believers refer to this realm as the third heaven. The third heaven represents that which is eternal, that which is true, that which is all knowing, that which is victorious and all powerful. It is an area that sin cannot enter. The Kingdom of God is perfect and divine. It is holy and righteous. In this dominion, God the Father, God the Son, God the Holy Spirit and all heavenly host abide. God has the highest dominion and authority over all things. I do not desire that you remain ignorant, "for Christ ascended above all principalities, powers, might, dominion and every name that is named, not only in this world, but also in that which is to come. God has put all things under Christ's feet. God has appointed Him head over all things to the church, which is His body, the fullness of Him that filleth all in all." Ephesians 1:21

If a person has accepted a cliché similar to reaching for the sky, then they have been deceived and have settled for less. The sky is not the limit! Jesus Christ is ultimate! He is the source of life and all creations. Through Christ Jesus all things are possible. There is nothing He cannot do. When a person takes it to the limit, they accept Jesus Christ as their personal Savior and they except Him as the Son of God. To know that He is coming back again to raise believers from the grave and give them eternal life or change them in the twinkling of an eye, is to also know that they will be caught up and be with Him in the great Kingdom, I Thessalonians 4:17. Do not conform yourselves to the standards of this world, but let God transform you inwardly by completely renewing your mind. With a renewed mind, a man and woman can begin to see that which is spiritual. They will also begin to understand the will of God. They will know what is good, what is pleasing to Him and what is perfect in His sight.

If any person would like to achieve true and gratifying success in life they need to offer themselves as a living sacrifice holy and acceptable to God, become dedicated to His service and be found pleasing to Him, Romans 12:1-2. This is the true worship that everyone should offer Jehovah the Creator.

The commonly used term "The sky is the limit" is a phrase that represents men and women who seek earthly treasures or things that are temporal. They aspire for things that gratify individuals only for the present moment. They fail to realize that the earth and the heavens are destined to pass away and will exist no more. Yet, the heavens and earth will be made a-new and only those that made Christ the ultimate in life will be able to abide with Christ in Paradise forever.

How do we know that the sky is not the limit? We know from the scripture given in Isaiah 14:14 that Lucifer had set his heart to ascending above the heights of the clouds. He desired to exalt his throne above the stars of God. Lucifer desired to climb to the highest of heights of the heavens. His sinful nature caused him to be judged by God, resulting in him being cast out of heaven. He was cut down to the ground. Lucifer is now known as Satan, the prince of the power of the air, the spirit that works in the children of immorality and disobedience.

Why A Person Chooses Christ

When a person chooses Christ, the enemy and his dominion no longer has authority over him or her because the individual has become a part of the third heaven. Believers no longer live under the laws of the second heaven's dominion. Now, the laws of the third heaven bind them. Physically they are a part of the earth and its atmosphere; yet, because their relationship has been re-established with God they have become aware of morality and all things associated with God's kingdom. A born again believer's mind becomes fixed on heavenly things. The Kingdom of God lives within believers. How can they know this to be true? Because the word of God governs their lives, believers communicate with the Father through the Son, and believers are given power to war against the enemy and minister the word of God. Believers are also given the same victory that

Christ has over death and sin. There is so much more added unto the believers when they become a part of the third heaven.

Previously mentioned the prince of the air has dominion over the earth and the first heaven. His authority and position is below that of God's. He abides in a lower realm because he was removed from heaven. The judgment the tempter received, including the multitude of angels that joined him in becoming disobedient, was a penalty of death and exile. All were cast down to a lower realm known as the first heaven. Luke. 10:18b. Christ said, "I beheld Satan as lightning fall from heaven." Also, Paul confirms the first heaven in his writing to the Ephesians when he writes, "For believers wrestle not against flesh and blood but against principalities, against powers, against rulers, of the darkness of this world, against spiritual wickedness in high places." High places refer to the first heaven, the second dominion, which is above the earth. Since the fall of Adam and Eve, Satan, through the power of sin has had authority over man and influenced the moral integrity of the land.

People must know that before the evil one can do anything against anyone, he brings forth an accusation or accuses the individual before God. He can no longer enter into the third heaven, but he can submit accusations and other types of indictments concerning humans on earth. God reviews these accusations or incriminating accounts. In so doing, God allows trials or certain tribulations to come upon people, especially for believers to prove their obedience and love. In Job, Chapter 1:8 it states "And the LORD said unto Satan, Hast thou considered my servant Job, that there is none like him in the earth, a perfect and an upright man, one that feareth God, and escheweth evil?" Tam (tawn), the Hebrew word for moral and upright in all aspects of man or according to the level of knowledge granted unto him should not be confused with the Greek term agathos (ag-ath-os) which means perfect in all things, for only God possesses such perfection. Whatever He allows is to benefit the individual in an effort to strengthen their relationship with Him. In reality people must take heed in knowing God allows judgment or trials to be administered for the sin persons willfully commit.

There are things that God protects, the believer and at times the unbeliever from when the accuser presents an accusation before Him. They need this protection because without it man would surely perish. Without it no one could stand against the evil one, his accomplishment and their accusations. No man or woman could withstand the power and dominion that the second dominion has over the earth and mankind. Why, because the dominion of the earth is lower than the dominion of the first heaven. Most men and women believe that their will can overcome spiritual warfare, but the facts are neither positive thinking nor motivational thought that can triumph over the authority or dominion the enemy has over mankind. To prevail in spiritual warfare, men and women must have Christ indwelling within them. For John 4:4 says, "Greater is He who is in you than he that is in the world."

What or who persuades a person to believe they can live without Christ and be victorious? What would make anyone believe that there is an authority more sufficient or as adequate as God the Father, God the Son, and God the Holy Spirit? What would make any man or woman believe that he or she can governor his or her life?

Though this chapter suggests that Christ is the limit and implies that Christ is the highest authorities; in no way does it promote ambivalence when it declares that there are no limits when people choose Christ. All things are possible when they believe on the name of Jesus. They have taken it to the limit when they accept Christ. Yes, He does make ways out of no way and He opens doors that were once closed. However, with freedom comes responsibility and accountability. And liberty does not warrant the right to live a life without limitations or restrictions. Christ has not delivered man and woman from the power of sin that they may live life without boundaries.

No Turning Back

God has equipped believers with everything they need to be victorious, to prosper even in this life. In this morally and ethically declining world, men and women must make the decision to remain faithful to God at all cost. The believer should never back down from his or her position of moral integrity and godliness. The believer should not back down even if it means to keep the peace. Christians have tolerated far too much sin. If it means his own death, he should not back down. If it means to be persecuted or to have people scandalize your name, you should never back down. Christ calls men and women to take a stand against social norms, to stir things up and ruffle some feathers. He said in the last days families will be divided, "Father against son and son against father, mother against daughter and daughter against mother, mother-in-law against daughter-in-law and daughter-in-law against mother-in-law." Luke 12:53

First Priority

Never back down. The kingdom of God should be everyone's first priority. Jesus said, "Seek ye, the kingdom of God and his righteousness, and all these things will be added unto you." Matthew 6:33. Too often, not only believers but also non-believers compromise their position.

Why Should We Not Back Down

Believers should not back down because they represent the highest authority in existence and He has given them the true means for becoming victorious. Christians are tasked with evangelizing the world and they must prevail in the ministry of spreading the Good News. Evangelism is not a matter of conscience, courage, and trust in God. It's a matter of obedience to the Great Commission. No one has to give a Christian permission nor can someone deny a Christian permission to witness to others. Believers must actively engage in the mission of witnessing.

Always remember, the heat of the battle is no place to start praying. We should have already prayed through before a situation or crisis occurs in our life. We should be filled with the Holy Spirit and ready for battle. Prayer allows the Holy Spirit to move in you, and fill you with a special anointing that over flows you with dunamis power. At the very moment that you receive this power, you should know that the battle is already yours for the taking. For God would

A Cry for Ethical and Moral Strength

have revealed to our spirit man in our relationship with him that he has given us victory. Within any spiritual conflict, we must confront Satan knowing that we have been called of God. We must also know that the battle is not ours, it is the Lords and He will deliver victory into our hands (I Samuel 17:47).

Moral Application: Believers are required to demonstrate the power that Jesus reveals when He defeated the enemy and destroyed the works of sin, sickness and death. He finished the works He had been sent to do. Let every man and woman finish the work that God has ordained for every believer to accomplish. God did not place men and women here on this earth simply because they are to praise Him, glorify His name and lift Him up. No, they have come forth of God to be victorious in the works He has pre-ordained for them. He has created each person complete and it is only through the leading of the Holy Spirit, through devoted prayer and fasting that you emerge victorious. Know that you have been called, appointed, and anointed. Stand on the fact that God has given believers the Helper to ensure the believer is victorious in all things. When believers hold to God's promised and complete word, nothing can cause them to back down. Take It To The Limit And Don't Back Down.

Chapter Twenty-Five
After All Is Said And Done, "The Shocker"
Moral Strength In Christian Accountability

> For we must all appear before the judgment seat of Christ, that each one may receive what is due him for the things done while in the body, whether good or bad. 2Cor 5:10

Many people of today believe and numerous doctrines teach that if the tempter were removed from this world the world would exist in complete utopia. That man would not sin because there would be no evil spirit of temptation. Therefore, there would be no sin. The same doctrines often teach that the world would become a paradise without the presence of the tempter, because man could rebuild and there would be no more war or crime. Many suggest that the earth would be placed in its original state and man could live forever because he would live in the perfect environment. Man would adhere to the will of God, and he would walk in perfection. Contrary to popular beliefs, this type of teaching sounds great but is not worth the paper it is printed on. It must be associated with all doctrines that have diverted from the true word of God. If any man has accepted any teaching that suggest without Satan's tempting of mankind this world and humanity could live in harmony and in peace and that they could live moral and ethical lives. Obviously, some men and women do not understand the meaning of salvation. They do not understand the true meaning of redemption. They can't understand the true purpose for the rapture nor have they comprehended the purpose for the judgment of God.

After It's All Said And Done

Christ said in his word that this world will come to past. Within II Peter 3:10-12, Peter said the Lord would come like a thief. On that day the heavens will disappear with a shrill noise, the heavenly bodies will burn up and be destroyed and the earth with everything in it will vanish. Knowing that the world will be destroyed by fire, what kind of person should you be? You should be a man of holiness, righteousness and dedicated to the service of God. You should be a believer of the complete word of God. Not accepting false teaching, not co-mingling teachings that are not consistent with the word of God and not trusting in your personal belief.

Though Peter was referring to the final destruction, men and women should be cognizant that a time of paradise will originate after a great battle. The battle of Armageddon where Satan will be defeated, bound and placed in a bottomless pit for 1000 years, Revelation 20:1, 2. Isaiah 66 has much to say about a world without sin and an environment without the tempter. That world is the restored earth; whereby, the tempter exists no more within its scope. He is bound for one thousand years prior to the destruction of the earth and the heaven. This period is termed the millennium. The scripture tells us, beginning at verse 1 of Chapter 20, an angel came down from heaven, having the keys of the bottomless pit and a great chain in his hand. He laid hold on the dragon, that old serpent which is the devil and Satan and bound him a thousand years, and cast him into the bottomless pit, and shut him up and set a sill upon him, that he should deceive the nations no more, till the thousand years come to past. The tempter will be bound and placed in a pit to prohibit him from deceiving the nation. He will no longer be able to tempt man or any creation of God's for one thousand years (a millennium).

The Shocker

Concerning man's conduct within paradise in the book of Isaiah located in Chapter 65:17, God said the behavior of man would be as such; there will be no weeping in the new paradise. The conduct of man will be proceedings of joy. Men and women will be having babies. There will be no death of infants. Men will build their own homes and enjoy their labor. No one else will enjoy the things that another man has labored for in his life. Men will live long lives such as that of the life of trees. Their children will not meet with disaster. Even when they pray, before they have finished praying God will have answered their prayers. The shocker is that during the era of utopia there is no tempter that men and women can blame for their sin. How shocking to discover that mankind is responsible for all of their sins. The shocker is discovering that each person is tempted by his or her own evil desires. He or she is dragged away from God and enticed by their personal lust. Unfortunately, after their desire is conceived it gives birth to sin. Don't be deceived; no temptation has seized anyone except what is common to the heart of mankind.

The Devil Didn't Make You Do It

"For, behold I create new heavens and a new earth: and the former shall not be remembered nor come into mind. But be ye glad and rejoice forever *in that* which create: for, behold I create Jerusalem a rejoicing, and her people a joy. And I will rejoice in Jerusalem, and joy in my people: and the voice of weeping shall be no more heard in her, nor the voice of crying. There shall be no more thence an infant of days, nor an old man that hath not filled his days: for the child shall die a hundred years old; but the sinner *being* a hundred years old shall be accursed. And they shall build houses, and inhabit *them*; and they shall plant vineyards, and eat the fruit of them. They shall not build, and another inhabit; they shall not plant, and another eat: for as the days of a tree *are* the days of my people, and mine elect shall long enjoy the work of their hands. They shall not labour in vain, nor bring forth for trouble; for they *are* the seed of the blessed of the LORD, and their offspring with them.

And it shall come to pass, that before they call, I will answer; and while they are yet speaking, I will hear. The wolf and the lamb shall feed together, and the lion shall eat straw like the bullock: and dust *shall be* the serpent's meat. They shall not hurt nor destroy in all my holy mountain, saith the LORD." Isaiah 65:17-25

Despite all of Gods efforts to provide mankind a way out from any level of sin and regardless of the perfect environment that He provided during the dispensation of the millennium, when we view the latter portion of Isaiah's writing, it is determined that death and sin remains among people that do not believe or accept Christ as their personal savior and among people living outside of the New Jerusalem, the true worship of God. It becomes clearer to the reader that theorist and philosophers are incorrect in their hypothesis because the findings reveal that even in a utopian environment man and woman are prone to sin if they have not placed Christ as head of their life. The shocker is knowing, even during the absence of the tempter in the lives of mankind, men and women will continue to sin because of the sinful nature of Adam and the power that the flesh has over them that have not accepted Christ.

The shocker is that the Devil cannot be blamed for anyone's sins. He and the fallen angels will be judged for their efforts to tempt mankind to sin. But because God does not permit mankind to be tempted above what they can handle and because He provides a way out of sin, each person is held accountable for all their actions whether they are good or bad. It is mankind's response to temptation that stands in judgment. The blame is not solely centered on the tempter. These findings may come as a shock; yet, God has openly revealed to the believer that salvation is essential, redemption is a necessity, repentance is a beginning and the blood of Jesus is the only thing that can wash away sin.

Carl L. Sweat, Jr., D. Min.

Chapter Twenty-Six
A Cry For Ethical And Moral Fortitude
Moral Strengthening In Patience

Habakkuk's Burden

"The burden which Habakkuk the prophet did see. O LORD, how long shall I cry, and thou wilt not hear! Even cry out unto thee of violence, and thou wilt not save! Why dost thou show me iniquity, and cause me to behold grievance? For spoiling and violence *are* before me: and there are those that raise-up strife and contention. Therefore the law is slacked, and judgment doth never go forth: for the wicked doth compass about the righteous; therefore wrong judgment proceedeth." Habakkuk 1:1-4

In a profound way Habakkuk reveals an answer from God concerning why He has not judged the diabolical corruption and immorality of mankind. Habakkuk was a prophet of the seventh century B.C. He lived during a period when the Babylonians ruled the nations. He was deeply disturbed by the violence that was originated by the cruel Babylonians against the righteous people and the immoral influence they had on the existing culture of Israel. The prophet complained to God. He questioned God, "Why are you silent?" He also asked, "How can you tolerate immoral people and evil doers?" Habakkuk inadvertently appealed to God for justice to be served. He desired God to keep his promise. The promise is God will judge the unjust and find them guilty of their sins. They will be sentenced to an eternal state of torment, Revelation 20:12-14.

Like many today, Habakkuk's complaints were conveyed directly to God. He asked how long does he have to cry out against violence and immorality before God would come to moral and ethical men and women's rescue. He approached God by inquiring how long would it be before He would save His people from all measure of trouble, wickedness, ungodliness, wrong doing and destruction that existed. Habakkuk wanted to know why must people of good moral and ethical character endure the harshness of witnessing a great decline in the moral state of society and why must they contend with the injustices of society? To the prophet, the law of the land appeared to be weak. The leaders that were selected to administer justice were not upholding the standard of the law and were not protecting the needy. Justice was not extended to the righteous. Evil men that followed immoral practices got the best of the God fearing people and those that attempted to live moral lives.

Though Habakkuk's words were of the past, they truly are applicable to men and women's lives today. When we look around the world by way of television, computers, various articles, books, and radios, we can agree that the world is filled with strife, war, contention, and destruction. Nothing has changed concerning injustice and oppression. Every manner of evil and immorality has rooted itself, taken hold, and flourished in this world.

God's Answer To Habakkuk Concerning Why He Has Not Judged

"And the LORD answered me, and said, Write the vision, and make it plain upon tables, that he may run that readeth it. For the vision *is* yet for an appointed time, but at the end it shall speak, and not lie: though it tarry, wait for it; because it will surely come, it will not tarry. Behold his soul *which* is lifted up is not upright in him: but the just shall live by his faith." Habakkuk 2:2-4

Believers are in need of crying out to God against immorality such as Habakkuk did when he approached God directly with his grievances. Similar to the widow in the parable of Luke 18:2, who took her grievance to the judge and requested he avenge her of her adversary Like Habakkuk, believers are to take their concerns and petitions to the highest judge and ask for justice to be served. His concerns prompted a response from God and believers' cries will also move the heart of God.

In response to the cry for justice and morality, God said write down the words He was about to reveal to him, make the writing plain and in large print so that people can read the good news at a glance. I want My words in writing because I know that placing them in writing affirms to the believer that whatsoever is written will be performed, will be a legal document, and is binding. Also, the written word holds individuals accountable. God wanted His promises to be conveyed plainly and communicated clearly. Even today He wants the believers to present His promises so effectively that a busy man or a man caught up in the hustle and bustle of this world can see God and hear what He has to say against immorality and injustice.

It's Not Time

God tells Habakkuk that it is not the appointed time for him to judge unjust men (Psalm 79:11). There is an appointed time for all things to take place. No act or event can occur without being filtered through the infinite wisdom of God. He knows and controls the time and season for the affairs of this world. Though it is not the time to judge unrighteousness or immorality, that day is coming very soon. It seems to be distant, but wait on it because in the end you will find God's word does come true (Hab.2:3).

Moral Application: The name Habakkuk is originally derived from the Hebrew language. It means to embrace. The prophet was known as "The Embracer", either for his love for God or because he wrestled with God. Each believer is to be known as "The Embracer". They are to be perceived as embracers because they are to cling to the word of God and embrace the promises of God with a grip that cannot be broken. The believer is to cherish the word of God, defend all of its principles and precepts, protect it and exult it above all things. They are to take a firm stand for godliness and cry out for morality. They are to never grow weary in well doing. Knowing that Christ's return is imminent, believers are to tarry in faith with anticipation that Christ's return could be immediate.

The day of the Lord has its own appointed time and the world grows closer to the moment when the trumpet will sound, Christ will pour out His wrath upon the earth in response to the many cries of the saints. When Christ returns He will initiate judgment upon the world. Therefore, plead with your neighbor, plead to him or her because he or she is not God's child; neither is God his or her Father. Plead to people to put away their immoral thoughts and deeds. Hosea 2:2

Chapter Twenty-Seven
War Waged Against Morality
Moral Strength In Knowing Truth Is Absolute

We know that the law is spiritual; but I am unspiritual, sold as a slave to sin. I do not understand what I do. For what I want to do I do not do, but what I hate I do. And if I do what I do not want to do, I agree that the law is good. As it is, it is no longer I myself who do it, but it is sin living in me. I know that nothing good lives in me, that is, in my sinful nature. For I have the desire to do what is good, but I cannot carry it out. For what I do is not the good I want to do; no, the evil I do not want to do-- this I keep on doing. Now if I do what I do not want to do, it is no longer I who do it, but it is sin living in me that does it. So I find this law at work: When I want to do good, evil is right there with me. For in my inner being I delight in God's law; but I see another law at work in the members of my body, waging war against the law of my mind and making me a prisoner of the law of sin at work within my members. What a wretched man I am! Who will rescue me from this body of death? Thanks be to God-- through Jesus Christ our Lord! So then, I myself in my mind am a slave to God's law, but in the sinful nature a slave to the law of sin. Rom 7:14-25

Deep within our humanness a great struggle exist. From the day of each individual's birth he or she is born into a pre-existing war with battles fought on all fronts. The war is known as the "War Against Morality." It is said that man and woman is born in sin and shaped in iniquity. Though mankind has a sinful nature, and the world's system teaches people to be benefactors and not givers, deceivers and not trustworthy, self orientated and not utilitarian, professional and not personal, one cannot negate the fact that an innate element causes men and women to seek morality and godliness. Despite the impediments of a fleshly nature and a world system, people strive to be godlike. Regardless of the struggle within and without each person, within this post-modern world prominent questions permeate the consciousness of humanity. Those questions are, "What is morality? Who draws the line between good and bad or wrong and right? Is there absolute truth? Where can we discover truth and upon what foundation is it established? How can a person gain moral strength?"

In the most logical sense the primary problem with understanding morality rests on the concept that an individual places upon the term "perfection". Humans are non-perfect beings. Yet, they are commanded by the Creator to strive to be perfect because He is perfect. With regret I submit that many perceive this calling to be a commandment for all humanity to live a faultless or errorless style of life. However, if that was the full intent or application of the term perfect, in the Creator's interpretation, then no man or woman could reasonably imagine that such a standard of life could be achieved.

Therefore, men and women are to view their life not so much through the eyes of perfection but more so through the intent of the term's implication and application. Mankind is sanctioned by the Creator to live a moral and ethical life. In doing so, with God's help, their life will be viewed as virtuous and godlike. Only then can perfection be accounted unto them. Perfection is not measured by the comparison of privations of an individual. No! The formula for perfection equates to God's provisions, grace and mercy, and man's submission to allow Him to become that innate element that strengthens him or her to fight in the war that has been waged against morality, godliness, and against perfection.

Dismantling Truth With Relativism

"I have much more to say to you, more than you can now bear. But when he, the Spirit of truth, comes, he will guide you into all truth. He will not speak on his own; John 16:12-13

In the war on morality one of the greatest fronts is a cooperative effort toward the dismantlement of Absolute Truth. For the most part, the enemy no longer engages in a direct assault on God (Truth). He has recently initiated a more subtle attack designed to undergird the very fiber and foundation of Christianity. His method is formulated to cause individuals to question the reality of absolute truth by advocating that all truth is relative.

I do not argue that truth is not relative. Truth must relate to the object or thing that a person(s) are identifying; however, I strongly advocate that there is a phenomenal truth that is absolute and can only become relevant to people at the certain level of revelation as it is granted unto each individual. Jesus said He is the Truth and if mankind would wholly accept Him we would begin to gain the awareness that there exists a truth that is absolute. A truth that is infallible, all knowing, and inclusive of all factors of the present, past and the future because He is a God that is, was and always will be. A truth that is ever present and everlasting. A truth that will judge the universe concerning the evil one and the angels that rebelled against God. A truth that will judge nationally. Identical to the nations destroyed by the flood during the days of Noah, the present world will reach a similar climax of immorality and be judged by the Word of God, a truth that will judge locally such as it judged the cities of Sodom and Gomorrah; and a truth that will judge individually for each individual will stand before God and give a personal account for all things committed in or out of his or her body.

Undoubtedly, Absolute Truth exists and can only be found through Christ. Christ was the word of God incarnated in the flesh. Christ not only knew all things, he understood all things. To deny Him is to deny that there is a greater level of knowledge and power. To deny Him is to presuppose that truth is relevant and is not given by the Spirit of God but is gained through methods of an empirical process. However, God said He gives all men and women knowledge that He, Absolute Truth, exists. Yet, many dispute the truth and wage war against it by committing immoral acts and falsely testifying against the word of God. Romans 1:18-2:2 confirms that many have refuted absolute truth by denying God.

"The wrath of God is being revealed from heaven against all the godlessness and wickedness of men who suppress the *truth* by their wickedness, since what may be known about God is plain to them, because God has made it plain to them. For since the creation of the world God's invisible qualities-- his eternal power and divine nature-- have been clearly seen, being understood from what has been made, so that men are without excuse. For although they knew God, they neither glorified him as God nor gave thanks to him, but their thinking became futile and their foolish hearts were darkened. Although they claimed to be wise, they became fools and exchanged the glory of the immortal God for images made to look like mortal man, birds, animals and reptiles. Therefore God gave them over in the sinful desires of their hearts to sexual impurity for the degrading of their bodies with one another. They exchanged the *truth* of God for a lie and worshiped and served created things rather than the Creator-- who is forever praised. Amen. Because of this, God gave them over to shameful lusts. Even their women exchanged natural relations for unnatural ones. In the same way the men also abandoned natural relations with women and were inflamed with lust for one another. Men committed indecent acts with other men, and received in themselves the due penalty for their perversion. Furthermore, since they did not think it worthwhile to retain the knowledge of God, he gave them over to a depraved mind, to do what ought not to be done. They have become filled with every kind of wickedness, evil, greed and depravity. They are full of envy, murder, strife, deceit and malice. They are gossips, slanderers, God-haters, insolent, arrogant and boastful; they invent ways of doing evil; they disobey their parents; they are senseless, faithless, heartless, and ruthless. Although they know God's righteous decree that those who do such things deserve death, they not only continue to do these very things but also approve of those who practice them. You, therefore, have no excuse, you who pass judgment on someone else, for at whatever points you judge the other, you are condemning yourself, because you who pass judgment do the same things. Now we know that God's judgment against those who do such things is based on *truth*."

A majority of men and women exchange the absolute truth that was given them from the creator for relative truth. A truth that is individualized and true only for their personal gain, a truth that is an adoption of ethical egoism, and a truth that has no foundation. Its basis is teleological. Relevant truth is not bound by precepts or rules. It is a truth that is customized or tailored for personal gratification and edification. It is a truth that is arrogant in nature and devised for self-will. These persons have waged war on God by contesting absolute truth, and they debate absolute truth through philosophical means such as Atheism, Deism and Pantheism.

Absolute Truth

Teach me your way, O LORD, and I will walk in your truth; give me an undivided heart, that I may fear your name. Ps 86:11

A Cry for Ethical and Moral Strength

Concerning absolute truth, mankind must be willing to accept that God is infinite in all things but they are finite in all aspects, especially in intellect and power. To search for and discover absolute truth, humans must be willing to embrace that God created the heavens and the earth. He has an interest in His creation's well being and has devised a complexly designed plan for the victory of all believers and for the demise of those that refuse to believe. This belief is called Theism.

There is no excuse for any man or woman to say that truth is not absolute because the Creator has made it plain to everyone. Though we are given an awareness of absolute truth, no human is expected or required to fully comprehend it for there are some things that mankind does not know nor will they ever understand until Christ reveals them to us at the appointed time or when He returns. However, people are commanded to walk by the measure of light given unto them. Perhaps such a statement means that the portion or level of absolute truth given to each individual by God and made relevant to him or her only through His enlightenment and revelation for application in each of their lives becomes the apportionment that God judges him or her. The measure of the word given and revealed to a person determines the measure of responsibility and accountability.

Therefore, truth is given by the individual's measure of faith because if a person is given knowledge and fails to apply it in their Christian journey or life they are held accountable. When much is given, in return, the giver requires much of the recipient. Undeniably, responsibility and accountability accompanies the gift of knowledge. Can a person then be thankful that absolute truth is given by process and not all at once? There is such a thing as being overwhelmed and a great possibility that if an infinite God revealed all factors of His complete plan to a finite people we all would fall prostrate in awe. This particular truth was revealed in the chapter titled "Biting Off More Than You Can Chew." The principle of moral decision-making addressed in the previous chapter demonstrates that often men and women are not mature or equipped enough to properly manage certain truths or the knowledge of God. This is why God did not give all the land to Israel at one time. They could not handle all of it at once. They had to receive the land little by little. If God had given them everything at once the land would have become desolate and the wild beast would have overtaken them.

> But I will not drive them out in a single year, because the land would become desolate and the wild animals too numerous for you. Little by little I will drive them out before you, until you have increased enough to take possession of the land. Exodus 23:29-30

The same principle must be applied to absolute truth. The implications of it, accountability and responsibility can cause many to become desolate and take over by the bestiality of life. This God is giving mankind absolute truth little by little.

Ultimately, faith is singled-out as a vital substance needed for the receiving and growing abundance of absolute truth. Growth or an increase in understanding of truth involves a deepening in the faith of God for if an individual loves God, he or she would be obedient to His word. When people of faith and communities of faith share in love, witnessing, and forgiveness, men and women are increased in their faith; thus, they enhance their understanding of absolute truth and live according to their commitment to do God's will.

The Holy Spirit Is An Active Agent

The Holy Spirit is the active agent in assisting mankind in growing in faith and understanding of the absolute truth (God). The Holy Spirit helps us to understand all things. Christ stated that He would send the Comforter, the spirit of the Father (absolute truth), and He would teach us all things. He will even bring into our remembrance the absolute truth that was taught us. As believers are being led by the Spirit of God they are being increased in becoming more like Him. They are encouraged and they possess a great hope that is imbedded in the Son's promise that when He returns they shall be like Him. The process that started at their rebirth will one day be complete and like the angels, believers will know Christ, the absolute truth, as they are known by Him. But for now, let all men acknowledge that absolutism precedes us and like Paul let mankind unify in agreement, "That we know in part and we prophesy in part, but when perfection comes, the imperfect disappears. When I was a child, I talked like a child, I thought like a child, I reasoned like a child. When I became a man, I put childish ways behind me. Now we see but a poor reflection as in a mirror; then we shall see face to face. Now I know in part; then I shall know fully, even as I am fully known." 1 Cor 13:9-12

Moral Application: Men and women are finite creatures that aspire to possess an infinite level of knowledge. Yet, absolute truth escapes their comprehension, but not their awareness. In the war against morality, individuals rarely blatantly attack God. However, they have organized covert operations whereby they advocate that truth is totally relevant and not absolute. These unbelievers fail to recognize that God is larger than man's apprehension; and that truth has a foundation and central point by which all things can be measured. Though humanity can only conceive reality in part and not in its entirety, they are on a journey and are engaged in a process designed for the understanding of absolute truth as they grow in faith. For those that deny Absolute Truth (God) or surrender their faith for a multitude of unacceptable reasons, the truth that they refuse to acknowledge and live by will serve as their judge. For if anyone claims to be without sin, they deceive themselves and the absolute truth is not in him or her. But if anyone confesses their sins, God is faithful and just and will forgive him or her of their sins and purify individuals from all immorality. I John 1:8-9

Undoubtedly, God has given revelation to all men and women concerning His existence and He has made clear through His creation that certain behaviors are moral or immoral. If this is true then let no man be as an infant, tossed back and forth and blown here and there by every wind of false teaching and by the cunning and craftiness of men in their deceitful scheming Eph 4:14. Know that there is an absolute truth and that truth is God. Similar to the perfect law given in ages past that could not be lived out of the fleshly body of mankind, I submit that the perfect, absolute truth, or word of God that lives within believers is not only impossible to be totally comprehend but also it is impractical to believe that anyone can live it completely out of their earthly flesh. The reason mankind cannot completely conform to the absolute truth is because of the war that is waged against them daily. This is why mankind requires the grace of God.

The Objective Of Relative Truth.

If it is true that mankind uses only ten percent of their brain, what then is the objective of the philosophy "Relative Truth." Obviously it is no more than a clandestine assault on God and the Christian Faith. Covertly, it aims to lower the standard of God's word that man can exalt himself to a level that he cannot reach or obtain without the aid of God. Contrary to popular belief, if mankind could exercise the full capacity of the brain, no one would refute that absolute truth would continue to evade his or her intellect. Thus, Relativism only serves those that have given-up the search to know and become more like God. To abandon the search of absolute truth is to relinquish God as truth and discard Him as the center of all things because all things find their beginning, existence and end in Him. The attributes of God fulfill the definition of Absolute truth, especially pertaining to a central foundation or fixed point used to measure all things.

This chapter started with a statement from the apostle Paul; therefore, we shall conclude with a thought from one of the great intellectualist and spiritual leaders of all time. Concerning the war against morality and absolute truth Paul encourages believers with the following words:

For the time will come when men will not put up with sound doctrine. Instead, to suit their own desires, they will gather around them a great number of teachers to say what their itching ears want to hear. They will turn their ears away from the truth and turn aside to myths. But you, keep your head in all situations, endure hardship, do the work of an evangelist, discharge all the duties of your ministry. For I am already being poured out like a drink offering, and the time has come for my departure. I have fought the good fight, I have finished the race, I have kept the faith. Now there is in store for me the crown of righteousness, which the Lord, the righteous Judge, will award to me on that day-- and not only to me, but also to all who have longed for his appearing. 2 Tim 4:3-8

A Cry for Ethical and Moral Strength

SECTION III

Diverse Teachings On Sexuality And Homosexuality

Rev. Paul H. Sherry: Former President of the United Church of Christ
David Runnion-Bareford: Executive Director of the Bible Witness Fellowship
Dr. Carlton Upton: Sr. Pastor of Tabernacle Christian Church

Carl L. Sweat, Jr., D. Min.

Chapter One
Now, No Condemnation

The Rev. Paul H. Sherry: Former President United Church of Christ

November 1998

A Pastoral Letter To The United Church Of Christ

The Rights Of Gay, Lesbian, And Bisexual Persons In Society And Their Membership And Ministry In the Church

"There is therefore now no condemnation for those who are in Christ Jesus." (Romans 8:1)

In recent months we have witnessed the continuance of hate crimes against gay, lesbian, and bisexual persons, while in the church discussion about their civil rights and the appropriateness of their membership and ministry in the life of the church has intensified. Several denominations in the United States, as well as some churches and bishops around the world, have adopted or reaffirmed policies that exclude gay, lesbian, and bisexual persons from sharing fully in the ministry of the church. Other Christian leaders have harshly suggested that gay, lesbian, and bisexual persons have no place at all in the life of the church and that their human rights do not deserve the full measure of legal protection. In addition, some political leaders, usually claiming religious support, have vigorously opposed efforts to secure these very rights. Sometimes these anti-gay positions have been justified by flawed scientific understandings of the nature of homosexuality. Underlying many of these convictions is the assumption, frequently untested, that the Bible in general, and Christianity in particular, teach that homosexuality is a sin.

In my role as pastor to the United Church of Christ, and in this season of theological reflection on "The Inclusive Church," I offer this Pastoral Letter to remind all of us that the church is to be a place where all are welcomed, where the gifts of all are recognized and received, and where the rights of all are defended and promoted. When so many in our society would reject and exclude, it is critical that we of the United Church of Christ bear witness to the conviction that it is possible to be deeply faithful to the Bible, profoundly respectful of the historic faith of the church and of its sacraments, and at the same time support the full inclusion and participation of all God's children in the membership and ministry of the church. Likewise, there can be no compromise that all persons in this society must enjoy equal protection under the law.

I write in deep gratitude for the journey of discernment and action that the United Church of Christ has taken over the past several decades. For all our difficulties and challenges, I believe the United Church of Christ is uniquely equipped to take on this complex but crucial vocation both in the public arena and among our ecumenical partners. Informed by the actions of several General Synods, by Biblical and theological reflection, and above all by countless pastoral encounters with members of our church, I am convinced that there must be and will be no turning back from our commitment, especially in the face of the current prejudice and misunderstanding prevalent in both the church and the society.

Contrary to what some assume or allege, the conviction of the General Synod of the United Church of Christ, along with the witness of many conferences, associations, and local churches, is not a superficial response to changing cultural norms or an easy reaction to certain social opinions. At their best, our commitments have grown out of a profound reflection on the meaning of our baptism and our participation in the sacrament of Holy Communion. Our commitments have grown as we have responded pastorally to the needs of many of our members and their families who have been the victims of prejudice or who have experienced rejection in the church.

We have been confronted and gifted by the presence in our church of gay, lesbian, and bisexual Christians who have been baptized in our sanctuaries, confirmed before our altars, and ordained by our associations. We have been confronted and gifted by men and women faithfully attentive to the Word, diligent in their sacramental life, forthright in their Christian witness and compassionate in their service. We have been confronted and gifted by parents and grandparents, sisters and brothers, daughters and sons, faithful members of our church, whose embrace by a loving God has enabled them to accept a gay, lesbian, or bisexual family member, and who yearn for that same loving embrace to be extended by the church to their child, their grandchild, their brother or sister, their parent. We have been confronted and gifted by faithful, mature, and able members who have experienced God's call to the ordained ministry of Word and Sacrament, who have sought and received the recognition and authorization of the church. We have been confronted and gifted by ordained men and women who have served faithfully and well for many years and who now wish to minister among us with renewed vitality openly affirming their same gender orientation. We have been confronted and gifted by gay, lesbian, and bisexual persons who have found love in the physical, emotional, and spiritual embrace of another, and are living in committed covenantal relationships of fidelity and trust which they yearn for the church to bless and the society to respect and protect. And we have been confronted and gifted by members of our church and those of other churches who have known the pain of rejection, the anguish of exclusion, and the fear of abuse, yet who remain faithful to their baptismal vows, seek to be fed at Christ's Table, and desire to be engaged in the mission of Christ's reconciling love in the world.

Confronted and gifted by these baptized persons, members of the United Church of Christ have been challenged to read the Bible again with new eyes and listen to the Holy Spirit with new ears. We have had to reexamine long held assumptions about those few passages of Scripture that appear to speak about homosexuality in the light of transforming interpretation from widely respected Bible scholars and teachers, and we have begun to recognize how our fears of those who are different, and our society's deeply entrenched bias against homosexual persons has often distorted and nearly silenced the Bible's liberating and inclusive voice. At the same time, encounters with hurting and excluded sisters and brothers have caused us to look to the whole of Scripture which speaks of a God who continually reaches out for those who are cast out for any reason, those who live at the margins of our lives. We have been reminded of our identity as disciples of the One who often ate with those rejected by the religious norms of the day, the One who sets before us all the Table of God's inclusive love, mercy, and grace.

In these encounters, we have remembered our own history, recalling ways we have been led to expand the church's welcome to others who have been excluded. We remember the Amistad and the story of our forebears, both enslaved and free, who rejected Biblical interpretations that supported slavery and whose new appreciation for the Gospel's mandate led them to fight for freedom for all. We remembered Japanese Americans driven from their homes during the Second World War, and those of our churches who spoke out for their rights. We remembered many women who refused to submit to a misuse of the Bible that denied them places of leadership or that conspired in their abuse, and who found affirmation and encouragement in our churches, our colleges, and our seminaries. We remembered ancestors of our Hungarian sisters and brothers who witness to the Reformed faith that led to their persecution as galley slaves and martyrs, as well as those who fled oppression in 1956 to find a safe haven among our churches. More recently we remembered our church's call for self-determination for Puerto Rican people, the championing of the rights of Chicano farm workers, the call for respect for the dignity of Native American people demeaned by caricature and stereotype, the recognition of the rights of Indigenous Hawaiians deprived of their land and culture, and solidarity with those who declared that the apartheid system erected and supported by other Bible reading Christians was idolatry, a denial of the very integrity of the church's confession. All of this has helped us discover that our church's concern for the rights and dignity of gay, lesbian, and bisexual people is not a break from our past, or a departure from Scripture, but is informed by our moments of greatest fidelity to the prophetic voice of the Bible and the Gospel's embrace for those who, with Christ, have been despised.

The encounters in our own church with each other over the subject of sexual orientation have not been easy and, for some, remain profoundly disturbing. We have experienced conflict; the covenants that bind us together have been tested. At times we have felt isolated from and misunderstood by some in the ecumenical community. But we have also experienced marvelous surprises:

- the growth and vitality of many local churches that have declared themselves open to and affirming of the gifts of gay, lesbian, and bisexual persons;

- the gracious perseverance of The United Church Coalition for Gay, Lesbian, Bisexual and Transgender Concerns which, for twenty six years, has been a prophetic presence in our church, clarifying concerns, challenging stereotypes, providing leaders for every setting of the church's life, gently and persistently changing hearts and minds, providing a refuge for those who have suffered wounds of prejudice and exclusion in church and society;

- the gratitude and encouragement of Christians in other churches who have found in our church's journey to new understandings a sign of hope amid discouragement;

- the growing self-esteem of lesbian, gay, and bisexual youth in our church who are able to worship in congregations that respect their full humanity, as well as the heterosexual youth in our churches who have found themselves called to confront the antigay prejudice so prevalent in their schools;

- the renewal that springs forth as we discover, again, that we are not trapped by the past but are part of a living tradition that is "reformed, yet always reforming," a people whose only comfort in life and in death is that they belong to Christ.

In these days we dare not be arrogant. The story of our pilgrimage with our gay, lesbian, and bisexual members at times has been marked by hesitation, fear, and frequent failures of nerve. At times prophetic voices, whether heard from inside or from outside the church, have been resisted. We have not always been properly respectful, or sought to understand with sincerity, those sisters and brothers among us who do not share our understanding or conviction or witness. At the same time, we have sometimes failed to recognize how the Bible has been used by some to perpetuate prejudice and to justify violence against homosexual persons.

But in these days we dare not be silent, either. I believe our voice among the churches and within our society is urgently needed, bearing witness to the belief that God cherishes all and dignifies all, and to our experience of gay, lesbian, and bisexual persons as gifts of God, called with us by their baptism into the fullest participation in God's mission of reconciliation in the world. I am convinced this voice will have power insofar as it is a voice shaped by the language of faith and the experience of worship, a voice in which the liberating truth of the Bible can be heard, and the courageous spirit of the saints will be echoed. By that voice, I believe, our churches will be renewed. More importantly, in that voice, I believe, the lonely will be called to companionship, the frightened will find comfort, the abused will know safety, and those sisters and brothers in Christ who have lost hope will rediscover the blessing of their baptism: Child of God, disciple of Christ, member of Christ's Church.

A Cry for Ethical and Moral Strength

Chapter Two
BWF Executive Director's Response

Open Letter to Rev. Paul Sherry

President of the United Church of Christ

December 1998

Dear Paul,

Certainly anyone of us who authentically seeks to follow Jesus Christ as Savior and Lord desires that all sinners come to repentance and be welcomed into the Church regardless of their human condition. This is not an issue among sincere Christians.

In your recent Pastoral Letter, however, you charge us to quite a different thing. You charge the church to accept persons who have sex outside of marriage and therefore are engaged in sexual sin to be placed in positions of spiritual authority in the church including that of pastors and teachers. Among your list of those you advocate placing in such positions are bi-sexuals; that is those who engage in sexual acts with both men and women and are therefore without questions engaging in sexual license. Lest anyone reading either of our letters be confused, we both know through long dialogue and engagement with those naming their identity by their sexuality that they emphatically make no distinction between orientation and behavior.

Your letter draws a false dichotomy between those who receive homosexuals into the church and defend their basic legal rights and those who reject and exclude. Jesus illustrated for us very clearly the embrace of sinners while condemning even the lust which leads to sexual sin and embracing the unchanging truth of God's righteousness. The love of Christ, calls us to love even at the expense of our own lives, but does not invite us to "change the grace of God into a license for immorality." (Jude 4)

I am especially alarmed by your criticism of our fellow denominations who have reaffirmed the historic Christian teaching on sexuality, placed in a sentence immediately following reference to 'hate crimes.' You are obviously making thinly veiled allusion to this summer's Lambeth Conference at which Anglican bishops representing 83 million Anglican Christians gathered and passed such a reaffirmation overwhelmingly. This testimony at Lambeth was largely the witness of 2/3 world church leaders to a sexually confused western church which has lost its way in the morass of a sexually deviant culture. You say, "we dare not be arrogant." I would charge you to accept your own challenge and submit to the wisdom of counsel from the large consensus of the global church on this matter. Have you considered that the positions taken in the UCC may well be in error?

We in the United Church of Christ are covenanted to be 'united and uniting,' and yet does not your letter, both in the tone and content of its criticism of those with whom you disagree, have the impact of being schismatic? Of what value is covenant relationship with other denominations and Christians if we are willing to consider that our positions on human sexuality may indeed be wrong and theirs right?

Is there any evidence to suggest that our culture is engaged in an enlightenment? Doesn't the reality that 1/2 our population has some sexually transmitted disease, 1/3 of our babies are aborted when they are conceived outside of marriage, 1 in every 5 of our women is raped, 1 in every 7 of our children is molested, and that we are saturated in pornography, indicate that we are a sex sick society engaged in delusion? Are we not living out the portrait of a dissolute culture pained so graphically in Romans 1 that includes the legitimization of homosexual behavior?

No one who sincerely follows Jesus Christ tolerates or justifies violence. To insinuate that those who uphold Godly standards of righteousness are somehow responsible for the Shepherd murder is as reprehensible as the insinuation that every child molested or murdered by someone of the same gender represents an indictment of all homosexual advocates on the ground that they have created an environment of acceptance for such acts.

As the father of a multi-racial family that has frequently engaged issues of racism at a deeply interpersonal level, I am especially offended by the comparison in your letter of those who may have suffered for their sexual lifestyle with those who have suffered injustice because of race or have been persecuted for their Christian conviction. This is a comparison every person of reason or experience rejects. It demeans those who have suffered in innocence for realities unrelated to their personal choice of behavior or lifestyle.

You refer in your letter to those who would justify their positions by "flawed scientific understandings of the nature of homosexuality." How many "flawed scientific understandings" have been offered to us in support of homosexual legitimacy including wide spread dissemination in UCC publications of the now infamous claim that 10% of the population was homosexual which is based on the discredited Kinsey research?

Your letter suggests that we reread the Bible "in the light of transforming interpretations from widely respected Bible scholars and teachers." May I remind you that these "scholars" come almost entirely from the liberal segment rather than the main stream of the Christian church. And many of those whose work has been most widely publicized have rejected the atonement and resurrection of Jesus Christ and have publicly confessed not having a personal faith in Jesus Christ as Savior and Lord of their own lives.

While I join you in prayer for reconciliation and unity in our churches, it is difficult to understand how your pastoral letter will lead us in that direction. May I respectfully suggest that your letter is theologically in error and that our Lord Jesus Christ who is the same yesterday, today and forever would be better served by a clear proclamation of the gospel.

Sincerely,

Carl L. Sweat, Jr., D. Min.

David Runnion-Bareford
Executive Director
Bible Witness Fellowship

Chapter Three
"Homosexuality In The Life Of The Church"
Romans 1:13-32

Periscope: verses 26-32

Dr. Carlton Upton
Sr. Pastor of Tabernacle Christian Church

The mainline church is facing a time bomb. There is pressure from within and without not only to respond to the homosexual crisis, but also to do it now. Gay liberationist and their sympathizers are hoping that the domino effect will be set in motion and result in support for their goals both within denominations and across denominational lines.

The most explosive issues of our day are those that have their roots in human rights -- the right to education, the right to work, the right to worship, as I may feel led. But should I have the right to do something you are convinced is morally wrong?

That is the crux of what is called the "gay rights" issue. Across the land, pressure is increasing to give homosexuals access to jobs of every kind, the right to be accepted as foster parents, and even the right to marry each other. Beneath it all is the insistence that the public change its thinking about the validity of homosexual pattern.

The first question to be faced is whether homosexuality is wrong, as most of us have been instructed through Biblical teachings. The answer, quite simply and on the authority of God's Word is --- yes, it is.

The big push of homosexuality today is to defend its practices as just another life-style. To support that position, homosexuals offer an amazing array of arguments. They say that homosexuals are born with their sexual preferences, just as others are born with heterosexual preferences. They cite the fact that sodomy is widespread, even common, and that when carried on in private it is no one's business but their own. They argue that other kinds of sexual indulgences are condoned or overlooked. In fact, within the past dozen or fifteen years the whole emphasis of homosexuals has been to defend the validity of their practice and press for what they call "gay rights."

Today, homosexuals are highly organized, having a network of regional conferences and a national clearinghouse to facilitate exchange of information. A national legal defense fund exists, and lawyers are instantly available to press the battle for gay rights wherever a need arises.

In all this, the Bible inevitably has come under sharp attack. Some homosexuals say the Bible should have no place in setting moral standards. Others seek to show by Scripture that the Bible itself justifies the homosexual life-style.

No Christian should be deceived. The Bible clearly tells us that homosexuality is without defense. Genesis 19 describes the homosexual lusts of the men of Sodom, which led to destruction of that city.

Homosexuals cite Ezekiel 16:49, which mentions Sodom's other sins --- "pride, fullness of bread, and abundance of idleness," as well as failure to help the poor and needy, but forget that the next verse goes on to say, "and they…committed abomination before me; therefore I took them away." So clearly is Sodom's destruction linked with the practice of homosexuality that the term *sodomy* today still has a single meaning.

The Levitical law expresses God's principles of righteousness. Here, in Leviticus 18:22, God's commandment says, "Thou shalt not lie with mankind as with womankind; it is abomination." The fact that is followed by a commandment against sexual acts with animals suggests the unthinkable nature of the homosexual relation.

There are other prohibitions in the Bible against homosexuality. One of the revealing New Testament statements is in Romans 1, which tells how men once knew Almighty God, but turned from Him to idols. The passage goes on to say that because men gave up God, God in turn gave men to "uncleanness through the lusts of their own hearts, to dishonor their own bodies between themselves."

Could this be homosexuality? The following verses make the fact too clear to miss.

"For this cause God gave them up into vile affections; for even their women did change the natural use into that which is against nature; and likewise also the men, leaving the natural use of the woman, burned in their lust one toward another, men with men, working that which is unseemly" (Romans 1:24, 26-27).

Does that mean that homosexuality is a curse on especially godless men? That is not what the Bible is saying. Paul is saying that homosexuality was brought into the race because man turned from God. It is one of many sins --- and others are enumerated in the closing verses of the same chapter.

Homosexuality, like alcoholism, cursing, or violence, gets its hold on an individual in many different ways. The only ultimate solution is the blood of Jesus Christ.

If homosexuality is sin, then man is ultimately responsible, not just for the sin but for rejecting deliverance from that sin through faith in Jesus Christ. And that is what the New Testament says in 1Corinthians 6:9-10 "Know ye not that the unrighteous shall not inherit the kingdom of God? Be not deceived: neither fornicators, nor idolaters, nor adulterers, nor effeminate, nor abusers of themselves with mankind, nor thieves, nor covetous, nor drunkards, nor revilers, nor extortioners, shall inherit the kingdom of God."

Homosexuality is a serious and offensive sin. But by far its worst effect is that it, along with other sins, can keep a man or woman outside of heaven forever. Today there are millions of homosexuals in our country --- some believe as many as 20 million. The degrading effect is beyond our understanding.

But the tragedy above all else is that they are letting their lust come between them and the blessing of salvation.

Most of the gay-rights leadership and the pressure producing the current gay crisis have come from New York City and San Francisco. In New York the gay movement began with riots following the Stonewall arrests in 1969. In 1972 the first avowed male homosexual was ordained of a known lesbian took place in New York City by the Episcopal Church.

There have been both gains and losses, from the gay viewpoint, within the church. To get a better perception of the issues in the church on homosexuality we need to view what different denominations respond to the issue.

In 1972 the Golden Gate Association of the United Church of Christ ordained a self-declared homosexual, William R. Johnson. They did so in spite of the advice against it by the denomination's Council on Church and Ministry. In the United Church of Christ's polity, the local association has the right of final decision. They used that right to get things going. William Johnson has not yet served a congregation as pastor, but he has worked extensively to further gay theology and gay rights within the United Church of Christ and other denominations.

In 1977 the Right Reverend Paul Moore, Jr., Bishop of New York for the Episcopal Church, ordained Ellen Marie Barrett, an avowed lesbian, to the priesthood. She had been active in the gay movement prior to that time and served as an officer of "Integrity", the Episcopal gay caucus. Bishop Moore received an avalanche of protest within the Episcopal Church, both from fellow bishops and from people within the diocese. Several dioceses expressed opposition at their annual conventions.

Many congregations have left the Episcopal Church because of the ordination of women, and much unrest has developed over the homosexual issue. The House of Bishops has ruled that homosexuals should not be married in the church nor be ordained priests.

The 1976 Book of Discipline of the United Methodist Church describes the sacred worth of all persons, including homosexuals, but then says, "Further, we insist that all persons are entitled to have their human and civil rights ensured, though we do not condone this practice incompatible with Christian teaching."

The General Assembly of the United Presbyterian Church, meeting in May of 1978 acted on the reports of ordination of homosexuals in the church. The majority report suggested that same sex love can be good and within the plan of God and, therefore, it would be proper for presbyters to ordain avowed, practicing homosexuals. It further states that there is nothing in the Constitution that hinders the ordination of practicing homosexuals.

The minority report sees homosexual acts as contrary to God's intention, that such acts are, therefore, sin. While it calls the church to be sensitive to the needs of gay persons in ministering to them, it recommends "that the General Assembly exercise its judicial role as the highest judicatory of the church and determine a definitive interpretation of the constitution which specifies that self-affirming, practicing homosexual persons may not be ordained to the professional ministry, on to the offices of ruling elder and deacon.

The Southern Baptist convention adopted their first resolution on homosexuality in 1976. It urged local congregations "not to afford the practice of homosexuality any degree of approval through ordination, employment, or other designations of normal lifestyle. The Orthodox Church has also rejected the idea of ordination of homosexuals. The Greek Orthodox Archdiocese, in its biennial meeting in 1976 in Philadelphia, "called homosexuality an insult to God; 'blasphemy,' and 'immoral and dangerous perversion,' and sinful failure."

The official Roman Catholic position is very clearly stated in a 1976 Vatican document on sexual ethics, reaffirming condemnation of homosexual acts. However, the Vatican has not ruled on the ordination of avowed homosexuals, and nothing in Canon law specifically prohibits it.

Is it an overstatement to say the time bomb of gay rights is about to be detonated in the church? I don't believe so. And as the time of decision rapidly approaches, no one can sit on the fence. Each member of these mainline churches needs to become more knowledgeable and personally ready for the impending decisions. Further, Christians need to enter into deliberations in appropriate constitutional ways designated by their church polity to help make these decisions. If not, decisions will be made for them.

The gay crisis is not "out there" in a vacuum. It is at our doorstep. The electronic and print media bombard us constantly with new developments. And instead of our witnessing to the culture, we have let the culture witness to us.

The crisis is primarily one of theology. But it is also a crisis of relationship in the church and in the life of the local congregation. It has to do with the ongoing health of established friend-ships, and it relates deeply to our unity in Christ.

Theologically, we are being asked to reinterpret the content of Scripture and to change our approach to Scripture. Some religious homosexuals have developed for themselves a systematic theology – even an apologetic – to attempt to biblically defend their position; it is popularly called gay theology. Gay theology calls for a total change in understanding of biblical texts that address homosexuality and for a redefinition of basic theological concepts concerning:

- Sexuality and the family;

- The holiness of God and His judgment on sin;

- The role of God's law for Christians who know God by grace;

- The relationship between justification and sanctification;

- The biblical meaning of love.

The debate has shown that some within the church don't have much biblical theology at all when it comes to believing. We have often falsely presumed that because we say the Bible is authoritative and because we ascribe to the creeds, we are firmly accepting the truth set forth in those documents. But we are finding in reality that, though we have drawn near with our lips, our hearts are far from Him.

Great value can come out of theological crises if Christian people take time to study the Scriptures and to speak the truth in love, making their convictions known within the life of the church. God's people cannot afford to flinch from facing difficult issues. Historically, the church has spoken its mind most clearly when forced to do so by theological or moral controversy. This is just such a time for us; it provides a wonderful opportunity for theological and biblical study, and for spiritual renewal – if we will pay the price for serious inquiry.

The crisis is not only theological; it's relational – involving ecclesiastical and congregational life. When the United Presbyterian Task Force report came out in favor of ordaining homosexuals, and a minority report was issued in opposition to such ordination, all manner of confusion broke loose in the denomination.

The homosexual crisis is a real crisis. The main issue before the church is not gay rights, but God's rights. God is God. As Creator of heaven and earth, He has ultimate authority over His creation. While man is the "crown" of God's creation, he is still the creature and under the Creator's authority.

Jesus Christ, God's son, "is the image of the invisible God ... all things were created through him and for him ... He is the head of the body, the church; he is the beginning, the first-born from the dead, that in everything he might be pre-eminent. For in him all the fullness of God was pleased to dwell, and through him to reconcile to himself all things, whether on earth or in heaven, making peace by the blood of his cross." And concerning the Son, the day is coming "… when he delivers the kingdom of God the Father after destroying every rule and every authority and power".

But until that day, Jesus 'provision in the earthly authority structure was first to the apostles, and through them He added the inspired New Testament to the Old Testament; then to leaders whom He raised up within the church throughout the ages (the shepherds of the flock); and finally to the body of Christ at large.

God the Father never abdicated His authority to Jesus; nor Jesus to the leadership of the church; nor the shepherds and elders to the sheep. God the Son clearly understood His accountability to His Father; in like manner, the shepherds are accountable to the Chief Shepherd; the flock is accountable to the under-shepherds.

God's rights as Creator and Redeemer are infinitely higher than our human rights. He is the one who initiated His relationship with man. It is His world and His church. Only because of His sovereign grace are we His people. Our "rights" must, therefore, yield to His.

God has established the channels through which He exercises His authority within the church. Those channels of authority in the New Covenant are the Lord Jesus Christ, the living Word; Holy Scripture, the written Word; and His appointed leaders in the church who are called to be obedient to Jesus Christ under the authority of Scripture through the leadership of His Spirit.

God's rights are communicated to us under the lordship of Jesus Christ through the Holy Spirit. When He speaks, we listen!

Our rights blossom as we bow to His authority within the church. Not to do so is sheer futility and folly as well as anarchy against our Monarch. He is the king who said, "Not every one who says to me, 'Lord, Lord,' shall enter the Kingdom of heaven, but he who does the will of my Father who is in heaven" (Matt. 7:21).

The Magna Carta of God's authority in the church is Holy Scripture. In Scripture He has made Himself known by His gospel of grace and has revealed His will for our lives. He continues to make His will

A Cry for Ethical and Moral Strength

known by the Holy Spirit speaking in Scripture, which is inspired and authoritative for all God's people.

The human channel through which God has chosen to exercise His authority is His appointed leaders. In virtually every Christian church, leaders are committed by their vows to being led by Scripture and by the Holy Spirit. In the United Presbyterian Church every ordained pastor and elder promises before God and their congregation to "obey Jesus Christ under the authority of Scripture."

The weight of responsibility is upon the shoulders of the pastor and in caring for the flock over which the Lord has appointed him. Pastors carry this heavy responsibility in the homosexual debate because the polity places the responsibility clearly on him. Pastors are responsible before God in their stewardship of leadership. He will hold us accountable and so will our flocks.

Listen to the writer of Hebrews: "Obey your leaders and submit to them; for they are keeping watch over your souls, as men who will have to give account. Let them do this joyfully, and not sadly, for that would be of no advantage to you" (Heb. 13:17).

Paul said to the Ephesians that ours is a divinely appointed office by which "to equip the saints for the work of the ministry, for building up the body of Christ" (Eph. 4:12). Peter tells us that we, as fellow elders, are to tend the flock of God willingly, not by domineering but by example, clothed with humility toward God and one another.

Paul warned the elders to Ephesus, "Take heed to yourselves and to all the flock, in which the Holy Spirit has made you overseers, to care for the Church of God which he obtained with the blood of His own Son."

Jesus set the pattern personally for all pastors and elders. He was the Good Shepherd who laid down His life for the sheep. He was not a hireling; His safety did not matter. He had counted the cost. In fact, the Shepherd Himself became the Lamb! The Good Shepherd who had power "to lay down His life and power to take it again" did not use that power for Himself, but used that power totally for the well-being of the sheep. Here was One who knew and loved His sheep so personally that He left the ninety and nine and searched for the one who was lost.

But note well the contrast between the Good Shepherd and those shepherds described by the ancient prophet Ezekiel.

The weak you have not strengthened, the sick you have not healed, the crippled you have not bound up, the stray you have not brought back, the lost you have not sought, and with force and harshness you have ruled them. So they were scattered, because there was no shepherd; and they became food for all the wild beasts. My sheep were scattered, they wandered over all the mountains and on every high hill; my sheep were scattered over all the face of the earth, with none to search or seek for them.

God's response was judgment. "Thus says the Lord God, Behold I am against the shepherds…" (Ezek. 34:10).

It is important to remind pastors that they are called to bring back the straying sheep. We are not called to wink at sin. We are not called to say the straying sheep are *"okay"* in their wandering and ordain their wandering ways as viable alternative lifestyles.

The Head of our church does call His shepherds and people to public morality – that is, to a ministry of compassion for people, to a respect for human rights, and to advocate social justice. He loves the weak, the broken, the oppressed, and the person in need.

But Jesus also calls us to private morality. Our words and our attitudes are important. He emphasized God's intention of fidelity. What Jesus thought about marriage and sexuality is of great importance for our study.

Jesus Christ was not soft on sexual sin as some want to say. He was a lover of sinners and treated them sensitively, even those whom He confronted strongly and directly. But as He forgave them, He then said, *"Go and sin no more" (John 8:11).* There is no evidence that Jesus' forgiveness ever left people in their sin. Instead, it led them to hate their sin and turn from it.

Jesus never spoke specifically to the issue of homosexuality. He didn't need to. The Old Testament was extremely clear on the subject, and the problem was not widespread in Israel because of that Old Testament teaching. But this is not to say that Jesus did not speak clearly about sexual morality. He spoke clearly and powerfully. "But what comes out of the mouth proceeds from the heart, and this defiles a man. For out of the heart come evil thoughts, murder, adultery, fornication, theft, false witness, slander. These are what defile a man … (Matt. 15:18-20)."

The church has not been taking Jesus seriously. Why not? For God's sake, why not? Because we are gutless. We are influenced by the numbers game. "But everybody's doing it." Since when did numbers determine morality? That is why we face the present crisis with homosexuality: Both the people and their leaders in the church are committing adultery with impunity. Do we respond? No, we're afraid we'll make some waves.

<u>The issue before us is not homosexuality, it is morality. The issue before us is not the ordination of homosexuals – gay rights. The issue before us is God's rights – God's right to call us to Himself, to call us to live as His obedient children, to call us to be holy (because He is holy), to call us to moral purity and integrity.</u>

There is considerable confusion in our society and in the church concerning homosexuality and homosexual practice. People are asking for a clear word rather than a muffled sound. They are asking for a biblical word, a word from the Lord, rather than the changing opinions of men. They want both firmness and compassion, which reflect the character of our Lord when confronting moral laxity and broken people.

I am mindful that a Scripture text out of context often becomes a pretext. However, a text in context and interpreted within the total perspective of Scripture becomes God's method of revealing truth. A proper discussion of the theological understanding of homosexuality must begin with the Creation and Fall narratives in Genesis 1:26-31, 2:18-25, and 3:1-24. The Creation narrative establishes us as persons who possess a specific sexual identity. "So God created man in his own image ... male and female he created them" (Gen. 1:27). His intention through this differentiation of the sexes was to complete the order of Creation. The point is this: Sexual differentiation is essential to understanding what is fully human. Don Williams says it well: "God does not create Man alone, neither does He create man/man or woman/woman. God creates Man as male and female, and only in community together is the image of God seen upon the earth. Thus the old myths of the androgenous (bisexual or unisexual) man are rejected and all ambiguity in the relationship between the sexes is removed. Man is created for another. That other is woman. Their relationship is ordered by God." Therefore, to be created in the image of God includes being in relationship as male and female. In Genesis 1 we discover that to be human is to share humanity with the opposite sex.

In Genesis 2 we find this theme of the complementary nature of male and female expanded. The incompleteness of creation is introduced when God says, " *'...It is not good that the man should be alone; I will make him a helper fit for him'" (2:28).* According to Williams, "Thus as god has directly made the man, so he directly makes the woman from man, and in her he receives the helper who makes him a complete person."

The purpose of sexual union is not only for procreation, but for the development of a deeper relationship. In Creation, humanity was *"one flesh"* because woman was taken from man (Gen. 2:21-23). In sexual intercourse a man and woman become one flesh again as they enter into their physical union.

In Genesis 3 we find the goodness of God's creation distorted by sin and the divine pattern for male – female relationship is marred. 'Genesis 3 talks about the serpent deceiving Eve, man's fall, God calls them into accountability, the serpent is cursed; his overthrow by the woman's seed, mankind's punishment; and the loss of paradise. Estrangement and alienation replaced God's intention. God's good gift to male and female was distorted through rebellion and pride. Strain between the sexes was the result.

Homosexuality is one result of this disjointedness. To be sure, it is not the only one. Adultery (see Gen. 26:10), incest (see Gen. 19:36), rape (see Gen. 34:2), and prostitution (see Gen. 38:15) also pose continual threats to sexual wholeness. It is in the light of the Fall and the damage done to our humanity and sexuality that homosexuality and the other deviations from God's created order must be understood.

From Genesis to Leviticus, from Romans and 1Corinthians to 1Timothy, the message is consistently the same: God created Man as male and female. Our sexuality is to be fulfilled in faithful heterosexual relationships within marriage. God does not alter His message to fit the culture. It is the same in every culture. He calls His people to live in contrast to the culture.

Everywhere in Scripture He condemns the objective behavior, not just the motives or subjective feelings. Everywhere He seeks to fulfill His original, pre-Fall purposes for marriage and family in the fabric of society. He constantly calls His people to be holy. "For I the Lord am Holy." It's the test in context.

My position on the issue of homosexuality in the life of the church is that I am against its practice in any form or shape in the church. I see no hope for the homosexual if the church of Jesus Christ changes its historical-biblical view of sexuality, morality, homosexuality as sin, or of the necessity to turn from that sin. If Christendom recants, the church will have "gained the whole world, but lost its soul." It would no longer have any authority in Scripture; it would cease following its Lord, Jesus Christ. It may feel somewhat better about itself for a time, but it would have provided only bogus grace, which is no grace at all. For God justifies the sinner, not the sin.

The good news for homosexuals begins with the bad news. Homosexuality is contrary to God's nature, which is holy. We have learned it is contrary to His purpose in creation. It is contrary to His plan for life, a fact that led to the destruction of Sodom and Gomorrah. It is contrary to His Law revealed through Moses. It is a perversion of God's intention and is not made right by the appeal to inversion, that is, to being a constitutional homosexual. It is not supportive of family life and the fidelity that Jesus so strongly emphasized. It does not lead to stronger moral character, but involves its victims in all kinds of deceit, manipulation, and lustful behavior.

The gay lifestyle is not only sinful, but it is also evidence of God's judgment against idolatry – worshiping other creatures rather than the Creator. The Scripture tell us that God allows homosexuals the "freedom" of doing what they want (see Rom. 1:18-28). This divine denunciation of homosexual sin is enlarged in the total fabric of Scripture concerning God's nature: holy, righteous, just, loving, gracious, and forgiving.

"God is light and in Him is no darkness at all. If we say we have fellowship with him and walk in darkness, we lie and not lie according to the truth (1John 1:5, 6)." And I'm glad John said in that very same text verse 9 "If we confess our sins, he is faithful and just to forgive us our sins, and to cleanse us from all unrighteousness."

But his law is given to bring us to Christ – to His grace. The law reveals the immeasurable gap between God and mankind. No one escapes the staggering dimensions of personal sin. God is not only holy, He is also love. This is the Good News. His nature includes liberating love. He loves homosexuals as much as He loves any other living person – including His Son! His love is unconditional. His love is not turned away by our sins; it is only turned away by our wills.

Homosexuals can receive Him or they can reject Him, but they cannot make His a different kind of love. They cannot come to God on their terms. They cannot put Him or His will into their mold. His love changes people. The more you receive that love, the more He liberates you. His love does not wink at our sin; He takes it more seriously than we do. He dealt with our sin through Jesus Christ's sacrifice at the cross. "Behold, the Lamb of God, who takes away the sin of the world!" (John 1:29).

The Good News includes Jesus' promise of His Holy Spirit. He has promised *"rivers of living water"*. Not just a trickle, or a stream, but rivers – more than enough. The Comforter, the Spirit of Truth, the Counselor, will come and live in your heart.

The Good News is that God invites you to come just as you are and promises to send you back into the world a changed person. II Corinthians 5:17 says, "Therefore if any man be in Christ he is a new creature: old things are passed away; behold all things are become new." There is hope for the homosexual because God never commands us to do anything without also offering to us the power and strength by which to obey.

There is a remedy for homosexuality, and God has put it in our hands. After declaring in I Corinthians 6:9-10 that no homosexual can inherit the kingdom of God, Paul goes on to say in verse 11, "And such were some of you: but ye are washed, but ye are sanctified, but ye are justified in the name of the Lord Jesus, and by the Spirit of our God."

What is this saying? The Word of God is telling us that although no one can hang on to homosexuality and still be accepted by Almighty God, some former homosexuals in the church at Corinth had found deliverance. They had entered a brand new life by faith in Jesus Christ.

The power of the blood of Jesus can take the dregs of humanity and make men out of them. It can take men lost to shame and make sons of God. No man can change himself, but Christ can change him.

About The Author

Rest assured that the stories and theology you receive in this book are Christ-centered. Rev. Carl Sweat, Jr. is Pastor of Laurel Hill United Church of Christ, a congregational setting of Christendom. He is the author of "Why Are Women In The Ministry?" an exciting and informative book. He is founder and Director of Graduate Studies at the United Christian Institute. The diversity he offers each reader is a B.A. in Sociology with a minor in Unbar Affairs, Virginia Union University, M.S. in Administrative Science, Central Michigan University, M. Div., Providence Theological Seminary, D. Min., Providence Theological Seminary and an Honorary D.D., awarded by the United Christian Institute. Rev. Carl Sweat, Jr. extends to you a realistic, practical and objective approach to the subject "A Cry for Ethical and Moral Strength."

Printed in the United States
26559LVS00005B/46-168